DEPRESSION AND THE SPIRITUAL IN MODERN ART

HOMAGE TO MIRÓ

DEPRESSION AND THE SPIRITUAL —— IN MODERN ART —— HOMAGE TO MIRÓ

Edited by

Joseph J. Schildkraut
Department of Psychiatry, Harvard Medical School,
The Massachusetts Mental Health Center,
Boston, USA

Aurora Otero
Department of Psychiatry, University of Barcelona
Clinic University Hospital of Barcelona
Barcelona, Spain

JOHN WILEY & SONS
Chichester · New York · Brisbane · Toronto · Singapore

Copyright © 1996 by John Wiley & Sons Ltd,
Baffins Lane, Chichester,
West Sussex PO19 1UD, England

National 01243 779777
International (+44) 1243 779777

Other Wiley Editorial Offices

John Wiley & Sons, Inc., 605 Third Avenue, New York, NY 10158-0012, USA

Jacaranda Wiley Ltd, 33 Park Road, Milton, Queensland 4064, Australia

John Wiley & Sons (Canada) Ltd, 22 Worcester Road, Rexdale, Ontario M9W
1L1, Canada

John Wiley & Sons (Asia) Pte Ltd, 2 Clementi Loop #02-01, Jin Xing
Distripark, Singapore 0512

Library of Congress Cataloging-in-Publication Data

Depression and the spiritual in modern art : homage to Miró / edited
  by Joseph J. Schildkraut, Aurora Otero.
    p.   cm.
  ISBN 0 471 95403 9 (alk. paper)
  1. Art and mental illness. 2. Spirituality in art. 3. Art,
Modern—20th century—Psychological aspects. I. Schildkraut,
Joseph J., 1934– . II. Otero, Aurora.
N71.5.D44   1996 *September 16, 1997*
701'.15—dc20   95-48035
                                                          CIP

British Library Cataloguing in Publication Data

A catalogue record for this book is available from the British Library

ISBN 0 471 95403 9

Typeset in 10/12pt Bookman by
Servis Filmsetting Ltd
Color reproduction by Daylight Colour Art Pte, Singapore
Printed and bound in Italy by New Interlitho, S.P.A.

CONTENTS

continued over

CONTRIBUTORS

Hagop S. Akiskal — Professor of Psychiatry, University of California at San Diego, Department of Psychiatry 0603, 9500 Gilman Drive, La Jolla, California 92093-0603, USA

Kareen K. Akiskal — Chief of Creativity Studies, The International Mood Clinic, La Jolla, University of California at San Diego, Department of Psychiatry 0603, 9500 Gilman Drive, La Jolla, California 92093-0603, USA

Nancy C. Andreasen — Andrew H. Woods Professor of Psychiatry, Mental Health Clinical Research Center, University of Iowa Hospital & Clinics, 200 Hawkins Drive (Room 2911 – JPP), Iowa City, Iowa 52242-1057, USA

Patricia C. Ballard — Museum Technician, National Gallery of Art, Washington D.C. 20565, USA

Eduardo Chillida — Sculptor, Intz-Enea, Paseo del Faro 26, 20008 San Sebastian, SPAIN

José Corredor-Matheos — Writer and Art Critic, Escorial, 50, 5–7, 08024 Barcelona, SPAIN

Cristóbal Gastó — Senior Lecturer of Psychiatry, University of Barcelona, Hospital Clinic i Provincial de Barcelona, Rossello, 140, 08036 Barcelona, SPAIN

Daniel Giralt-Miracle — Historian and Art Critic, Av. Princep d'Asturies, 16, 08012 Barcelona, SPAIN

Alissa J. Hirshfeld — Psychotherapy Intern, The Marina Counselling Center, San Francisco, California 94123, USA

Kay Redfield Jamison — Professor of Psychiatry, Johns Hopkins University School of Medicine, Department of Psychiatry, 600 N. Wolfe Street, Baltimore, Maryland 21205, USA

William Jeffett — Assistant Keeper Exhibitions, Sainsbury Centre for Visual Arts, University of East Anglia, Norwich NR4 7TJ, UK

David Lomas — Lecturer in Art History, Department of Art History, University of Manchester, Oxford Road, Manchester, M13 9PL, UK

Rosa Maria Malet — Director, Fundació Joan Miró, Barcelona, Parc de Montjuïc, 08038 Barcelona, SPAIN

Jane M. Murphy — Professor of Psychiatry, Harvard Medical School, Massachusetts General Hospital, 705 Warren Street, Boston, Massachusetts 02114, USA

Konrad Oberhuber — Director, Graphische Sammlung Albertina, Augustinerstrasse 1, A-1010 Wien, AUSTRIA

Jordi E. Obiols — Professor of Psychopathology, Department of Personality Measure and Psychopathology, Autonomous University of Barcelona, 08193 – Bellaterra, Barcelona, SPAIN

Aurora Otero — Associate Professor of Psychiatry, University of Barcelona, Clinic University Hospital of Barcelona, 08036 Barcelona, SPAIN

Barbara Rose — Research Professor in Art History, American University, Washington D.C. 20016, USA

Robert Rosenblum — Professor of Fine Arts, New York University, 100 Washington Square East, 303 Main Building, New York, NY 10003-668, USA

Carl Salzman — Professor of Psychiatry, Harvard Medical School, Massachusetts Mental Health Center, 74 Fenwood Road, Boston, Massachusetts 02115, USA

Joseph J. Schildkraut — Professor of Psychiatry, Harvard Medical School, Massachusetts Mental Health Center, 74 Fenwood Road, Boston, Massachusetts 02115, USA

Antoni Tàpies — Painter, Fundació Antoni Tàpies, Aragó, 255, 08007 Barcelona, SPAIN

PREFACE

The Editors first met through our mutual friend and colleague Hagop Akiskal. Shortly thereafter, one of us (AO), then President of the Catalan Society of Psychiatry, invited the other (JJS) to speak on the biochemistry of depression at the University of Barcelona. During this visit to Barcelona, birthplace of the great Catalan artist Joan Miró, JJS revealed his longstanding love of Miró's art and his dream of organizing a symposium on "Mood Disorders and Spirituality in Twentieth-Century Artists" to be held in Barcelona in homage to Joan Miró. This idea captured the imagination of many of the members of the Catalan Society of Psychiatry and planning for the symposium was begun immediately with the cooperation of Rosa Maria Malet, Director of the Miró Foundation in Barcelona, and with the encouragement of David Fernández Miró, the artist's grandson, who sadly died before the symposium took place.

The symposium was held in Barcelona in May 1993, during that city's celebration of the 100th anniversary of the birth of Joan Miró, while the Miró Foundation was holding its centenary retrospective exhibition of Miró's art. This book grew out of that symposium.

Many people have helped us in organizing the symposium and editing this book. We are grateful to all of them. First, we want to thank the members of the organizing committee for the symposium, Drs Joan Obiols, Jordi E. Obiols, Josep M. Menchón, Rocío Martín-Santos, Joan Serrallonga, Laura Gómez, Carles García and Roser Guillamat. Their hard work and devoted efforts over many months made the symposium happen. We would also like to thank Rosa Maria Malet, Miquel Tàpies, John Zvereff, Professor Carles Ballús, Carolee Heileman, Carles Taché and especially Vicenç Altaió, commissioner of Miró Year, for the support they gave us.

We appreciate the contributions of all of the participants in the symposium: Hagop S. Akiskal, Kareen K. Akiskal, Nancy C. Andreasen, Carles Ballús, Maria Lluïsa Borràs, Eduardo Chillida, José Corredor-Matheos, Mihaly Csikszentmihalyi, Mariano de la Cruz, Cristóbal Gastó, Daniel Giralt-Miracle, Miguel Gutiérrez, Joan Hernández Pijoan, Kay Redfield Jamison, William Jeffett, David Lomas, Juan José López-Ibor, Rosa Maria Malet, Joan Massana, Konrad Oberhuber, Joan Obiols, Jordi E. Obiols, Antoni Porta, Miquel Porter Moix, Joaquim Pujol, Albert Ràfols Casamada, Barbara Rose, Robert Rosenblum, Antoni Tàpies and Jaume Vilató.

We are grateful for the generous support provided by the Direcció General de Recerca—Generalitat de Catalunya, Charlene Englehard Troy and the Englehard Foundation, Cavas Raventós i Blanc and the Arco Chemical Company, and the Karen Tucker Fund. Additional support for the symposium came from Astra-Ifesa and Upjohn Duphar as well as Alonga, Beecham, Ciba-Geigy, Esteve, Juste, Lilly and Wyeth Orfi pharmaceutical companies.

We owe a large debt of thanks to Ana Curiel of C&C Convenciones y Servicios, who was kindly available in Barcelona to provide assistance with this project at all times. We also express our thanks and appreciation to the dedicated staff of our US editorial office: Gladys C. Rege, who provided invaluable assistance at the beginning of this project; Patsy Kuropatkin, who cheerfully helped us obtain manuscripts from even our most over-committed and frequently-flying group of authors, and who labored conscientiously to keep our editorial office organized; Gail Bursell, who assumed responsibility for the financial operations of the US editorial office; and Kathleen M. Pappalardo and Nancy L. McHale for their generous assistance whenever it was needed. A special thanks goes to Patricia C. Ballard, who did a phenomenal job in locating and obtaining reproductions of the works of art requested by the authors.

We are extremely grateful to SmithKline Beecham for sponsoring the publication of this book through a generous educational grant; and to Michael Davis, Hilary Rowe, Elaine Hutton, Mandy Collison and their colleagues at John Wiley & Sons Ltd for their help in publishing this book.

We also would like to express our appreciation for the enthusiasm and encouragement we received from Margarita Mejía, Manuel Porter, Sergi Porter, Peter Schildkraut and Michael Schildkraut.

Finally, we want to thank Betsy Beilenson Schildkraut, who was with us from the very conception of the idea for the symposium and who assisted us in so many ways, particularly in the editing of this book.

For all of their help we are most grateful.

Joseph J. Schildkraut
Aurora Otero

FOREWORD

JOSEPH J. SCHILDKRAUT

". . . there exists a relationship between the deepest conflicts that reveal themselves in religion and in art forms and the depressed mood or melancholic illness" (D.W. Winnicott, 1965, p. 25).

"[The] innate receptivity [of the creative man] makes him suffer keenly. . . . [T]his suffering . . . is not only a private and personal suffering but at the same time a largely unconscious existential suffering from the fundamental human problems. . . . As the myth puts it, only a wounded man can be a healer. . . . Because in his own suffering the creative man experiences the profound wounds of his collectivity and his time, he carries deep within him a regenerative force . . ." (E. Neumann, 1959/1974, p. 186).

A relationship between depression or melancholia and artistic creativity has been noted throughout history: from ancient Greece with its speculations concerning a link between creativity and madness; to the Renaissance with its idiosyncratic, creative personalities; to the Romantic Period with its introspective and moody poets and painters; down to the Modern Era (Wittkower & Wittkower, 1963; Richards, 1981; Hershman & Lieb, 1988; Andreasen & Glick, 1988; Rothenberg, 1990; Jamison, 1993; Ludwig, 1995). Through historical, biographical and systematic empirical diagnostic studies, the link between depression and artistic creativity has been the focus of considerable research during the past several decades (Andreasen, 1978, 1987; Andreasen & Canter, 1974, 1975; Andreasen & Powers, 1974; O'Connor, 1986, 1987; Jamison, 1989, 1990, 1993; Schildkraut & Hirshfeld, 1995; Schildkraut, Hirshfeld & Murphy, 1994; Ludwig, 1995); some scholars have used psychoanalytic theory to explain the connection (Storr, 1985; Kuspit, 1993). Concurrently, many scholars have come to recognize the spiritual strivings and yearnings for transcendence inherent in the works of many of this century's greatest artists, as they have in the works of many of the great artists of the past (Rosenblum, 1975; Schildkraut, 1982; Tuchman & Freeman, 1986; Lipsey, 1988).

Artists themselves have recognized and explored the interrelatedness of melancholia or depression, spirituality and artistic creativity. One of the first to do so was Albrecht Dürer, in his enigmatic engraving *Melencolia I* (1514), probably the most famous portrayal of melancholia in the history of art (Figure 0-1). In this work filled with mystery, the winged Melencolia sits immobilized by sorrow, her head resting on her clenched fist, her eyes in a fixed stare. Her hair is dishevelled and her robes are rumpled. Surrounded by the symbols and tools of creative work, she suffers from "the tragic unrest of human creation" (Panofsky, 1955, p. 156), destined to lose in her competition with God. Erwin Panofsky, who has written extensively on Dürer, calls this an "Artist's Melancholy" (Panofsky, 1955, p. 162), the paradoxical union of genius and despair.

0-1 (right)
ALBRECHT DÜRER
MELENCOLIA I, 1514
Engraving, 9⅝ × 7⅜ in
(24.3 × 18.7 cm)
Gift of Miss Ellen T. Bullard. Courtesy, Museum of Fine Arts, Boston

Set into the building wall, directly behind the winged Melencolia, is a Jupiter square, a so-called magic square of 16 fields, with all the horizontal, vertical, and diagonal lines summing to 34, the Jupiter number (Schimmel, 1993, pp. 30–32 and Plate 2), believed to signify a palliative "against Saturn [the planet associated with melancholia] and against Melancholy" (Klibansky, Saxl & Panofsky, 1964, pp. 325–327). Leaning against the building behind the figure of Melencolia is a wooden ladder, a symbol of the incompleteness of man-made structures and the desire to transcend the human condition on earth (Eliade, 1991).

Dürer's *Melencolia I* can be seen to reflect the inertia of the creative artistic genius, withdrawing from that which can be attained on earth, immobilized by the failure to ascend to aspired heights. "Dürer himself . . . was, or at least thought he was, a melancholic in every possible sense of the word", Panofsky wrote. "He knew the 'inspirations from above', and he knew the feeling of 'powerlessness' and dejection" (Panofsky, 1955). Of the engraving, *Melencolia I*, Panofsky noted:

"It typifies the artist of the Renaissance . . . who [felt] 'inspired' by celestial influences and eternal ideas, but suffer[ed] all the more deeply from his human frailty and intellectual finiteness. . . . [I]n doing all this it is in a sense a spiritual self-portrait of Albrecht Dürer" (Panofsky, 1955, p. 171).

The interrelatedness of melancholia, spirituality and artistic creativity is also recognized in the engraving, *Allegory: An Old Philosopher Seated on Globe*, also known as *Melancholy*, by Jacob de Gheyn (1569–1629) (Figure 0-2). In this work we see a melancholic man "brooding on the terrestrial globe" (Wittkower & Wittkower, 1963, p. 9) under a somber night sky, as if pondering his place on earth and in the heavens. The Latin inscription (by Hugo Grotius) says:

"Atra, animaeque, animique lues atterima bilis
Saepe premit vires ingenii et genii."

(Melancholy, the most calamitous affliction of soul and mind
Often oppresses men of talent and genius)
(Wittkower & Wittkower, 1963, p. 9).

In Spanish art of that time, the association between depression and artistic creativity is depicted in *The Poet* (1620–1621), an etching by Jusepe de Ribera (Figure 0-3), perhaps "the first work of art to link poetry and melancholy" (Reed & Wallace, 1989, p. 281). Inspired by poetry, and surrounded by poets during his formative years in Paris, Joan Miró, the twentieth-century Spanish (Catalan) artist whose work provided the inspiration for this book, thought of himself as a painter-poet for whom painting was a vehicle for expressing his inner self—his soul.

0-2
JACOB DE GHEYN
ALLEGORY: OLD PHILOSOPHER SEATED ON GLOBE (also known as MELANCHOLY)
Engraving
Metropolitan Museum of Art, The Elisha Whittelsey Collection; The Elisha Whittelsey Fund, 1949

As his grandson David Fernández Miró wrote in 1989, providing us with selected glimpses of the artist, "Miró's relationship with poetry was born with him. He never made any distinction between poetry and painting, except in their material forms of expression. . . ." (D.F. Miró, 1989, p. 240). And he went on to note, "The work of Miró was the plastic equivalent of the work of his poet friends. His titles themselves are pure poetry. . . ." (D.F. Miró, 1989, p. 241). In the words of the artist, ". . . paintings with very poetic titles. Creating a parallel between poetry and painting . . ." (J. Miró, 1936, cited in D.F. Miró, 1989, p. 240).

Further, describing Miró, his grandson David noted:

"In his youth, he was impressed by the Spanish mystics, in particular, Teresa

0-3
JUSEPE RIBERA
THE POET, 1620–21
Etching, 6⅜ × 5 in
(16.2 × 12.6 cm)
Metropolitan Museum of Art, Harris Brisbane Dick Fund, 1930

of Jesus and John of the Cross, who were always with him in spirit—no unusual thing in a personality such as that of Miró, gifted with a brilliant sense of perception of the universe around him: from a blade of grass to the tallest tree, from the light of a glow-worm to the moon and the sun, everything made a strong and yet tender impression on him and he was unable to avoid expressing this in his work. . . . the magic instant caught in flight, and the achievement of something transcendental and perceptible with that magic that is here but that most mortals scarcely catch—these constitute the essence and the truth, partners in the ceaseless evolution—with all its doubts and anxieties—of true artists like Miró who appear so infrequently. . . ." (D.F. Miró, 1989, p. 240).

Concerning Miró's first visit to Paris, his grandson David wrote: "Miró was overcome by Paris. . . . he was unable to paint, though he knew that the fire was being kindled in his tragic and taciturn nature that was beset with moments of profound sadness, doubt and loneliness" (D.F. Miró, 1989, p. 240). He goes on to note that Miró spoke of the ". . . need to escape from the deeply tragic side of [his] temperament . . ." (J. Miró, cited in D.F. Miró, 1989, p. 240). "However, despite this inner tension", his grandson continued, "Miró believed in predestination, in the unknown, in magic, in oriental wisdom, which circulated through his soul like a gift of Providence that he had not asked for but which was there and which he could sense" (D.F. Miró, 1989, p. 240). Although not commonly associated with Albrecht Dürer, many of the themes found in Dürer's master engraving *Melencolia I*—isolation, loneliness, despair, depression, dissatisfaction with earthbound limitations

and the yearning to ascend to celestial heights—are issues with which Miró struggled in his life and which he captured in his art.

This book, conceived and produced as an homage to Joan Miró, consists of four parts. Part I, on the relationship between "Mood Disorders and Artistic Creativity", provides an overview of this subject that may help to inform future scholarship on Miró and his art. In recognition of the central role of spirituality in the art of Joan Miró, Part II presents a series of essays by artists, art historians and art critics on "The Spiritual in Modern Art". Part III "Joan Miró" deals with aspects of the life and work of this master of twentieth-century art, focusing on his spirituality, his temperament, his depression and his struggles with his identity, both as a person and as an artist, that went on for much of his life. Part IV is on the "Abstract Expressionists of the New York School", a group of artists who rose to prominence in the middle of this century. Profoundly influenced by Miró, their work stands as a lasting tribute to the great Catalan master.

Homage to Joan Miró.

REFERENCES

Andreasen, N.C. & Glick, I.D. (1988). Bipolar affective disorder and creativity: implications and clinical management. *Comprehensive Psychiatry*, **29**(3), 207–217.

Andreasen, N.C. (1978). Creativity and psychiatric illness. *Psychiatric Annals*, **8**, 113–119.

Andreasen, N.C. (1987). Creativity and mental illness: prevalence rates in writers and their first-degree relatives. *American Journal of Psychiatry*, **144**(10), 1288–1292.

Andreasen, N.C. & Canter, A. (1974). The creative writer: psychiatric symptoms and family history. *Comprehensive Psychiatry*, **15**, 123–131.

Andreasen, N.C. & Canter, A. (1975). Genius and insanity revisited: psychiatric symptoms and family history in creative writers. In *Life History Research Psychopathology*, Eds R. Wirt, G. Winokur and M. Roth, pp. 187–210. University of Minnesota Press, Minneapolis.

Andreasen, N.C. & Powers, P.S. (1974). Creativity and psychosis: a comparison of cognitive style. *Archives of General Psychiatry*, **32**, 70–73.

Eliade, M. (1991). *Images and Symbols, Studies in Religious Symbolism*. Princeton University Press, Princeton, NJ.

Hershman, D.J. & Lieb, J. (1988). *The Key to Genius: Manic-depression and the Creative Life*. Prometheus Books, New York.

Jamison, K.R. (1989). Mood disorders and patterns of creativity in British writers and artists. *Psychiatry*, **52**, 125–134.

Jamison, K.R. (1990). Manic-depressive illness, creativity and leadership. In *Manic Depressive Illness*, Eds F.K. Goodwin & K.R. Jamison, pp. 332—367. Oxford University Press, New York.

Jamison, K.R. (1993). *Touched with Fire: Manic-depressive Illness and the Artistic Temperament*. Free Press Macmillan, New York.

Klibansky, R., Saxl, F. & Panofsky, E. (1964). *Saturn and Melancholy*. Basic Books, New York.

Kuspit, D. (1993). *Signs of Psyche in Modern and Postmodern Art*. Cambridge University Press, New York.

Lipsey, R. (1988). *An Art of Our Own: The Spiritual in Twentieth-century Art*. Shambhala, Boston.

Ludwig, A.M. (1995). *The Price of Greatness—Resolving the Creativity and Madness Controversy*. Guilford Press, New York.

Miró, D.F. (1989). Jottings: literature as a constant factor in the life of Joan Miró. In *109 llibres amb Joan Miró*. Fundació Joan Miró, Barcelona.

Neumann, E. (1959/1974). *Art and the Creative Unconscious*. Bollingen Series LXI, Princeton University Press, Princeton, NJ.

O'Connor, F.V. (1986). Depressive elementalism and modernism: a postmodern meditation. *Art Criticism*, **2**, 43–56.

O'Connor, F.V. (1987). The psychodynamics of modernism: a postmodernist view. In *Psychoanalytic Perspectives on Art*, Ed. M.M. Gedo, Analytic Press, Hillsdale, NJ.

Panofsky, E. (1955). *The Life and Art of Albrecht Dürer*. Princeton University Press, Princeton, NJ.

Reed, S.W. & Wallace, R. (1989). *Italian Etchers of the Renaissance & Baroque*. Museum of Fine Arts, Boston, MA.

Richards, R. (1981). Relationship between creativity and psychopathology: an evaluation and interpretation of the evidence. *Genetic Psychology Monographs*, **103**, 261–324.

Rosenblum, R. (1975). *Modern Painting and the Northern Romantic Tradition: Friedrich to Rothko.* Harper & Row, New York.

Rothenberg, A. (1990). *Creativity and Madness—New Findings and Old Stereotypes*, Johns Hopkins University Press, Baltimore.

Schildkraut, J.J. (1982). Miró and the mystical in modern art: problems for research in metapsychiatry. *American Journal of Social Psychiatry*, **II**(4), 3–20.

Schildkraut, J.J. & Hirshfeld, A.J. (1995). Mind and mood in modern art I: Miró and "Melancolie". *Creativity Research Journal*, **8**(2), 139–156.

Schildkraut, J.J., Hirshfeld, A.J. & Murphy, J.M. (1994). Mind and mood in modern art II: depressive disorders, spirituality and early deaths in the Abstract Expressionist artists of the New York School. *American Journal of Psychiatry*, **151**, 482–488.

Schimmel, A. (1993). *The Mystery of Numbers.* Oxford University Press, New York.

Storr, A. (1985). *The Dynamics of Creation*, Atheneum, New York.

Tuchman, M. & Freeman, J. (1986). *The Spiritual in Art: Abstract Painting 1890–1985.* Los Angeles County Museum of Art/Abbeville Press, New York.

Winnicott, D.W. (1965). *The Maturational Process and the Facilitating Environment.* International Universities Press, New York.

Wittkower, R. & Wittkower, M. (1963). *Born under Saturn.* Norton, New York.

PART I
MOOD DISORDERS AND ARTISTIC CREATIVITY

INTRODUCTION

JOSEPH J. SCHILDKRAUT

In Part I the evidence for an association between mood disorders (depression and manic-depressive illness) and artistic creativity is presented by Nancy Andreasen in her chapter, "Creativity and Mental Illness: A Conceptual and Historical Overview", and by Kay Jamison in her chapter, "Mood Disorders, Creativity and the Artistic Temperament". The findings they present demonstrate that mood disorders and artistic creativity tend to co-occur, and that this association appears to be familial and possibly genetically transmitted. Andreasen proposes the hypothesis that underlying traits related to personality and cognitive style might help to account for the co-occurrence of mood disorders and artistic creativity. While plausible, this hypothesis remains to be tested and, in any event, it clearly does not exclude other possible contributing factors. Jamison, in her chapter, comments on how difficult it has been for many individuals to accept the association between mood disorders and artistic creativity despite the mounting evidence supporting this association. This issue, particularly in relation to Miró, arose on many occasions during the course of planning for the symposium in Barcelona, and it remained unresolved throughout the symposium.

In his chapter "Art and Creativity: Neuropsychological Perspectives", Jordi Obiols provides a scholarly, broad-ranging, speculative dissertation drawing on the fields of ethology, psychology and neurophysiology. Cristóbal Gastó then presents a case study of the influential Catalan artist, J.M. de Sucre. In the last chapter of Part I, Carl Salzman considers the issues involved in "Treating the Depressed Artist".

CHAPTER 1

CREATIVITY AND MENTAL ILLNESS: A CONCEPTUAL AND HISTORICAL OVERVIEW

NANCY C. ANDREASEN

THE ACT OF CREATION

"Ἐν αρχη ην ο λογοσ,
και ο λογοσ ην προσ τον θεον,
και θεοσ ην λογοσ."

*(In the beginning was the word,
And the word was with God,
And the word was God.)
(John **i**.1, 2).*

As the above quotation reminds us, the process of creation may be considered the most fundamental component of the universe. "Logos", translated as "word" in the King James Bible, really means something like "elemental plan, conceptual structure, rational principle, generative power". The textured concept of logos is both a part of "the ground of all being" (as Paul Tillich referred to God), and ultimately *is* the ground of all being.

This presentation grows both from my experience as a humanist engaged in a variety of literary pursuits and from my experience as a psychiatrist engaged in the study of the structural and functional activity of the normal brain and its disruptions in a variety of mental illnesses. Consequently, the presentation will link these two interests, beginning with a consideration of the nature of creativity itself, followed by a discussion of the relationship between creativity and psychopathology.

THE NATURE OF THE CREATIVE PROCESS

Contemplating the nature and process of creativity raises three basic questions: What causes it? What nurtures it? What destroys it? Although we do not have any definitive answers to these questions, they are worth stating simply because they raise issues that are fundamental to understanding what are the best and worst capacities in human nature.

In addition, there is a variety of associated questions which are more accessible through empirical investigation. Raising these questions may provide us with a secondary entry into the three primary questions raised above, which are less accessible to direct investigation and more in the realm of philosophy. Do creative people have a characteristic cognitive style? Do creative people have a characteristic personality style? Is creativity a unitary concept or a basic substrate, like general intelligence? If so, what causes it to differentiate? Do people in different creative fields differ in cognitive or personality style? The implied answer to many of these rhetorical questions is "Yes". Since traits such as cognition and personality are difficult to measure precisely, these questions will be addressed using informal observations based on interviews with a series of creative individuals—principally writers—conducted over the past several decades. These informal observations were gleaned during a more formal structured study of the relationship between creativity and mental illness, described in the second section of this chapter.

THE CREATIVE PROCESS AND PERSONALITY

A recent interview that I did with a well known writer summarized especially clearly some of the traits that define the interaction between the creative process and personality. Four quotations from this interview, which articulates some of the features of the creative process, are listed in Table 1-1.

"*I slip into a state that is apart from reality.*" In order to create many writers and other artists slip into a state of intense concentration and focus. In psychiatric terms, this would be described as a "dissociative state," that is, the person in a sense separates from himself or herself and metaphorically "goes to another place". In ordinary language the person might be said to be no longer "in touch with reality". In a subjective sense, however, the creative individual is moving into another reality, which is a deep shaft of consciousness into which he or she disappears. This experience of "disengagement", "intense focus" or "being in another place" is probably somewhat analogous to the altered states described by the great mystics. Once there, the artist may remain for hours on end, living in a world that is a mixture of nebulous floating concepts and forms that are gradually turned into a material object that ultimately becomes the creative product, be it a poem, a play or a painting. This capacity to focus intensely, to dissociate and to realize an apparently remote and transcendent "place" is one of the hallmarks of the creative personality when in the midst of the creative process.

T A B L E 1 - 1

CHARACTERISTICS OF THE CREATIVE PERSON AND PROCESS

"I slip into a state that is apart from reality".

"I don't write consciously— it is as if the Muse sits on my shoulder".

"My mind wanders—even when I talk".

"I've always felt as if I'm invisible".

"*I don't write consciously—it is as if the Muse sits on my shoulder.*" Creativity is not a rational logical process. Although organization, structure and planning do contribute to designing the overall shape of a play, a building or a painting, the essence of a creative product cannot be consciously planned or willed into existence. The notion of the muse, or the need for inspiration, is much more than a metaphor. Most creative individuals express over and over the fact that during the process of creating an idea, which occurs in "that place", they are simply expressing unconscious thoughts and processes. They are prone to make statements such as "I don't know where it comes from; it just happens". The particular writer whose specific remarks appear in Table 1-1 actually stated that he never knows how the particular play that he is writing is going to end until he finishes the last few scenes and bits of dialogue. He smiled and said, "If I knew how it was going to come out in advance, it would probably ruin the play, since I would be giving the audience clues that would tip them off and spoil the psychological suspense that builds to the final ending".

"*My mind wanders—even when I talk*". Creative people are more prone to be flooded with ideas and thoughts, and also less likely to censor them, since they are the stuff of which their art is made. As we understand more and more about how the brain works in our current age of neuroscience, we may observe that creative individuals have a different quality or quantity of attentional mechanisms mediated through midline brain structures such as the reticular activating system, the thalamus or the cingulate gyrus. In the older language of cognitive psychology, the inability to censor input either from within or from without has been referred to as a defective or altered "filtering mechanism". Whatever the process, within the creative individual this is experienced as producing a steady input of ideas which may be somewhat fragmented and formless. To an outside observer, the person may seem to move rapidly from one topic to another. In viewing the external world, this same mechanism may lead to heightened perceptions, greater sensitivity to external stimuli and a heightened intensity of experience.

"I've always felt as if I'm invisible". Just as creative people have a tendency to concentrate intensely to the point of dissociation, they also often have the capacity to be a disengaged and dispassionate observer. To others they may seem aloof, detached or even cold and hard. To themselves they often feel as if they are watching the rest of the world without others even knowing about it. This may seem to run counter to the flamboyance displayed by some creative individuals, which may appear to be seeking attention rather than invisibility; nevertheless, many creative people, even when flamboyant, express a subjective sense that they can see into other people without being watched. In a sense, they have the ability to spy on the universe.

CREATIVITY, COGNITION AND PERSONALITY TRAITS

These various aspects of the creative process can be described through a set of adjectives that loosely define the temperament and cognitive style of creative people. These traits appear to represent a basic substrate that defines the creative individual and are relatively independent of the medium of creativity. That is, these traits are common to creative individuals who work in fields as diverse as mathematics, physics, poetry or the visual arts. These personality and cognitive traits are fundamental to the creative process, are linked to the subjective experiences described above, and make the creative individual more vulnerable to fluctuations in mood and perhaps to developing mood disorders.

Personality traits that define the creative individual include adventuresomeness, rebelliousness, individualism, sensitivity, playfulness, simplicity and persistence. Creative people are prone to engage in exploratory behavior, which may push the limits of social conventions. They dislike externally imposed rules, seemingly driven by their own set of rules derived from within. Paradoxically, however, this indifference to conventions is combined with sensitivity. Conceptually, sensitivity may take two forms, either sensitivity to what others are experiencing or sensitivity to what the individual himself or herself is experiencing. Creative people tend to be high on both aspects. Inevitably, this combination of pushing the edge and experiencing strong feelings will lead to a sense of injury and pain. Nevertheless, creative people also have traits that make them durable and capable of perseverance. The adventuresomeness and rebelliousness are coupled with playfulness, which possesses an inherent joyfulness. Creative people also have an ability to persist in spite of repeated rebuffs. Persistence is absolutely fundamental, since creative people typically experience repeated rejection because of their tendency to push the limits and to perceive things in a new way. Young poets, playwrights or painters must experience being turned down, and they must retain the capacity to keep going in spite of very little external validation of their worth. These traits are joined to a basic simplicity, which is defined by a single-ness of vision and dedication to their art. At some levels, their work is really all they care about.

These personality traits are combined with a characteristic set of cognitive traits. These include a lack of preconceptions (or ego boundaries), intellectual openness, intense curiosity, intense concentration, obsessionality, perfectionism and high levels of energy. Clearly, these cognitive traits are related to personality and may explain many of the personality characteristics that creative people possess, as well as their vulnerability to fluctuations in mood.

Creative people tend to approach the world without preconceptions. The obvious order and rules that are so evident to less creative people, and which give a comfortable structure to life, often are not there for the creative individual, who tends to see things in a different and original way. This lack of commonalty with the rest of the world may produce feelings of alienation or loneliness. In addition, the lack of evident and obvious standards of perception or information produces a blurring of the boundaries of identity, sometimes referred to in psychoanalytic terminology as ego boundaries. Creative people also tend to be intensely curious. They like to understand how and why, to take things apart and put them back together again, to move into domains of the mind or spirit that conventional society perceives as hidden or forbidden. Their curiosity also has a driven and energetic quality. Once absorbed in an idea or topic, they pursue it with a dogged intensity. This intellectual persistence can move into a preoccupation with detail that has an obsessional and perfectionistic quality to it. They must work on a topic, project or idea until they "get it right".

INTERVENING VARIABLES AND THE MANIFESTATION OF CREATIVITY

A predisposition to creativity may be defined by these various traits. But whether the capacity for creativity is ever brought to fruition, and the nature of the creative product, may be a matter of chance. The soil upon which the seed falls may be barren or infertile. Teachers and family members may treasure the creative spirit or find it abhorrent. A great mind or spirit may be born in a time or place that overwhelms it with the stifling effects of ignorance, poverty or oppression. Fifth-century Greece or fifteenth-century Florence nurtured creativity, while twentieth-century Bosnia or Somalia would be likely to destroy it. Gender may have an inhibiting or mediating effect as well. Although women are almost certainly born with as much innate creative ability as men, the striking paucity of women who have achieved at high levels down through the centuries probably reflects the social oppression to which they have been subject. Fortunately, twentieth-century society, at least in some regions of the world, is rectifying this inequity, which could potentially double our available human creative capacities.

Other variables may intervene in

order to determine how creativity is expressed in a given individual. Specific forms of training may shape particular individuals to move in a given direction, such as music versus science. Intellectual abilities, which are probably distinct from creative capacities, may also shape creativity. That is, some individuals are more gifted in verbal skills, while others are more gifted in visual or spatial skills, potentially leading the former to express their creative abilities as writers and the latter as visual artists. Finally, simple physical abilities such as eyesight, stature or motor coordination may shape creativity. A creative person who is born into an athletically graceful body or endowed with dextrous hands is more likely to become a dancer or musician than a person born into a handicapped or clumsy body. Toulouse-Lautrec could never have become Nijinsky.

CREATIVITY AND MENTAL ILLNESS

A predisposition to mental illness has often been discussed as a possible factor that could also be related to creativity. This association has been noted for many centuries. For example, Aristotle (trans. 1953) commented in the *Problemata* that "Those who have been eminent in philosophy, politics, poetry and the arts have all had tendencies toward melancholia". The near proverbial statement that "there is a fine line between genius and insanity" was perhaps first stated in heroic couplets by John Dryden (cited in Bredvold et al, Eds, 1956) in *Absalom and Achitophel*:

"Great wits are sure to madness near allied;
And thin partitions do their bounds divide."
(pp. 163–4)

The upsurge of romanticism in the nineteenth century led to a widespread preoccupation with the possible association, as many writers and artists pushed the limits by experimenting with alcohol and drugs and sometimes experienced premature and tragic deaths. Poems such Keats' *Ode to Melancholy* or Coleridge's *Kubla Khan* seem to suggest that the road to Xanadu is paved with pain and suffering. Cesare Lombroso (1891) wrote a widely quoted book on hereditary genius, arguing that the capacity for creativity was closely linked to psychopathology and tended to be transmitted as a "hereditary taint". Many famous families seem to prove the rule—the Coleridges, the James', the Huxleys and the Mills, for example.

Anecdotal studies do not, however, constitute compelling evidence. If one starts with a hypothesis and looks only for proof to support it, credibility is suspect if subjected to the scrutiny of scientific skepticism. Havelock Ellis (1926) was among the earliest to attempt an objective empirical study of the association. This early study appears weak in retrospect, but it was the first attempt to identify a sample of individuals in a relatively unbiased manner. Ellis used as his sample the 1020 individuals who were cited in the *Dictionary of National Biography*. Among these 1020 individuals, he noted that 4.2% were "insane", that 5% had personality disorders, that 8% were melancholic, and that 16% had been in prison. Viewed retrospectively, this study clearly has many limitations, a perhaps inevitable consequence of being the first empirical and scientific study of the topic. Diagnostic evidence is minimal, and terminology is imprecise. The choice of the *Dictionary of National Biography* as the resource for identifying individuals with "genius" is a weak strategy, since it is likely to identify people who are eminent, but not necessarily people who are creative. This bias is reflected, for example, in the large numbers of individuals who had been in prison.

Several studies attempted to rectify some of these weaknesses, and as well to determine the truth of Lombroso's original hypothesis that genius and insanity were transmitted together as a hereditary taint. Working in Germany, Adel Juda (1949) studied both individuals who were eminent in the arts and those who were eminent in the sciences. She noticed relatively high rates of illness in both groups, as well as a hint that mental illness might be transmitted in the families of creative individuals. For example, among creative artists (writers, painters, etc.), she noted a 2.7% rate of schizophrenia, a 22% rate of personality disorders, and a 1.8% rate of suicide. Rates of psychosis in parents and siblings ranged from 3 to 4%, while both groups of first degree relatives had approximately a 13% rate of personality disorders. Given that the study lacked a control group, however, the numbers are somewhat difficult to interpret.

In a study published in *Hereditas*, J.L. Karlsson (1970) used epidemiological methods similar to those implemented by Ellis, but took advantage of the population registries available in Scandinavian countries in order to improve diagnostic precision. In this particular study Karlsson used patients suffering from psychosis in Iceland, as identified by population registries, as his primary sample. He then determined how many of their relatives were creative, using a listing in Iceland's *Who's Who* as his objective measurement. He noted that 13% of the relatives of schizophrenics were listed, while 23% of the relatives of manic depressives were listed. These rather high rates suggest a possible genetic transmission for creativity, as well as a strong association between manic depressive illness and creativity, but also a remarkably high association with schizophrenia. The major disadvantage of this study was its relatively weak method for identifying creativity, in that a listing in Iceland's *Who's Who* is not a particularly powerful measure.

During this era when scientific and empirical strategies began to be applied to the study of the association between mental illness and creativity, a major debate arose as to whether the association was with a particular type of mental illness. Karlsson's data showed a rather strong association with both schizophrenia and manic depressive illness, but a preferential increase in manic depressive illness. At around this same time, Leonard Heston (1966) completed a well-designed study of the genetics of schizophrenia, using a powerful paradigm known as the "adopted offspring technique". This particular technique attempts to separate nature and nurture by looking at the adopted children of people who have a particular condition; in Heston's study the condition was schizophrenia. Heston evaluated the adopted children of mothers who suffered from schizophrenia, comparing their rates of schizophrenia with those of the adopted children from mothers not known to have any mental illness. In this study he noted that the adopted children of schizophrenic mothers, who were reared in families without psychopathology, had an increased rate of schizophrenia as compared to adopted children of normal mothers. As a peripheral observation, Heston also noticed that the adopted children of schizophrenic mothers seemed to have an increased rate of creative or artistic hobbies as compared to the children from the control group, and he proposed that people who were creative and people who were schizophrenic might share a similar genetic endowment, with the severe manifestations being expressed as schizophrenia and the mild as creativity.

In this context, Thomas McNeil (1971) conducted a particularly good study in Scandinavia using the adopted offspring paradigm. This study was given a slightly different twist, however, in that McNeil studied adopted individuals who pursued creative or semi-creative occupations as his primary sample. He then determined the prevalence of mental illness in these individuals, as well as the prevalence of illness in their biological and adoptive parents. This study has contributed a variety of observations. First, among the adopted individuals themselves (known as "probands" in epidemiological jargon), he noted that the probands had a high rate of mental illness. He subdivided his subjects into two groups; the "highly creative" individuals had achieved a high level of success in a particular field, as documented by playing in major orchestras, publishing a number of books of poetry or novels, or producing art objects hung in major galleries. "Semi-creative" individuals included journalists, photographers, music teachers, and others who were less clearly high achieving. Among the highly creative probands, 30% were noted to have some type of mental illness, with the majority being given diagnoses of "constitutional psychotopathy". The rate among the semi-creative individuals was 10%. In addition, McNeil noted a very high rate of illness in the biological parents of these adopted individuals (28% among the highly creative and 8% among the semi-creative), while the adoptive parents who raised these children had a relatively low rate, as did

their siblings (5 and 0%). These results appear to provide rather strong support for a familial transmission of both creativity and mental illness, which is independent of environmental factors. One of the major strengths of the adopted offspring paradigm is that it separates nature and nurture by examining individuals who potentially carry a genetic trait (i.e. as measured in the biological parents) but who are reared in an environment not predisposed to the development of that trait (i.e. as measured in the adoptive parents).

These studies set the stage for our own work on the relationship between creativity and mental illness. They had suggested a somewhat strong association, but also had a variety of methodological weaknesses that we sought to correct. Weaknesses included the lack of a carefully selected control group, lack of standardized diagnostic criteria, and lack of an objective definition of creativity that most individuals would accept. Our studies of the relationship between creativity and mental illness were conducted at the University of Iowa Writer's Workshop between approximately 1970 and 1985. The Writer's Workshop is the oldest creative writing program in the USA, as well as the best recognized. Many famous writers have served in this program either as students or faculty. Examples include Robert Lowell, John Cheever, Kurt Vonnegut, Philip Roth, Stanley Elkin, John Irving and Anthony Burgess. The workshop has a small permanent faculty and a large number of rotating faculty, who come to teach for a semester or a year. The opportunity to interview and evaluate workshop faculty provides a microcosm for studying artistic creativity in a particular genre, such as poetry or novels. Although the sample is clearly not random, it probably has a reasonably limited bias, since faculty are selected primarily on the basis of eminence.

The study was conducted in two phases. During Phase I, published in 1974, both faculty and teaching/writing fellows (i.e. candidates for doctoral degrees) were evaluated (Andreasen & Canter, 1974). During Phase II, subjects were limited primarily to rotating faculty members (Andreasen, 1987). Phase I was conducted prior to the development of the Diagnostic and Statistical Manual (DSM) of the American Psychiatric Association; it was also initiated prior to the publication of the Research Diagnostic Criteria (RDC) (Spitzer et al, 1978; American Psychiatric Association, 1980). Consequently, a set of predefined diagnostic criteria were developed in order to make diagnoses in this sample. In addition, a structured interview was developed, which was specifically tailored to the study of creativity and the assessment of psychopathology in creative individuals. A control population was identified that consisted of individuals known to be educationally equivalent to the writers, but not to have any specific creative interests or abilities. The occupations of the control sample included a diversity of fields, such as hospital administration, social work and medicine.

The goals of the workshop study were to determine whether creative writers had an increased incidence of psychopathology and whether their first-degree relatives (i.e. parents and siblings) had an increased incidence of either psychopathology or creativity. Diagnoses among family members were made using the Family History Research Diagnostic Criteria (Andreasen et al, 1977). The hypotheses that informed Phase I of the study derived from the prevailing ethos of the time. That is, the working hypothesis was that the writers themselves would have a low rate of mental illness, but that their first-degree relatives would have an increased rate of schizophrenia. As the writers were interviewed successively, a striking and surprising finding emerged. The writers themselves had a high rate of mood disorder rather than schizophrenia, and their first-degree relatives had very high rates of both mood disorders and creativity. The results of Phase I were published in *Comprehensive Psychiatry* and provided the first empirical documentation for an association between mood disorders and creativity, as well as the first careful empirical documentation that creativity and mood disorders tend to co-occur familialy (Andreasen & Canter, 1974). The results of Phase II, which built on the strengths of Phase I and added the use of widely standardized diagnostic criteria (i.e., DSM-III), are summarized in Tables 1-2, 1-3 and 1-4 (Andreasen, 1987).

As Table 1-2 indicates, the writers had a significant increase in any type of bipolar disorder, any type of mood (affective) disorder and alcoholism, as compared to the control group. Bipolar disorder refers to a type of mood disorder in which individuals experience both "highs" and "lows". Although these fluctuations may be mild and therefore considered subclinical, the majority of the subjects in this study required treatment of some type. The majority of the patients with a bipolar disorder were "bipolar II", which refers to a condition where depressions are relatively severe but the highs are not sufficient to require hospitalization. Thirteen per cent were, however, "bipolar I", a very severe form of mood disorder that usually does require hospitalization. None of the subjects had schizophrenia.

TABLE 1-2
LIFETIME PREVALENCE OF MENTAL ILLNESS IN WRITERS AND CONTROL SUBJECTS

RDC diagnosis	Writers (N = 30)		Control subjects (N = 30)		χ^2	P
	N	%	N	%		
Any affective disorder	24	80	9	30	13.20	0.001
Any bipolar disorder	13	43	3	10	6.90	0.01
Bipolar I disorder	4	13	0	0		n.s.
Bipolar II disorder	9	30	3	10		n.s.
Major depressive disorder	11	37	5	17		n.s.
Schizophrenia	0	0	0	0		n.s.
Alcoholism	9	30	2	7	4.01	0.05
Drug abuse	2	7	2	7		n.s.
Suicide	2	7	0	0		n.s.

Entries with no χ^2 value had expected frequencies less than 5; Fisher's exact test was used in these cases. From Andreasen (1987), © 1987, the American Psychiatric Association, reprinted by permission.

Turning to family members of writers, one notes that they also have a very high rate of mood disorder. As compared to the control subjects, the writers have a significant or near-significant increase in bipolar mood disorder, depression, any mood disorder, and any illness in their first degree relatives (Table 1-3). As shown in Table 1-4, however, not only do the writers have an increased rate of mood disorder, but they also have an increased rate of creativity in their first-degree relatives. As in the McNeil study, subjects were divided into those that had mild or moderate levels of creativity and those who had high levels of creativity. Although the relatives did not differ in the former, they did differ in the latter and also when all levels of creativity were pooled. If one looks at a "genetic map" of the family members of each writer, then it becomes clear that the families of these writers were virtually "shot through" with either creativity or mood disorder. Very few of the writers in the sample were free of what might be called either the "hered-

itary taint" or the "hereditary gift". Most writers had at least one family member who was either creative or had a mood disorder.

This sample contained a number of families in which various family members displayed different kinds of creativity. The "probands", or "index cases", were writers, but the types of creativity observed in family members were quite diverse. Some were dancers, others were musicians, others were painters, others were inventors and still others were mathematicians or physicists. This observation lends credence to the hypothesis that creativity is a cognitive or personality trait that is transmitted, and that its specific manifestation may vary according to environmental influences and physical endowments.

A final topic explored in Phase I of the study was the relationship between creativity and intelligence. The results of this facet of the study are summarized in Table 1-5. All subjects were given two different IQ tests, the Weschler Adult Intelligence Scale

TABLE 1-3

MENTAL ILLNESS IN FIRST-DEGREE RELATIVES OF 30 WRITERS AND 30 CONTROL SUBJECTS

	All relatives						Parents						Siblings					
	Of writers (N = 116)		Of control subjects (N = 121)				Of writers (N=60)		Of control subjects (N = 60)				Of Writers (N=56)		Of control subjects (N = 121)			
Family history RDC diagnosis	N	%	N	%	χ^2	P	N	%	N	%	χ^2	P	N	%	N	%	χ^2	P
ANY AFFECTIVE DISORDER	21	18	3	2	14.21	0.001	10	7	1	2	6.41	0.001	11	20	2	3	6.35	0.01
BIPOLAR DISORDER	4	3	0	0		0.056	1	2	0	0		n.s.	3	5	0	0		n.s.
MAJOR DEPRESSION	17	15	3	2	9.84	0.01	9	5	1	2	5.35	0.05	8	14	2	3		0.05
ALCOHOLISM	8	7	7	6	0.01	n.s.	5	8	4	7		n.s.	3	5	3	4		n.s.
SUICIDE	3	3	0	0		n.s.	2	3	0	0		n.s.	1	2	0	0		n.s.
ANY ILLNESS	49	42	10	8	34.77	0.001	25	42	5	8		0.00003	24	43	5	8	17.00	0.001

Entries with no χ^2 value had expected frequencies less than 5; Fisher's exact test was used in these cases. From Andreasen (1987), © 1987, the American Psychiatric Association, reprinted by permission.

TABLE 1-4

PREVALENCE OF CREATIVITY IN FIRST-DEGREE RELATIVES OF 30 WRITERS AND 30 CONTROL SUBJECTS

	Relatives of writers		Relatives of control subjects			
Relatives' creativity[a]	N	%	N	%	χ^2	P
ALL RELATIVES	116	100	121	100		
+CREATIVE	20	33	11	18		n.s.
++CREATIVE	12	20	5	8	4.85	0.05
TOTAL CREATIVE	32	53	16	27	9.10	0.01
PARENTS	60	100	60	100		
+CREATIVE	5	8	3	5		n.s.
++CREATIVE	7	12	2	3		n.s.
TOTAL CREATIVE	12	20	5	8		n.s.
SIBLINGS	56	100	61	100		
+CREATIVE	15	27	8	13		n.s.
++CREATIVE	8	14	3	5		n.s.
TOTAL CREATIVE	23	41	11	18	6.44	0.01

[a]+Creative = somewhat creative; ++creative = well-recognized level of achievement. Entries with no χ^2 value had expected frequencies less than 5; Fisher's exact test was used in these cases. From Andreasen (1987), © 1987, the American Psychiatric Association, reprinted by permission.

TABLE 1-5
SCORES ON INTELLIGENCE TESTS OF 15 WRITERS AND 15 CONTROL SUBJECTS

| | Score | | | | | |
| | Writers | | Control subjects | | | |
Test	Mean	SD	Mean	SD	t	P
WAIS	123.7	9.3	121.2	7.1	0.82	n.s.
Verbal IQ	126.4	10.6	122.8	3.5	1.25	n.s.
Performance	116.9	13.5	116.1	13.7	0.16	n.s.
Verbal minus performance	9.5	16.6	6.7	13.4	0.51	n.s.
Similarities scale	13.8	2.4	14.3	1.7	−0.61	n.s.
Vocabulary scale	15.3	1.8	13.1	1.2	3.89	0.0006
Picture completion scale	12.4	2.7	12.0	1.6	0.49	n.s.
Raven Progressive Matrices (advanced set)	25.3	7.1	25.6	7.3	−0.11	n.s.

From Andreasen (1987), © 1987, the American Psychiatric Association, reprinted by permission.

(WAIS) and the Raven Progressive Matrices (RPM) (Raven, 1977; Wechsler, 1983). The WAIS is the most widely used intelligence test in the USA, while the RPM was developed in the UK and is designed to be a "culture-free" IQ test. The results of these two studies are essentially identical. Both the writers and controls had IQs in the "high normal" range, with means around 125. The WAIS can be divided into two components, a verbal component and a performance component. The verbal component is weighted toward verbal skills and information that is coded in verbal materials (e.g. ability to define words, verbal abstraction) while the performance component tests primarily skills that are spatial and visual. There are no differences between the writers and the control subjects on verbal and performance IQ. The only significant difference is in vocabulary, a very expected finding, given that the writers work in a medium that requires fine honing of skills for selection and

knowledge of word meaning.

SUMMARY AND CONCLUSION

These findings suggest that there is indeed a link between creativity and mental illness. The early Iowa work has now been replicated by many other investigators, such as Jamison and Akiskal, whose work is represented in other chapters in this volume. Creativity and mental illness appear to co-occur within individuals and also in their family members, suggesting that there is a hereditary predisposition to both traits. What does this association mean?

Based on both empirical data and on personal interviews with writers about their personality and cognitive style, I suspect that the predisposition to creativity and mental illness tends to co-occur because it reflects an underlying personality and cognitive style which predisposes to both creativity and mood disorder. This personality and cognitive style is characterized by traits that make an individual original, open and exploratory, but also leaves them vulnerable to suffering. These traits have been discussed earlier, and include a lack of ego boundaries, intellectual openness, intense curiosity, intense concentration, obsessionality, perfectionism, high levels of energy, adventuresomeness, rebelliousness, individualism and sensitivity. People with such traits tend to be both original and highly productive, but they also tend to be physiologically and emotionally vulnerable. When these traits function well, they lead to art and science. When they function badly or excessively, they may lead to the highs and lows of mania and depression. To be endowed with these traits can be both a great gift and a great burden.

ACKNOWLEDGEMENTS

This research was supported in part by NIMH Grants MH31593, MH40856 and MHCRC 43271, The Nellie Ball Trust Fund, Iowa State Bank and Trust Company, Trustee; and a Research Scientist's Award, MH00625.

REFERENCES

American Psychiatric Association, Committee on Nomenclature and Statistics (1980). *Diagnosis and Statistical Manual of Mental Disorders (DSM-III)*. American Psychiatric Association, Washington, D.C.

Andreasen N.C. (1987). Creativity and mental illness: prevalence rates in writers and their first-degree relatives. *Am. J. Psychiat.*, **144**(10), 1288–1292.

Andreasen, N.C. & Canter, A. (1974). The creative writer: psychiatric symptoms and family history. *Compr. Psychiat.*, **15**, 123–131.

Andreasen, N.C. Endicott, J., Spitzer, R.L. et al (1977). The reliability and validity of the family history method using Family History Research Diagnostic Criteria (FH-RDC). *Arch. Gen. Psychiat.* **34**, 1229–1235.

Aristotle: (Translated by W.S. Hetts, 1953). *Problemata*, Vol 2. Cambridge, Cambridge University Press.

Dryden, J. (1956). *Absalom & Architophel*, in *Eighteen Century Poetry and Prose*, 2nd Edn, Eds, L.I. Bredvold, A.D. McKillop & L. Whitney. Ronald Press: New York.

Ellis, H.A. (1926). *A Study of British Genius*. London, Houghton-Mifflin.

Heston, L.L. (1966) Psychiatric disorders in foster home reared children of schizophrenic mothers. *Br. J. Psychiat.*, **112**, 819–825.

Juda, A. (1949). The relationship between highest mental capacity and psychic abnormalities. *Am. J. Psychiat.*, **106**, 296–307.

Karlsson, J.L. (1970). Genetic association of giftedness and creativity with schizophrenia. *Hereditas*, **66**, 177–182.

Lombroso, C. (1891). *The Man of Genius*. London, Walter Scott.

McNeil, T.F. (1971). Prebirth and postbirth influence on the relationship between creative ability and recorded mental illness. *J. Personality*, **39**, 391–406.

Raven, J.C. (1977) *Advanced Progressive Matrices*. Psychological Corporation, Harcourt Brace Jovanovich, New York.

Spitzer, R.L. Endicott, J. & Robins, E. (1978). Research Diagnostic Criteria: rationale and reliability. *Arch. Gen. Psychiat.* **35**, 773–782.

Wechsler, D. (1983). Wechsler Adult Intelligence Scale. The Psychological Corporation, Harcourt Brace Jovanovich, New York.

CHAPTER 2

MOOD DISORDERS, CREATIVITY AND THE ARTISTIC TEMPERAMENT

KAY REDFIELD JAMISON

A possible link between madness and genius is one of the oldest and most persistent of cultural notions; it is also one of the most controversial. There are several ways to examine the relationship. Biographical studies focus on life-study investigations of prominent writers, artists and composers. Research in the late nineteenth and early twentieth centuries, for example, provided anecdotal but suggestive evidence of significantly increased rates of mood disorders and suicide in eminent writers and artists and their first-degree relatives. Recently, more systematic biographical research has given strong support to a much higher rate of mood disorders in artistic populations than could be expected from chance alone. Diagnostic and psychological studies of living writers and artists, conducted during the past 20 years, give more scientifically meaningful estimates of the rates and types of psychopathology in groups of artists and writers. Finally, studies of creative and related achievement in affectively ill patients provide corroborating evidence from a different perspective, as do family studies of psychopathology and creative accomplishment. We shall examine, in turn, the findings from each of these types of investigations.

There are, of course, many problems in studying the relationship between mood disorders and artistic achievement. Biographical studies—while intrinsically fascinating and irreplaceable, deeply instructive sources of information about moods, their extremes and their roles in the lives of artists—are fraught with difficulties. Writers and artists, however brutally honest they may be in some of their self-assessments, are frequently blinded and biased as well. The reliability of their letters, journals and memoirs can be limited because they are written from a single perspective or fully mindful of future biographers and posterity. Biographers, too, write with strong slants and under the influence of prevailing or idiosyncratic viewpoints. Historical context and existing social customs also determine which behaviors are culled out or emphasized for comment. Certain life-styles provide cover for deviant and bizarre behavior, and the arts, especially, have long given latitude to extremes in behavior and mood. The assumption that within artistic circles madness, melancholy and suicide are somehow normal is prevalent, making it difficult at times to ferret out truth from expectation. Biographical or posthumous re-

This chapter is based on K.R. Jamison (1993). Could it be madness—this? In *Touched With Fire: Manic-depressive Illness and the Artistic Temperament.* Copyright © 1993 by Kay Redfield Jamison. Reprinted with permission of The Free Press, an imprint of Simon & Schuster, New York.

search carries with it other problems as well. Any historical perspective necessarily dictates that a listing of highly accomplished, affectively ill individuals will be only a partial one—illustrative but by no means definitive. Always, in the analysis of individual lives, problems arise. It is fairly easy to identify any number of major nineteenth-century British or American poets who were manic-depressive, for example, but it is more difficult to determine what proportion of the total pool of "great poets" they represent. (In many instances, of course, the individuals under study are sufficiently important to be interesting in their own right, independent of any general grouping.) Also, more detailed information exists for some individuals than for others (for example, those more in the public eye, those existing in relatively recent times, or those writing more extensively about themselves).

The tendency for highly accomplished individuals to be, almost by definition, inordinately productive and energetic creates problems of another sort—a bias toward the under-diagnosis of the manic side of manic-depressive illness. Biographical studies indicate that writers, artists and composers often describe in great detail their periods of melancholy or depression, but that other aspects of mood swings, such as hypomania, and even at times overt psychosis, are subsumed under "eccentricity", "creative inspiration" or "artistic temperament". Thus, many individuals with clear histories of profound or debilitating depressions are labeled "melancholic" rather than manic-depressive, despite their episodic (and often seasonal) histories of extremely high energy, irritability, enthusiasm and increased productivity levels (periods often also accompanied by costly lapses in financial, social and sexual judgment).

Paradoxically, the more chronically hypomanic the individual, the more noticeable and relatively pathological the depression will appear. Diagnostic biases in the opposite direction also occur. Some researchers have tended to overdiagnose manic-depressive illness because they observe patterns of behavior common to both hypomania and normal accomplishment (for example, enthusiasm, high energy and the ability to function with little sleep) and then label as manic-depressive anyone displaying these "symptoms".

Despite the difficulties in doing diagnostic studies based on biographical material, valid and highly useful research can be done by using in a systematic way what is known about manic-depressive illness: its symptomatic presentation (for example, pronounced changes in mood, energy, sleep, thinking and behavior), associated behavior patterns (such as alcohol and drug abuse, pathological gambling, pronounced and repeated financial reversals and chaotic interpersonal relationships), suicide (70–90% of all suicides are associated with manic-depressive or depressive illness; therefore, if an individual has committed suicide, it is almost always the case that a mood disorder was at least contributory), its natural course (an episodic, cyclic course of symptoms, with normal functioning in between; usual onset of symptoms in the late teens or early twenties, with temperamental signs often exhibited much earlier; seasonal aspects to the mood and energy changes; and, if untreated, a worsening of the illness over time), and, very important, a family history, especially in first-degree relatives (parents, siblings or children), of depression, mania, psychosis or suicide. Other psychiatric and medical conditions that can have similar symptoms (for example, thyroid and other metabolic disturbances, drug-induced states, organic brain syndromes or complex partial seizures and related epileptic conditions) need to be considered, and ruled out, as well. Making a retrospective diagnosis is, in many ways, like putting together the pieces of an elaborate psychological puzzle or solving a mystery by a complicated but careful marshaling of elements of evidence. Biographical diagnoses must ultimately, of course, be more tentative than diagnoses made on living individuals, but they *can* be done, reliably and responsibly, and with an appreciation of the complexities that go into anyone's life, most especially the life of an artist. (Ultimately it should prove possible to extract DNA from hair or tissue samples and make more definitive posthumous diagnoses.)

Several case-history studies of psychopathology in eminent writers and artists were conducted during the late nineteenth and early twentieth centuries—for example, those done by Francis Galton, Cesare Lombroso, J.F. Nisbet and Havelock Ellis—but it is only more recently that systematic biographical research has been carried out. Adele Juda, who studied 113 German artists, writers, architects and composers, was one of the first to undertake an extensive, in-depth investigation of both artists and their relatives (Juda, 1949). Her research was hampered somewhat by ambiguous inclusionary criteria (that is, how the subjects were chosen) as well as inadequate diagnostic methods, which led to an inevitable confusion between schizophrenia and manic-depressive illness.

Juda's study remains an important one, however, both for its scope (more than 5000 individuals were interviewed during the course of 17 years) and its attempt to bring rigor to a highly subjective field. Juda found that although two-thirds of the 113 artists and writers were "psychically normal", there were more suicides and "insane neurotic" individuals in the artistic group than could be expected in the general population. The highest rates of psychiatric abnormality were found in the poets (50%) and musicians (38%); lower rates were found in painters (20%), sculptors (18%) and architects (17%). The brothers, sisters and children of those in the artistic group were much more likely to be cyclothymic, commit suicide or suffer from manic-depressive illness than were individuals in the general population; psychosis was far more common in the grandchildren of the artistic group as well.

In another biographical study, Colin Martindale (Martindale, 1972, 1990) examined the lives of 21 eminent English poets (born between 1670 and 1809) and 21 eminent French poets (born between 1770 and 1909). More than one-half (55%) of the English poets and 40% of the French had a history of significant psychopathology (for example, "nervous breakdowns", suicide or alcoholism), and fully one in seven poets had been institutionalized in an asylum or had suffered from severe "recurring and unmistakable symptoms" such as hallucinations or delusions. Combining the expected general population rates for the two major psychoses, schizophrenia and manic-depressive illness, yields a combined rate of only 2%; because, as we shall see, virtually all of the psychosis in creative individuals is manic-depressive rather than schizophrenic in nature, an expected base rate of 1% is probably a more appropriate comparison. Whichever figure is used, the expected rate is far less than that shown by the poets in Martindale's sample. Other researchers, including W.H. Trethowan, who looked at the lives of 60 composers (Trethowan, 1977), and Joseph Schildkraut, A.J. Hirshfeld and

J.M. Murphy, who studied 15 visual artists from the Abstract Expressionists of the New York School (Schildkraut & Hirshfeld, 1990; Schildkraut et al, 1994), have found that approximately one-half of their subjects suffered from depressive or manic-depressive illness. Trethowan found that approximately one-half of the composers had a "melancholic temperament", and that mood disorders were "easily the commonest and most important of psychiatric illnesses". This represents an almost tenfold increase in affective illness over what could be expected by chance alone. That 40% of the artists in the study by Schildkraut et al (1994) actually received psychiatric treatment is significant as well, as research indicates that only one person in three with affective illness seeks help for it. Likewise, the suicide rate among the artists (2 out of 15) is at least 13 times the general rate; it is considerably higher (another 13%) if single-vehicle car accidents are thought of as suicide equivalents (which they may be in some instances).

Arnold Ludwig's recent study of individuals, biographies of whom had been reviewed in the *New York Times Book Review* over a 30-year period (1960–1990), is impressive for both its scope and careful methodology (Ludwig, 1992). Consistent with Juda's findings in German artists and mine in British writers and artists, Ludwig found that the highest rates of mania, psychosis and psychiatric hospitalizations were in poets; most significantly, a staggering 18% of the poets had committed suicide. Composers also showed high rates of psychosis and depression. Overall, when Ludwig compared individuals in the creative arts with those in other professions (such as businessmen, scientists, and public officials), he found that the artistic group showed two to three times the rate of psychosis, suicide attempts, mood disorders and substance abuse. The rate of forced psychiatric hospitalization in the artists, writers and composers was six to seven times that of the non-artistic group.

To study the occurrence of mood disorders and suicide in a consecutive sample of poets born within a 100-year period, I examined autobiographical, biographical and medical records (where available) for all major British and Irish poets born between 1705 and 1805. As might be expected, a wide range of biographical, medical and family history information was available within this group of 36 poets. For some, such as Lord Byron, both the quantity and quality of the material was excellent; for others, such as Robert Fergusson, John Bampfylde and William Collins, the information, especially of a psychiatric nature, was far less complete. The available letters, books and medical records were examined for symptoms of depression, mania, hypomania and mixed states; seasonal or other patterns in moods, behavior and productivity; the nature of the course of the illness (for example, age of onset, duration and patterns of recurrence over time); and evidence of other psychiatric or medical illnesses (for example, syphilis) that might confound the diagnostic picture. A strong emphasis was placed upon both the severity and the recurrence of symptoms; in all cases it was the *patterning* of mood, cognitive, energy, sleep and behavioral symptoms that formed the focus of study. The family histories of the poets, although more difficult to ascertain, were similarly analyzed.

A strikingly high rate of mood disorders, suicide and institutionalization occurred within this group of poets and their families. Six (William

Collins, Christopher Smart, William Cowper, Robert Fergusson, John Codrington Bampfylde and John Clare) were committed to lunatic asylums or madhouses, a rate easily 20 times that of the general population living during the same time period. Two others (Thomas Chatterton and Thomas Lovell Beddoes) committed suicide. More than one-half of the poets showed strong evidence of mood disorders. Fourteen, or more than one in three of the poets, seem likely to have suffered from manic-depressive illness (Christopher Smart, William Cowper, George Darley, Robert Fergusson, Thomas Chatterton, William Blake, Samuel Taylor Coleridge, George Gordon, Lord Byron, Percy Bysshe Shelley, John Clare, Hartley Coleridge, Thomas Lovell Beddoes and James Clarence Mangan). Of these 14 poets, the majority exhibited psychotic symptoms at one time or another, two committed suicide, and four were committed to asylums. William Collins and John Codrington Bampfylde, who also were committed to asylums, were probably manic-depressive as well, but only the melancholic side of Collin's illness is unequivocally documented and few details are available about the nature of Bampfylde's problems. Six poets—Oliver Goldsmith, Robert Burns, Walter Savage Landor, Thomas Campbell, John Keats and Robert Stephen Hawker—probably had milder forms of manic-depressive illness (cyclothymia or bipolar II disorder), although Keats and Burns died before it became clear what the ultimate severity and course of their mood disorders would have been. Samuel Johnson, Thomas Gray, George Crabbe and Leigh Hunt suffered from recurrent depression. A comparison with rates of manic-depressive illness in the general population (1%), cyclothymia (1–2%) and major depressive disorder (5%) shows that these British poets were 30 times more likely to suffer from manic-depressive illness, 10–20 times more likely to be cyclothymic or to have other milder forms of manic-depressive illness, more than five times as likely to commit suicide, and at least 20 times more likely to have been committed to an asylum or madhouse. These rates, while markedly elevated, are consistent with findings from the other biographical studies that we have reviewed; they are also consistent with results from more recent studies of living writers and artists that are discussed later in this chapter. The genetic nature of mood disorders is underscored by the family histories in many of the poets of depression, mania, suicide, violence or insanity (for example, in the families of Byron, Gray, Cowper, Chatterton, Bampfylde, the Coleridges and Campbell; and, suggestively, in the families of Johnson, Crabbe, Blake, Clare, Beddoes and Mangan). Not without reason did Robert Burns (see Bett, 1952) write: "The fates and character of the rhyming tribe often employ my thoughts when I am disposed to be melancholy. There is not, among all the martyrologies that ever were penned, so rueful a narrative as the lives of the poets".

Biographical studies such as the ones we have been discussing provide one kind of evidence, persuasive in its own right, about the link between mood disorders and artistic creativity. Modern studies of living writers and artists give a different perspective; their findings are, however, quite consistent with those obtained through the case-history, or biographical, methods. Nancy Andreasen and her colleagues at the University of Iowa were the first to undertake scientific diagnostic inquiries into the relationship between creativity and psychopathology in living writers (Andreasen & Canter, 1974; Andreasen & Powers, 1975; Andreasen, 1987). Their studies, using structured interviews, systematic psychiatric diagnostic criteria and matched control groups, represented a marked methodological improvement over prior anecdote-based research, as well as over the earlier studies that failed to distinguish adequately between types of psychopathology (especially manic-depressive illness and schizophrenia). The size of the sample of writers was relatively small (30), and the writers were at varying levels of creative achievement (all were participants in the University of Iowa Writers' Workshop, one of the most prestigious in the nation; some were nationally acclaimed but others were graduate students or teaching fellows not yet at the level of national or international recognition). Andreasen notes that because she studied only writers, her results cannot be generalized to other groups of creative individuals, such as philosophers, scientists or musicians. Although this is true, and writers may be disproportionately likely to have affective disorders, the homogeneity of her sample is certainly valuable in its own right.

The writers demonstrated an extraordinarily high rate of affective illness. Fully 80% of the study sample met formal diagnostic criteria for a major mood disorder. By contrast, 30% of the control sample (individuals whose professional work fell outside the arts but who were matched for age, education, and sex) met the same criteria. The statistical difference between these two rates is highly significant, $P < 0.001$; that is, the odds of this difference occurring by chance alone are less than one in a thousand. Although the lifetime prevalence of mood disorders in the control group is much less than in the group of writers, it still represents a rate much greater than could be expected in the general population (5–8%). It is unclear whether this is due to an over-representation of affective illness in the sample (for example, it could reflect the tendency, discussed later, for individuals who are better educated and from the upper social classes to suffer disproportionately from manic-depressive illness) or because the diagnostic criteria were over-inclusive for both the creative and control groups. Of particular interest, almost one-half the creative writers met the diagnostic criteria for full-blown manic-depressive illness, bipolar I, or its milder variant, bipolar II (major depressive illness with a history of hypomania). Over one-third of the writers had experienced at least one episode of major depressive illness, and two-thirds of the ill writers had received psychiatric treatment. The writers' suicide rate was also greatly in excess of the general population's. Indeed, all five of the suicides that were reported occurred in either the writers or their first-degree relatives; none occurred in the control group. None of the writers or control subjects met the diagnostic criteria for schizophrenia; this is scarcely surprising, given the generally disorganizing and dementing quality of the illness, but it is significant in light of earlier claims that schizophrenia and creativity were closely allied. In fact, Andreasen, a prominent schizophrenia researcher, went into her study of writers in the belief that she would find a correlation between schizophrenia and creativity, not between mood disorders and creativity.

Other studies of living writers and artists have also found a greatly elevated rate of mood disorders in the artistically gifted, thus confirming the work of Andreasen and her colleagues. Hagop Akiskal and his wife Kareen, for example, have recently completed extensive psychiatric interviews of twenty award-winning European writers, poets, painters and sculptors. Their study, which has not yet been published, found that recurrent cyclothymic or hypomanic tendencies occurred in nearly two-thirds of their subjects; all told, 50% of the writers and artists had suffered from a major depressive episode. Preliminary data from another study by the Akiskals (done in collaboration with David Evans of Memphis State University), show similar findings in blues musicians (Hagop Akiskal, personal communications, September 20 1988 and February 1 1990).

Several years ago, while on sabbatical leave at St George's Medical School in London and the University of Oxford, I studied a group of 47 eminent British writers and artists (Jamison, 1989). I was interested in looking at rates of treatment for mood disorders within these groups, as well as seasonal patterns of moods and productivity, the nature of intensely creative episodes, the similarities between such episodes and hypomania, and the perceived role of very intense moods in the work of the writers and artists. The poets, playwrights, novelists, biographers and artists in my study were selected on the basis of their having won at least one of several major prestigious prizes or awards in their fields. All the painters and sculptors, for example, were either Royal Academicians or Associates of the Royal Academy, honors established by King George III in 1768 and held at any given time by a very limited number of British painters, sculptors, engravers and architects. Literary prizes used as selection criteria included the Queen's Gold Medal for Poetry, and the Hawthornden, Booker and James Tait Black Memorial prizes. Significantly,

nine of the 18 poets were already represented in *The Oxford Book of Twentieth-Century English Verse*. Of the eight playwrights, six were winners of the New York Drama Critics' Award or the Evening Standard (London) Drama Award; several had won both, had won one of these awards more than once, or had also received Tony awards.

The focus of the study was on the role of moods in the creative process, not on psychopathology; this fact was made clear to all potential subjects in order to minimize the possibility that individuals with mood disorders would be more likely to participate. Although my study required a considerable amount of time and effort on the part of highly successful and busy individuals, the rate of acceptance was surprisingly high, more than matching the standards for rates of response for such types of research. All the writers and artists were asked detailed questions about a history of treatment for depressive or manic-depressive illness; seasonal or diurnal patterns, if any, in their moods and productivity; behavioral, cognitive and mood correlates of their periods of most creative work; and their perceptions of the role of very intense moods in their work. Specific psychiatric diagnostic criteria were not used in this study, as the aim was to determine the actual rates of treatment; this is a more stringent criterion of illness severity than whether or not an individual meets the diagnostic criteria for mood disorders.

A very high percentage of the writers and artists (38%) had been treated for a mood disorder. Of those treated, three-quarters had been given antidepressants or lithium or had been hospitalized. Poets were the most likely to have required medication for their depression (33%) and were the only ones to have required medical intervention (hospitalization, electro-convulsive therapy, lithium) for mania. Fully one-half of the poets had been treated with drugs, psychotherapy and/or hospitalization for mood disorders. The playwrights had the highest total rate of treatment for depression (63%), but a relatively large percentage of those treated, more than half, had been treated with psychotherapy alone. It is unclear whether this was due to a difference in the severity of illness or to treatment preference.

With the exception of the poets, the artists and writers reported being treated for depression only, not mania or hypomania; the design of the study did not allow systematic diagnostic inquiry into the frequency of mild manic or hypomanic episodes. Approximately one-third of the writers and artists reported histories of severe mood swings that were essentially cyclothymic in nature. One in four reported having experienced extended elated mood states. Novelists and poets more frequently reported the prolonged elated states; playwrights and artists, on the other hand, more often reported severe mood swings. The relatively low rate of treatment for affective illness in those individuals in the predominantly non-verbal fields (painting and sculpture) is interesting, and it may be that they are less inclined than writers to seek psychiatric help. The total number of painters and sculptors in my study is small, however, and it is difficult to generalize from preliminary findings.

Virtually all the creative writers and artists (89%) said they had experienced intense, highly productive and creative episodes. This included all the poets, novelists and artists, and all but one of the playwrights. Only one of the five biographers, however, reported experiencing such episodes. The most fre-quent duration of these episodes was two weeks, with half of them lasting between one and four weeks. These "intensely creative" episodes were characterized by pronounced increases in enthusiasm, energy, self-confidence, speed of mental association, fluency of thoughts and elevated mood, and a strong sense of well-being. A comparison of these changes with the DSM-III criteria for hypomania reveals that mood, energy and cognitive symptoms show the greatest degree of overlap between the intensely creative and hypomanic episodes. Several of the more behavioral changes typically associated with hypomania (hypersexuality, talkativeness, increased spending of money) were reported by only a minority of subjects.

In summary, the rate of treatment for affective illness (38%) was extremely high in this sample of distinguished British writers and artists. Lifetime prevalence rates for manic-depressive and depressive illness in the general population (as determined by the ECA study) are 1 and 5% respectively. The proportion of individuals who actually seek or receive treatment, even though they meet the formal diagnostic criteria for affective illness, is far smaller. Therefore, the findings of this study represent a conservative estimate of the actual rate of mood disorders in the sample. Myrna Weissman and her colleagues, for example, found that only 20% of individuals with a current psychiatric disorder had seen a mental health professional in the previous year (Weissman et al, 1981); other researchers have concluded that only one-third of affectively ill patients actually make a mental health visit of any kind (Shapiro et al, 1984). Similarly, although lithium is the presumptive treatment of choice for approximately 1% of the adult population, the actual utilization rate, as determined by R.G. McCreadie and D.P. Morrison in Scotland, is only 0.77 per 1000 (McCreadie & Morrison, 1985). Javier Escobar and his associates found that lithium was used by only 0.15% of the general population (Escobar et al, 1987). Both studies clearly indicate a gross under-utilization of lithium relative to the established prevalence of manic-depressive illness. Antidepressants, more frequently prescribed, were used by 2.5% of the ECA community sample of 15 000 individuals. These drug treatment figures are in marked contrast to those of the British writers and artists I studied, 6.4% of whom reported the use of lithium (this included 16.7% of the poets), and 23.4% of whom acknowledged having used antidepressants. The contrast in rates is even more pronounced if one considers that antidepressant use in general is far more common in women than men, yet the sample of writers and artists was predominantly male.

The British study revealed many overlapping mood, cognitive and behavioral (especially sleep) changes between hypomania and intense creative states, despite the fact that questions regarding one state were asked independently of those regarding the other and in a manner designed to minimize possible effects of suggestion. Cognitive and mood changes shared far more overlap than behavioral ones, indicating that the milder forms of hypomania may represent the more productive phases of affective illness. The affective continuum that ranges from normal states through hypomania and then mania is very important, but poorly understood. It remains unclear whether the overlap in cognitive and mood changes represents etiologically related syndromes or phenomenologically similar but causally unrelated patterns of expression. It also remains unclear the extent to which writers and artists are simply more sensitive than the general population to their own mood states, and therefore more able—and perhaps also more willing—to articulate and report them.

Ruth Richards and her colleagues at Harvard used a very different research design to study the relationship between creativity and psychopathology (Richards et al, 1988). They hypothesized that a genetic vulnerability to manic-depressive illness would be accompanied by a predisposition to creativity which, according to this hypothesis, might be more prominent among close relatives of manic-depressive patients than among the patients themselves. Such a compensatory advantage, they speculated, would be roughly analogous to the resistance of malaria found among unaffected carriers of the gene for sickle-cell anemia. To test their hypothesis, Richards and her associates selected 17 manic-depressive and 16 cyclothymic patients, along with 11 of their normal first-degree relatives, using criteria that would ensure inclusion of a spectrum of disorders. These patients and their relatives were compared with 15 normal control subjects and 18 controls who had a psychiatric diagnosis but no personal or family history of major affective disorder, cyclothymia, schizoaffective disorder, schizophrenia or suicide. Unlike other studies, which limited the definition of creativity only to significant, socially recognized accomplishment in the arts or sciences, this one attempted to measure the disposition toward originality manifested in a wide range of everyday endeavors. These investigators administered the Lifetime Creativity Scales, a previously validated instrument that assesses the quality and quantity of creative involvement in both work and leisure activities.

Richards and her colleagues found significantly higher combined creativity scores among the manic-depressive and cyclothymic patients, and their normal first-degree relatives, than among the control subjects. The normal-index relatives (of manic-depressive and cyclothymic patients) showed suggestively higher creativity than did the manic-depressive patients, and the cyclothymic patients were close to the normal relatives. The authors concluded:

"Overall peak creativity may be enhanced, on the average, in subjects showing milder and, perhaps, subclinical expressions of potential bipolar liability (i.e. the cyclothymes and normal first-degree relatives) compared either with individuals who carry no bipolar liability (control subjects) or individuals with more severe manifestations of bipolar liability (manic-depressives). . . . There may be a positive compensatory advantage . . . to genes associated with greater liability for bipolar disorder. The possibility that normal relatives of manic-depressives and cyclothymes have heightened creativity may have been overlooked because of a medical-model orientation that focused on dysfunction rather than positive characteristics of individuals. Such a compensatory advantage among the relatives of a disorder affecting at least 1% of the population could affect a relatively large group of people."

Somewhat related, though as yet still preliminary, research has also found an unusually high incidence of special abilities (for example, outstanding artistic, language and mathematical abilities) in a sample of children with manic-depressive illness (DeLong & Aldershof, 1983). Two British studies, one of architecture students and the other of chemistry students, found that higher academic and creative performance was associated with greater psychological disturbance and an increased use of mental health facilities (Lucas & Stringer, 1972; Banks et al, 1970). Neither study, however, specified diagnosis or types of psychopathology.

Further support for a link between creativity and mood disorders comes from several family studies. Andreasen, in her study of writers from the University of Iowa Writers' Workshop, also investigated the family histories of the writers and the control subjects. Consistent with the higher rate of mood disorders in the writers, her findings showed the rate of mood disorders in first-degree relatives (parents and siblings) was much higher for the writers than the controls. The overall rate for any type of psychiatric disorder was also much higher in the relatives of the writers than in the controls. Additionally, more first-degree relatives of writers (20%) showed histories of creative accomplishment than did relatives of the controls (8%).

The familial association between mental illness and creativity has been found in many other studies as well. Early, far less systematic investigations by Lombroso (1889), Galton (1891), Lange-Eichbaum (1932) for example, strongly suggested that both psychopathology and creative accomplishment permeated the family histories of eminent writers, composers and artists. Likewise, the pedigrees of several writers and composers—for example, those of Byron, Schumann, Woolf, Mary Shelley, Tennyson and the Jameses—also support a pronounced pattern of co-existing mood disorders and creative abilities, at least in certain highly accomplished families (Jamison, 1993). Juda's research findings, which were discussed earlier, are consistent with a familial association between mental illness and creativity as well. More recently Jon Karlsson, at the Institute of Genetics in Iceland, has shown that the first-degree relatives of psychotic patients, as well as the patients themselves, are far more likely than the general population to be eminent across many fields of artistic and intellectual endeavor (Karlsson, 1970, 1981, 1984). He also found that there was a significantly increased risk of mental illness in distinguished Icelandic scholars and their relatives. Although Karlsson has posited a familial relationship between schizophrenia and creativity, several researchers (Richards, 1981; Andreasen & Glick, 1988; Melvin & Mossman, 1988) have pointed out that his data actually show a very strong relationship between mood disorders, especially manic-depressive illness, and creativity.

These studies demonstrate that creativity and mental illness, especially mood disorders, tend to aggregate in certain families and not in others, but they do not decisively show that genetic factors are operating; that is, they show a family association but not necessarily that the characteristics under discussion are heritable. It could be, for example, that the family and its environment are exerting the primary influence, rather than the genetic inheritance itself. Thomas McNeil, using an adopted offspring research design, attempted to clarify this nature-versus-nurture problem (McNeil, 1971). All of McNeil's subjects were adults who had been adopted shortly after birth and were part of a larger Danish psychiatric genetics study. They were classified as being "high creative" (most of the individuals in this group had achieved national prominence in the arts), "above average", or "low creative"; their rates of mental illness were then compared with those found in their biological and adoptive parents. The rates of mental illness were highest in the "high" creative group and in their biological parents. The rates of psychopathology in the adoptive parents did not vary significantly from one level of adoptee creativity to another.

Despite the inevitable methodological problems that exist in all the studies discussed so far—the small number of individuals studied, types or lack of control groups, variable diagnostic and selection criteria and flawed measurement techniques—there is an impressive consistency across the findings. Many lines of evidence point to a strong relationship between mood disorders and achievement, especially artistic achievement. Biographical studies, as well as investigations conducted on living writers and artists, show a remarkable and consistent increase in rates of suicide, depression and manic-depressive illness in these highly creative groups. Figures 2-1 and 2-2 summarize these findings in a visual way. It can be seen that artistic groups, when compared with the expected rates for suicide and mood disorders in the general population, demonstrate up to 18 times the suicide rate, 8–10 times the rate of major depressive illness (indeed, because the Epidemiologic Catchment Area study found that major depression was more than twice as common in women, 7%, as in men, 2.6%, the rates of depression in the primarily male samples represented in Figure 2-1 are even more striking), and 10–40 times the rate of manic-depressive illness and its milder variants. (Although only 6.4% of the writers and artists in my 1989 study are represented in Figure 2-1 as

2-1
Mood disorders in writers
and artists.
Adapted from K.R.
Jamison, *Touched with
Fire*, 1993

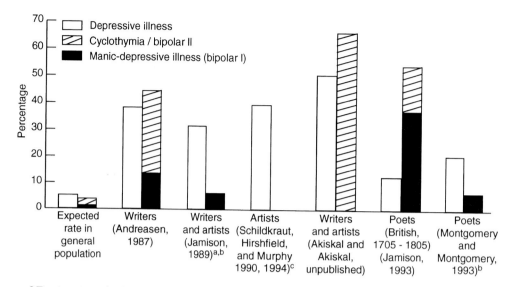

a Treatment rate (estimated to be one-third of the rate of illness). b Bipolar II and cyclothymia rates not ascertained. c Bipolar I, Bipolar II, and cyclothymia rates not ascertained

2-2
Suicide rates in writers
and artists.
Adapted from K.R.
Jamison, *Touched with
Fire*, 1993

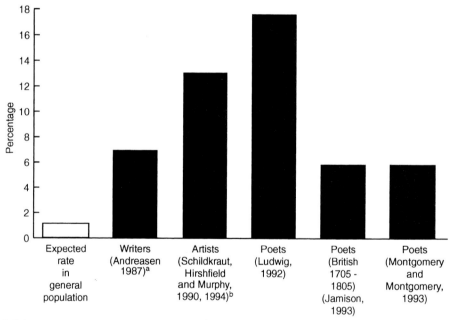

a Suicide rate at time of study completion. b Two other artists died in single vehicle accidents

having bipolar I illness, this is a spuriously low estimate; all of them had received medical intervention for mania, and epidemiological research indicates that only one person in three who meets the diagnostic criteria for manic-depressive illness actually seeks and receives treatment for it). Findings from other types of studies also point to a strong association between mood disorders and creativity. Manic-depressive patients, cyclothym-

ics and their first-degree relatives show higher levels of creativity than normal individuals, for example, and both creativity and affective illness have been found to co-exist at higher rates than expected in the first-degree relatives of writer and artists.

Given the historical as well as modern research support for a strong relationship between mood disorders and artistic creativity—"that fine madness" described centuries ago—

why does such heated controversy continue? The major resistance to an association between psychopathology, or mental illness, and creativity seems to focus on a few central points. The first is that many writers, artists, and composers are, or were, perfectly sane; therefore, the argument goes, the presumption of a strong link between mental illness and creativity is, on the face of it, absurd. Harold Nicolson (1947), in discussing the health of writers, makes the extreme point rather dryly:

"The theory that there exists some special connexion between literary genius and mental derangement is one which, to my mind, has been seriously exaggerated. It is true that a few creative writers have in their later years become demonstrably insane; it is also true that almost all creative writers have at some moments of their lives been panic-stricken by the conviction that their imagination was getting the better of their reason; but it is not in the least true that all creative writers have been mad all the time."

But of course no one would argue that all writers or artists, or even most of them, are actually mad; and, equally obviously, no one would seriously argue that even one, much less all creative writers had been mad all the time. But the fact that there is only a partial correlation does not mean that there is no correlation at all. Clearly there are many artists, writers and composers who are perfectly normal from a psychiatric point of view. The argument here is not that such people do not exist, for they obviously do. Rather, the argument is that a much-higher-than-expected rate of manic-depressive illness, depression and suicide exists in exceptionally creative writers and

artists. It is this discrepant rate that is of interest and that ultimately needs to be explained.

Another argument set forth against an association between "madness" and artistic creativity is that a bit of madness and turmoil is part and parcel of the artistic temperament, and that artists are just more sensitive to life and the experiences of life than are other people. This is almost certainly true, and it would be foolish to diagnose psychopathology where none or little exists. Such an argument, however, begs the issue. It is precisely this overlap between the artistic and manic-depressive temperaments that we are interested in looking at.

What is to be made of this tendency to deny a link between psychopathology and genius, to regard bizarre—and occasionally dangerous—behavior as somehow normal if it occurs in writers and artists? Is it simply an admirable tolerance for deviant and eccentric behavior if it occurs in individuals who are, by definition, already far from the normal temperamental and intellectual standards of human society? Or does it reflect a belief that artists may just be fulfilling society's and their own expectations that they ought to act the part of the "tormented genius"? Do the strains and anxieties of being an artist somehow create a special type of melancholy and oddness? These possibilities, while no doubt true to a certain extent, tend to disregard the possibility that individuals with temperaments liable to emotional extremes may be more likely to choose artistic careers, thereby increasing the chances of an interaction between a biological vulnerability and psychological stress. Likewise, they do not take into account the fact that the artists and writers under discussion here generally have shown emotional instability prior to the onset of their artistic careers and manifested a severity of psychiatric symptoms, an age of onset, and a pattern of mood disturbances highly characteristic of manic-depressive illness; they also have had greatly increased rates of depression, manic-depressive illness and suicide in their first-degree relatives.

Most of the controversy surrounding the "mad genius" versus "healthy artist" debate, however, arises from confusion about what is actually meant by "madness", as well as from a fundamental lack of understanding about the nature of manic-depressive illness. These two issues—controversy over the meaning of "madness" and confusion about the nature of one of the major "madnesses" (that is, manic-depressive illness)—are inevitably and closely bound together. Any attempt to arbitrarily polarize thought, behavior and emotion into clear-cut "sanity" or "insanity" is destined to fail; it defies common sense and it is contrary to what we know about the infinite varieties and gradations of disease in general and psychiatric illness in particular. "Madness", in fact, occurs only in the extreme forms of mania and depression; most people who have manic-depressive illness never become psychotic. Those who do lose their reason—are deluded, hallucinate, or act in particularly strange and bizarre ways—are irrational for limited periods of time only, and are otherwise well able to think clearly and act rationally. Manic-depressive illness, unlike schizophrenia or Alzheimer's disease, is not a dementing illness. It may on occasion result in episodes of acute psychosis and flagrant irrationality, but these bouts of madness are almost always temporary and seldom progress to chronic insanity. Yet the assumption that psychosis is an all-or-

nothing sort of phenomenon, and that it is stable in its instability, leads to tremendous confusion: Van Gogh, it is said, could not have been mad, as his paintings reflect lucidity of the highest order. Lucidity, however, is not incompatible with occasional bouts of madness, just as extended periods of normal physical health are not incompatible with occasional bouts of hypertension, diabetic crisis, hyperthyroidism, or any other kind of acute exacerbation of an underlying metabolic disease.

There is a great deal of evidence to suggest that, compared to "normal" individuals, artists, writers and creative people in general are both psychologically "sicker"—that is, they score higher on a wide variety of measures of psychopathology—and psychologically healthier (for example, they show quite elevated scores on measures of self-confidence and ego strength) (Jamison, 1993, pp. 300–301, n 78). Manic-depressive illness is an inherited vulnerability to a disease that can manifest itself in a wide range of fluctuating emotional states, behaviors, thinking patterns and styles and energy levels. Heightened passions and partial derangement of the senses tend to come and go, as Byron so drolly described: "I can never get people to understand that poetry is the expression of *excited passion*, and that there is no such thing as a life of passion any more than a continuous earthquake, or an eternal fever. Besides, who would ever *shave* themselves in such a state?" (George Gordon, Lord Byron, quoted in Marchand, 1978). The temperaments associated with manic-depressive illness are also part of the affective continuum, forming in turn a natural bridge between a virulently psychotic illness on the one hand and the moody, artistic temperaments on the other.

Finally, many critics who are opposed to the idea that psychopathology is linked to artistic ability express concern that labeling artists as mentally ill ignores the enormous discipline, will and rationality that are essential to truly creative work. In speaking of Goethe, for example, Thomas Carlyle (1971) wrote:

"This man rules, and is not ruled. The stern and fiery energies of a most passionate soul lie silent in the centre of his being; a trembling sensibility has been inured to stand, without flinching or murmur, the sharpest trials. Nothing onward, nothing inward, shall agitate or control him. The brightest and most capricious fancy, the most piercing and inquisitive intellect, the wildest and deepest imagination; the highest thrills of joy, the bitterest pangs of sorrow; all these are his, he is not theirs."

This emphasis on the need for control calls to mind the ancient admonition of Longinus (1965), who argued that "sublime impulses are exposed to greater dangers when they are left to themselves without the ballast and stability of knowledge; they need the curb as often as the spur". Poets, while beholden to the spur, have also been mindful of a need for the curb. John Keats (see Rollins, 1958), in response to a poem sent to him by Shelley, wrote:

"You, I am sure, will forgive me for sincerely remarking that you might curb your magnanimity and be more of an artist, and "load every rift" of your subject with ore. The thought of such discipline must fall like cold chains upon you, who perhaps never sat with your wings furl'd for six Months together. And is this not extraordina[r]y talk for the writer of Endymion? whose mind was like a pack of scattered cards. . . ."

Coleridge (see Watson, 1975), no stranger to the idea of scattered thoughts and unfurled wings, also underscored the absolute necessity for order and reason. "Poetry", he wrote, "even that of the loftiest, and seemingly, that of the wildest odes, [has] a logic of its own as severe as that of science; and more difficult, because more subtle, more complex, and dependent on more and more fugitive causes. In the truly great poets . . . there is a reason assignable, not only for every word, but for the position of every word".

The need for clear and logical thought is obvious but, as we discussed earlier, clarity and logic are perfectly compatible with the ebbings and flowings of manic-depressive illness and its associated temperaments. Indeed, whether out of a need to impose order upon a chaotic internal universe, or for other as yet unexplained reasons, many individuals with manic-depressive illness are inclined to be unusually obsessive and highly organized. And, while many ideas may be generated during mildly manic states, much of the structuring, editing, and fine-tuning of artistic work is carried out during normal or mildly depressed periods. Seamus Heaney (1980) described Robert Lowell's extraordinary ability to forge the raw material of his mind and emotions into finished art. Lowell, he wrote:

". . . had in awesome abundance the poet's first gift for surrender to those energies of language that heave to the fore matter that will not be otherwise summoned, or that might be otherwise suppressed. Under the ray of his concentration, the molten stuff of the

psyche ran hot and unstaunched. But its final form was as much beaten as poured, the cooling ingot was assiduously hammered. A fully human and relentless intelligence was at work upon the pleasuring quick of the creative act. He was and will remain a pattern for poets in this amphibiousness, this ability to plunge into his amphibiousness, this ability to plunge into the downward reptilian welter of the individual self and yet raise himself with whatever knowledge he gained there out on the hard ledges of the historical present."

REFERENCES

Andreasen, N.C. (1987). Creativity and mental illness: prevalence rates in writers and their first-degree relatives. *Am. J. Psychiat.*, **144**, 1288–1292.

Andreasen, N.C. & Canter, A. (1974). The creative writer: psychiatric symptoms and family history. *Compr. Psychiat.*, **15**, 123–131.

Andreasen, N.C. & Glick, I.D. (1988). Bipolar affective disorder and creativity: implications and clinical management. *Compr. Psychiat.*, **29**, 207–217.

Andreasen, N.C. & Powers, P.S. (1975). Creativity and psychosis: an examination of conceptual style. *Arch. Gen. Psychiat.*, **32**, 70–73.

Banks, C., Kardak, V.S., Jones, E.M. & Lucas, C.J. (1970). The relation between mental health, academic performance and cognitive test scores among chemistry students. *Br. J. Educat. Psychol.*, **40**, 74–79.

Bett, W.R. (1952). *The Infirmities of Genius*, p. 147. Philosophical Library, New York (with reference to Robert Burns' *Common Place Book*).

Carlyle, T. (1971). Goethe, in *Thomas Carlyle: Selected Writings*, Ed. A. Shelston, p. 37. Penguin, Harmondsworth.

DeLong, G.R. & Aldershof, A. (1983). Associations of special abilities with juvenile manic-depressive illness. *Annals of Neurology*, **14**, 362.

Escobar, J.I., Anthony, J.C., Camino, G., Cotler, L., Melville, M.L. & Golding, J.M. (1987). Use of neuroleptics, antidepressants and lithium by U.S. community populations. *Psychopharm. Bull.*, **23**, 196–200.

Galton, F. (1891). *Hereditary Genius: An Inquiry Into Its Laws and Consequences*, 5th Edn. Alexander Moring, London.

Heaney, S. (1980). Robert Lowell: A Memorial Address, *Agenda: Robert Lowell Special Issue*, **18**, 26.

Jamison, K.R. (1989). Mood disorders and patterns of creativity in British writers and artists. *Psychiatry*, **52**, 125–134.

Jamison, K.R. (1993). *Touched With Fire: Manic-depressive Illness and the Artistic Temperament*. Free Press, New York.

Juda, A. (1949). The relationship between highest mental capacity and psychic abnormalities. *Am. J. Psychiat.*, **106**, 296–307.

Karlsson, J.L. (1970). Genetic association of giftedness and creativity with schizophrenia. *Hereditas*, **66**, 177–182.

Karlsson, J.L. (1981). Genetic basis of intellectual variation in Iceland. *Hereditas*, **95**, 283–288.

Karlsson, J.L. (1984). Creative intelligence in relatives of mental patients. *Hereditas*, **100**, 83–86.

Lange-Eichbaum, W. (1932). *The Problem of Genius* (Trans. E. Paul and C. Paul). Macmillan, New York.

Lombroso, C. (1889). *L'Homme de Genie*. Alcon, Paris.

Longinus. (1965). On the sublime, in *Classical Literary Criticism: Aristotle, Horace, and Longinus* (Trans. T.S. Dorsch), p. 101. Penguin, Harmondsworth.

Lucas, C.J. & Stringer, P. (1972). Interaction in university selection, mental health and academic performance. *Br. J. Psychiat.*, **120**, 189–195.

Ludwig, A.M. (1992). Creative achievement and psychopathology: Comparisons among professions. *Am. J. Psychother.*, **46**, 330–356.

McCreadie, R.G. & Morrison, D.P. (1985). The impact of lithium in Southwest Scotland. I. Demographic and clinical findings. *Br. J. Psychiat.*, **146**, 70–74.

McNeil, T.F. (1971). Prebirth and post-birth influence on the relationship between creative ability and recorded mental illness. *J. Personality*, **39**, 391–406.

Marchand, L.A. (Ed.) (1978). *Byron's Letters and Journals*, Vol. 8, p. 146. John Murray, London.

Martindale, C. (1972). Father's absence, psychopathology, and poetic eminence. *Psychological Reports*, **31**, 843–847.

Martindale, C. (1990). *The Clockwork Muse: The Predictability of Artistic Change*. Basic Books, New York.

Melvin, J.A. & Mossman, D. (1988). Mental illness and creativity. *Am. J. Psychiat.*, **145**, 908.

Nicolson, H. (1947). The health of authors. *Lancet*, **11**, 709–714.

Richards, R.L. (1981). Relationships between creativity and psychopathology: an evaluation and interpretation of the evidence. *Genet. Psychol. Monographs*, **103**, 261–324.

Richards, R.L., Kinney, D.K., Lunde, I. & Benet, M. (1988). Creativity in manic-depressives, cyclothymes, and their normal first-degree relatives: a preliminary report. *J. Abnormal Psychol.*, **97**, 281–288.

Rollins, H.E. (Ed.) (1958). *The Letters of John Keats, 1814–1821*, Vol. 2, p. 323. Harvard University Press, Cambridge, MA.

Schildkraut, J.J. & Hirshfeld, A.J. (1990). Mind and mood in modern art: The New York School. *CME Syllabus and Proceedings Summary, American Psychiatric Association Annual Meeting*, New York, pp. 255–256.

Schildkraut, J.J., Hirshfeld, A.J. & Murphy, J. (1994). Mind and mood in modern art II. Depressive disorders, spirituality and early deaths in the abstract expressionist artists of the New York School. *Am. J. Psychiat.*, **151**, 482–488.

Shapiro, S., Skinner, E.A., Kessler, L.G., Von Korff, M., German, P.S., Tischler, G.L., Leaf, P.J., Benham, L., Cotler, L. & Regier, D.A. (1984). Utilization of health and mental health services: three epidemiologic catchment area sites. *Arch. Gen. Psychiat.*, **41**, 971–978.

Trethowan, W.H. (1977). Music and mental disorder. In *Music and the Brain*, Eds. M. Critchley and R.E. Henson. Heinemann, London.

Watson, G. (Ed.) (1975). *Biographia Literaria*, p. 3. Dent, London (with reference to Samuel Taylor Coleridge).

Weissman, M.M., Meyers, J.K. & Thompson, W.D. (1981). Depression and treatment, in a U.S. urban community, 1975–1976. *Arch. Gen. Psychiat.*, **38**, 417–421.

Chapter 3

ART AND CREATIVITY: NEUROPSYCHOLOGICAL PERSPECTIVES

Jordi E. Obiols

INTRODUCTION

In this chapter I will begin with certain general assumptions about the essence of artistic phenomena. Three suppositions, though arguable, I consider fundamental:

1. Among the deep roots of art we find ancestral behavior, which is primitive and archaic. Also, at the base and the origin of artistic phenomena we find a profound combination of special psychological states of an emotional character (transcendence, ecstasy and others) that relate art to the sacred and the religious experience.

2. Art entails, at a cognitive level, a duality between the creative and receptive, aspects of which would be the apprehension of general features or perception of totalities on one hand, and the appreciation of details which allows the analysis of distinct parts, on the other. This dialectic has been stated in different ways (intuition/reason, synthesis/analysis, sensibility/intellect).

3. Finally, and specific to artistic creativity, there must be an interaction between two elemental dimensions of the psychological world: the processes of control and spontaneity, of inhibition and release, and of adherence to a standard and its violation. No great art may be created without this fundamental dichotomy.

These three points will be respectively examined in light of the relationship between human behavior and: (a) subcortical neural structures; (b) differences in function of the two cerebral hemispheres; (c) the most anterior and the "highest" part of the brain, i.e. the prefrontal lobe. Finally, in the last section, a neurophysiological approach to creativity will be proposed.

ARCHAIC BEHAVIOR, TRANSCENDENT EXPERIENCE AND ART: RELATIONSHIP TO SUBCORTICAL STRUCTURES OF THE HUMAN BRAIN

"Let them paint with their heart, yes, with their heart, let them paint with suffering, with struggle. Let them paint with the brain but let the brain be dominated by the grand force of the sensible heart" (Joan Miró, 1977).

"Each of us is a living fossil, carrying within our genes a history that goes back to the beginning of humanity, and far beyond". This sentence from the geneticist Jones (1991) reminds us what many thinkers have felt for a long time. The human being, every human being, is not a "tabula rasa" when he or she is born. We carry something inside which appears throughout our lives, a phylogenetic load of behaviors, subjective experiences and neural structures which bind us, as individuals, to the rest of humanity and to the animal world.

In the field of psychology, it is probably C.G. Jung who, with his notion of the "archetypes", has dealt most deeply with this subject. To Jung, the archetypes are the sources of constitutionally predetermined behaviors; they are unconscious, genetically encoded dispositions that contribute, among other things, to the creation of "primordial images", common to all cultures and periods (Arnheim, 1980).

Ethology shows us, on the other hand, basic animal behaviors that have interesting relationships with what humans call "aesthetic", for example bird-song, with all its melodic and structural complexity. We know that this complexity is related to biological and social functions essential to the individual and to the species (territorial protection, group cohesion and recognition, warning about dangers, guidance for the younger animals, coupling, etc). The strategies for sexual seduction also involve a large variety of expressions (plumage, dances, movements, "decoration" of nests, etc.) that we may consider related to human seductive behaviors (make-up, hairdo, dressing, perfume, tone of voice, etc.) in what has been considered a real "art of pleasing" (Vigouroux, 1992).

Homologies can also be found in the structure of human and animal brains. Paul MacLean (1990) has emphasized the relevance of three anatomic–functional systems in the human brain, which he named the "triune brain"—a primitive or reptile brain, a paleomammal brain and a neomammal brain. To sum up, the reptile brain is formed by the striatal complex or basal ganglia, the paleomammal by the limbic system, and the neomammal by the neocortex of the cerebral hemispheres. The fundamental points of

MacLean's contribution which are relevant here are:

1.   Every formation represents a stage of the phylogenetic development of the central nervous system (CNS) and has its own intelligence and subjectivity, its own sense of time and space, its own memory.

2.   The three evolutionary formations can be imagined as three interconnected biological computers.

3.   The two oldest formations (mentalities) do not have the necessary apparatus for verbal communication. The neomammal formation is oriented primarily towards the outside world, with a progressive capacity for learning and problem-solving, and constitutes the neural substratum for the linguistic communication of subjective states.

Thus, the human brain has been developed to its large volume, while retaining the chemical traits and the anatomic organization of the three basic formations (reptile/paleo-mammal/neomammal). MacLean's view explains the survival of human behaviors that we end up calling "instinctive", "unconscious", "irrational", and that we can observe in the child, the primitive man and even the modern human adult.

As examples of prototypical behaviors, we can think about territorial behavior, regulated by paleomammal structures, which includes marking with urine by animals like dogs and cats; also, the protector visual marking that certain primates evidence by showing (the sentinel animal) the sexual member with a partial erection. MacLean reminds us that in mythology, the gods Pan, Priap, Amon and others are often described with a large phallus which is superstitiously given a protective power (see Figure 3-1). In

scendence and the sacred. A duality has been suggested in artistic activity: the particularity of the piece itself, of the individual who creates it, of his or her temporal circumstances and, at the same time, the universality, this inherent perennial quality that goes beyond the artist, his or her collectivity and his or her time. "A profoundly individual expression is anonymous. By being anonymous, it allows us to reach the universal. I am sure of it: the more local a thing is, the more universal it becomes", said Joan Miró (1959). This transcendence evokes the sacred and divine aspect of each human being.

3-1
MIN AMUN, c. 3000 BC
Egyptian Museum, Cairo.
© PA Jürgen Liepe

But what is the transcendent experience from the psychobiological point of view? Can we approach scientifically this human experience, which is, in essence, subjective, intimate and ineffable? Does it have a cerebral base? We must also ask ourselves: how can this "sacred" component of an experiential and emotional character, that we see as tied to the artistic experience, relate to the more thoughtful, rational components of the human being?

certain primitive cultures, stone statues that show the phallus in erection have been used to mark territorial limits. It is as if the urogenital visual symbol is a substitute for the urinary territorial marks of smell of the lower animals. Another example, in the case of defying behavior, is the tribe of the Asmat, where men and boys, when frightened, excited, euphoric or surprised, start a dance showing their penis which follows the same sequence as certain primates do (Gajdusek, 1970).

So we see how primitive behaviors, phylogenetically conditioned, are at the base of phenomena (visual marking, dancing) that we could classify as *proto-artistic*. Territory, sexuality (preservation of species) and death underlie founding myths and sacred feelings, and all of them constitute the source of art.

On the other hand, the study of the origins of human culture suggests a very close relationship between artistic activity and another fundamental component of the human spirit, the religious experience, the sense of *tran-*

Let us recall the triune brain concept, suggesting three anatomic–functional levels. In this structure, it is possible that "emotions" and "thoughts" may occur in an "independent way because they are products of different cerebral mechanisms" (MacLean, 1990). The limbic system can be understood as a modulator or generator of feelings involved in guiding behaviors required for self-preservation and preservation of the species. "It is of special significance that the limbic cortex has the capacity to generate feelings (free-floating, unspecific) that give a sense of what is real, true and important" (MacLean, 1990, p. 17). This idea draws evidence from the phenomenology of temporal lobe epilepsy (TLE) that can affect the inner part of the temporal lobe. During partial seizures, patients suffering from this kind of epilepsy experience a variety of symptoms, some of which are subjective or "experiential" and involve intense emotional states including paranoid type feelings, fear associated with depersonalization, derealization and strangeness, as well as gratifying sensations such as pleasure, ecstasy and triumph. As aspects of an interictal behavior syndrome or Geschwind Syndrome (Benson, 1991), some patients with long-standing TLE experience clairvoyance, certainty, conviction and revelations of truth. The latter are associated with a sense of cosmic, mystical consciousness and "discovery" experiences (such as the "eureka feeling"). These are sometimes "floating" experiences, that the epileptic cannot refer to specific contents.

It must be recalled here that schizophrenic patients can also experience "revelations"; normally they will integrate them in a more or less elaborated belief-system, i.e. the delusion. It is interesting to point out that recent research suggests, with increasing precision, that the temporal lobes are an important location of schizophrenic pathophysiology (Andreasen, 1986). In fact, a number of TLE patients have been described that show a "schizophreniform" syndrome or typical psychotic personality traits (Trimble, 1988).

A.J. Mandell (1980), following William James' ideas in *The Variety of Religious Experience* (James, 1985), defends the daring proposition that God is in the brain, that is, that we can track the neurophysiological basis of transcendent experience in the human brain. The TLE phenomenology, described above, is useful to demonstrate a relationship between activation of structures of the limbic system, such

as the amygdala, and subjective experiences of ecstasy, illumination, contact with God and religiousness. The pathophysiologic mechanisms of epilepsy could affect patients during simple partial seizures but, more frequently, through alterations of emotions and personality during the interictal period (Tisher et al, 1993).

We find an example of this with the great Russian writer Dostoyevsky. There is evidence to document his epilepsy (Gastaut, 1984). In his case, the loss of consciousness was preceded by an unusual premonitory aura, ". . . a brilliant feeling of ecstasy, of contemplation of God, associated with an exaltation of intellectual power, a sensation of infinite happiness". There are grounds for believing that Mohammed, St Paul, Moses and Van Gogh also suffered limbic seizures. As Bear (1991) puts it: "It appears that a temporal lobe focus in the superior individual may spark an extraordinary search for that entity we alternatively call truth or beauty".

The evidence of such mechanisms does not come exclusively from the study of TLE. Certain chemical substances with psychoactive properties such as amphetamines, cocaine and LSD (hallucinogenics in general) represent, for Mandell (1980), the "pharmacological bridge to transcendency". These drugs, as is known, have the capacity to provoke states of pleasure, excitement, ecstasy and also, especially with LSD, religious experiences of a transcendental nature. The fact that high doses of these drugs produce such effects in normal subjects suggest that these feelings are not only aspects of the pathology of TLE or schizophrenia but also characteristics of *latent mental mechanisms* of the *normal* human brain.

Therefore, we see that, under certain conditions, the activation or release of specific brain areas causes the sudden, "unexplainable" appearance of intense emotional states, of an ecstatic, transcendent nature and of "pure" feelings of revelation.

We find other examples of emotion–cognition dissociation in studies of cortical stimulation with electrodes (Penfield, 1975) and in particular cases of specific brain injuries: a syndrome of "visuo-emotional hyporeactivity" has been described as a consequence of a visual-limbic disconnection (right hemisphere damage together with a small injury in the deep left occipital lobe). Thus, an intact visual perception (left occipital hemisphere), failing to activate the limbic structures, loses emotional significance (Habib, 1986).

In sum, we have seen how certain subcortical structures, especially the amygdaloid complex within the limbic system and the basal ganglia, contribute to the anatomical and functional basis of primitive and emotional behaviors and how these may underlie artistic phenomena.

HEMISPHERIC SPECIALIZATION AND ARTISTIC ACTIVITY

One of the most fascinating discoveries of modern neuropsychology is hemispheric specialization. Paul Broca and Carl Wernicke opened this field in the last century by discovering the relationship between specific *language* problems and discrete injuries of the left hemisphere. What do we currently know about the specific and differential capacities of both brain hemispheres? And what relationship does this phenomenon have with art and creativity?

The following are some of the relevant facts in this field:

1. Injuries in the left hemisphere cause, in a majority of individuals, disorders in language (aphasia, alexia, agraphia).

2. Right hemisphere injuries tend to cause spatial perception problems.

3. In positron emission tomography (PET) scanner brain images, stimulation with music shows greater activation in the right hemisphere.

Since the 1950s, and starting from the first discoveries of the left hemisphere linguistic functions, different dichotomies have been proposed about hemispheric specialization: linguistic functions versus spatial functions; verbal functions versus non-verbal functions; analytic versus synthetic; detailed versus gestalt processing; serial versus parallel processing; propositional mind versus apositional mind; logical, abstract versus creative, imaginative; categorical organization versus organization in spatial coordinates (Cutting, 1990).

The study of brain-injured patients is instructive. Maurice Ravel, the great French musician, suffered from neurological injury from a traffic accident in 1932, at age 56. His musical production was practically arrested and he suffered apraxia: he could not swim and he increasingly lost the ability to play the piano. Afterwards, he kept on experiencing problems with writing and speaking. Nevertheless, his spatial orientation remained intact. Ravel's memory and judgment as well as his esthetic sense were also intact up until his death. He was unable to write or play music but his thought and musical perception were untouched and he was able to pick up in a quick and precise way slight errors (either in musical notes, measure or rhythm) in the execution of musical pieces. Yet he could not recognize written musical notation, neither could he write. He himself said: "I feel my own music but I will no longer ever be able to write it".

Ravel had surgery in 1937 and a lesion of the left hemisphere was discovered. He died as a consequence of the operation (Alajouanine, 1968).

The drawings of patients with damaged right hemispheres are typically different from those who suffer left hemisphere damage. In the first group (with damaged right hemisphere) we observe an accumulation of details and motives, as well as great difficulty in giving them coherence. The drawing is fragmented, and the artist's style is lost. In the second group (with damaged left hemisphere), we find a simplification of the forms, the "whole" is preferred to the details, the work is well organized and the style remains intact (Gardner, 1982).

In the past several decades new studies have appeared that point out the importance of the right hemisphere in such linguistic aspects as metaphor, humour, creativity and social nuance. There are published cases of "loss of creativity among professional writers with right hemisphere injuries" (Critchley, 1962). Right hemisphere damage alters the metaphoric comprehension, increasing the probability of literal interpretations of language (Winner & Gardner, 1977). Other authors (e.g. Diggs & Basili, 1987) have shown the loss of creative thought in right hemisphere-injured patients.

Another relevant aspect of our subject is the possible interhemispheric differences in mood states and emotional reactions. The intracarotid injection of a short-acting barbiturate causes for a few minutes the anesthesia and the consequent functional inhibition of the hemisphere on the same side as the injected carotid artery. On the left side, the injection almost invariably causes a depressive state, while right hemisphere paralysis generally causes euphoria. It has been confirmed that right hemisphere damage causes either euphoria or indifference, while left hemisphere damage causes depression and "catastrophic" reactions (Gainotti, 1972). Furthermore, the ability of expressing emotions through the voice—emotional prosody—is affected by right-sided injuries, but not by left-sided injuries. The left side of the face generally expresses more emotions than the right side, and this asymmetry disappears if there is a right-sided injury. The right hemisphere is also superior to the left hemisphere in detecting emotional signals or qualities of faces and voices (Cutting, 1990).

A remarkable opportunity to study hemispheric specialization is manifested in "split-brain" patients, i.e. patients whose corpus callosum (the fibrous bridge that connects the two hemispheres) has been sectioned to treat epilepsy and who, therefore, remain with disconnected hemispheres. This condition enables investigators to study separately the specific reactions of each hemisphere. In these patients we can also examine the lateralization of emotions: terror movies are seen as more disturbing if they are presented to the right hemisphere. Erotic films projected to the left hemisphere are described in an analytical way, without much emotion; however, the projection of the same stimulus to the right hemisphere leads to pronounced emotional changes (Gazzaniga & LeDoux, 1978).

Therefore, it has been proposed that there is a right hemispheric advantage for the emotional aspects of perceptions. However, the left hemisphere has more capacity for semantic and categorial analysis ("knowing" more than "feeling") (Kosslyn & Koenig, 1992). These are two interacting ways of understanding the world as well as the artistic object. We need our right hemisphere to interpret and convey feelings and emotional nuances. It is likely, therefore, that the right hemisphere is involved in basic musical processing and "first impressions" (so decisive!) in the grasping of the art work. It is also likely that the most sublime and pure artistic forms, particularly in the modern era, imply the use of analytic processes, heavily loaded with categorizations and linguistic formulations that require a fully functioning left hemisphere.

PREFRONTAL LOBE AND "ART BRUT"

"I used to paint like Raphael. But it has taken me a whole life to learn how to draw like a child" (Pablo Picasso, in Gardner, 1982).

It is not uncommon to hear at an art museum, in front of a Miró painting, a comment such as: "My five-year-old child can do the same thing". As I see it, this comment reveals on one hand a certain amount of naiveté of this prototypical parent and, on the other, something more interesting, the evident proximity between certain forms of the best art of the twentieth century and the productions of children (Figure 3-2).

Beyond personal opinions, our present conception of art allows us to talk about "children's (plastic) art", "psychopathological art" and even about the study of "primates' painting" (Lenain, 1990).

Great figures of twentieth-century art (Picasso, Miró, Dubuffet, Klee, the surrealists, and many others) have shown an enormous interest in the artistic production of psychotic patients, children, and "primitive" man. Some schools and avant-garde artistic movements such as Surrealism, Tachisme and Action Painting, have considered them as important influences, and they even have consti-

3-2
JOAN MIRÓ
LITHOGRAPH VIII, from the
ALBUM 13 LITHOGRAPHIES,
1948
14⅝ × 10⅜ in
(37.2 × 26.5 cm)
Fundació Joan Miró,
Barcelona. © 1996 Artists
Rights Society (ARS),
NY/ADAGP, Paris

tuted the essence of the so called "Art Brut" (Thévoz, 1981). Do these different forms of unofficial or "non-cultural" art, as Dubuffet (1967) would say, have any relation among them? And if so, why? Is there any relationship with respect to brain functioning?.

Educators and child psychologists agree in accepting the existence of a "golden age" of children's creativity, approximately between three and six years of age. At these ages children act with an enviable freedom and exhibit a plastic and linguistic imagination and an inventiveness that adults marvel at. A few years later, things start to change. Children's activities tend to yield to convention, to the identification with their peers. Submission to rules in games as well as in the use of symbols tend to discriminate experimentation and novelty (Gardner, 1982). At this stage, the child initiates a creative productivity marked by literality and realism.

Cerebral maturation processes, especially the cortical ones, develop postnatally, well into adolescence. The prefrontal lobe regions and the inter- and intrahemispheric fibers of association are, among all the brain regions, the slowest ones in maturing. Yet we know that these structures play a crucial role in the mental and behavioral processes involved in planning, the estimation of future reinforcement or punishment, and the introjection and assimilation of norms.

"The human prefrontal cortex takes care of, integrates, formulates, executes, monitors and modifies all the activities of the nervous system. The majority of mental functions can be sustained without the prefrontal lobe, although the responses become automatic and lack the most inherently human qualities . . . The frontal lobes are the key to the highest human functions." (Stuss & Benson, 1986).

Also, the regulation of playing and laughing behavior is related to the frontal neocortex (MacLean, 1990). The dysfunction in certain areas of these lobes causes the appearance of a psychopathological syndrome, the *orbito-frontal syndrome*, characterized by uninhibited, antinormative and antisocial behaviors. The lowered frontal function, i.e. "hypofrontality", may lead thus to a pathological infant-like condition.

Schizophrenia is a brain disease that has been traditionally related to art and creativity. Certainly, there have been schizophrenics who have produced remarkable works even if most of these patients are, in general, quite uncreative. Nevertheless, a tendency to very idiosyncratic and anticonventional productions can be recognized in these patients when they are encouraged to draw or paint or when we analyze their linguistic production.

Yet, we know that in schizophrenia brain pathology resides probably in the limbic system structures, in the inner temporal lobe and in its connections with the frontal lobes. A "hypofrontality" state has been detected (Weinberger, 1991) in many schizophrenic patients that can be compared in some cases to the hypofrontal syndromes mentioned above. The frontal–limbic disconnection that takes place could give way to the loss of social inhibitions and conventions that we can observe in the behavior (including the artistic behavior) of schizophrenic patients. "Art and insanity have, to begin with, one thing in common, the resurgence of the unconscious in the conscious life" (Vigouroux, 1992, p. 36). A neuropsychological translation of this psychodynamic expression could be: in a psychotic condition, the regulation and inhibitory mechanisms of cortical (especially frontal) structures over the subcortical (emotional) structures are altered.

Therefore, it is quite possible that the prefrontal lobes, through their multiple (and well documented) connections with the subcortical and limbic system structures (that "produce" emotions, motivations and desires) act as real "inhibitors" and "modulators" of the "instinctive" and "primitive" subcortical behaviors.

At the *phylogenetic* level, the frontal structures are the most different with respect to the brains of other species. This makes possible, among other things, the appearance in humans of very complex conventions (morality, law) that articulate and allow the existence of the intricate structure of human societies. At the *ontogenetic* level, the maturing of these structures probably runs parallel to the so-called "socialization" processes. This "frontalization" would gradually stop the child's "anarchic" behavior, including creativity.

All considered, why does the artist, as we have seen in Picasso's statement, strive after this state of childlike creativity? At this point it is worth remembering that the modern conception of art and creativity gives preference, above other values, to its individual and subjective aspects and to *originality*. Picasso's statement is a good metaphor of the artist's struggle for liberation from anything related to norms, guidelines, or the influences of peers or schools that every adult artist certainly harbors. The artist's quest for the most "hidden", "profound", "unconscious", "primitive" forces has been, in fact, pervasive in history. If we acknowledge that emotion and the archaic components are essential in art, it is understandable that artists strive to free the emotional forces constrained by the influences of the frontal hemispheres. The norm is, in essence, anti-individual and anti-creative. This is why it is, to a certain extent, anti-artistic.

At this point, we might be concluding that the frontal lobe is the first enemy of the artist, the repressor of creative forces, the great ruler! But let us not forget that, in spite of all we have seen, art (especially contemporary art) is a highly distilled product of the human spirit, a peak of human culture and civilization. This means that, at least in the highest forms of artistic achievement, man develops his most refined intellectual abilities. In this sense art is not only a "rough" manifestation of an emotional drive or an elementary intelligence, but the final result of a highly sophisticated elaboration. The critical attitude of the artist towards reality and his own work (see Figure 3-3) seems to be an inherent element of the creative process. Sometimes this attitude of self-analysis and self-censure reaches painful extremes—how many artists confess

3-3
EDWARD QUINN
*PICASSO WITH PAINTING,
LA GAROUPE*
© *Edward Quinn, Nice*

they literally destroy their writings or paintings! (Figure 3-3).

On the other hand, many twentieth-century artistic forms are directly and voluntarily linked by their creators to political, social or aesthetic issues; this, again, shows the highly intellectual elaboration of artistic work.

All these intentional, premeditated, critical contents of artistic creation and evaluation necessarily imply the highest brain functions, i.e. the ones that are related to the language areas and the frontal lobes. The failure of these structures impairs goal-directed behavior, reduces flexibility of atten-

41

tion in the face of external stimuli and impairs critical judgment, all of them fundamental elements in the artistic process. The assimilation of norms, apparently despised in some contemporary artistic trends, is, in spite of all, pervasive in art history. From the "auric proportion" of classical art up to the varied sets of norms of differing artistic schools, who would dare to contest the importance of a learned normative component in many of the great masterpieces in history? Even in today's art, in which we find an eager search for individuality, the craftsman's training persists in many cases as a basis for artistic creation, and these skills are undoubtedly the basis of the assimilation of norms and the acquisition of ordered techniques.

A final comment: we started this section referring to the existence of children's art and psychopathological art. From a neuropsychological perspective we can certainly understand the obvious differences—in spite of the naive reaction on the part of those parents whose "children paint like Miró"—between these forms of art and art itself: a thoughtful elaboration, the projecting of all kinds of learning and experiences, a critical filtering, and finally an intellectual effort of analysis, all of which defines "cultural" art. We may thus state that "l'art brut" does not need a finely integrated frontal activity, while cultural art does.

SPECULATIONS ABOUT CHAOS, ORDER AND CREATIVITY

A pareidolia is an abnormal perception, an illusion of the senses that makes us see concrete forms (or integrate sounds) where there is only an amorphous mass of stimuli. Examples are seeing animal contours in clouds, or fantastic figures in the shadows of a wall, at the bottom of a cup of turkish coffee or in the ink blots of the Rorschach test.

The cloud, or the blot, is a messy, nonsensical and *chaotic* group of forms. The human mind projects over this ensemble a vision that is free, individual and new. This implies the making of a new order that did not exist *a priori*. Therefore this process, which we must call creative, takes place in the interaction of the chaotic mass with the ordering mechanisms, generated within the individual mind.

The starting point is the idea that *order* is a basic component in the work of art. The observer needs to discover it (it may not be obvious!—especially in many forms of contemporary art) to appreciate the content and obtain some kind of pleasure. Aesthetic pleasure has been related to classification and categorization.

"The need for organization is a requirement of art, and the aesthetic sense can open a way to taxonomy and can even anticipate some of its results" (Lévi-Strauss, 1962).

The interesting point is, however, that the creator doesn't proceed in an "ordered", logico-sequential way to arrive at this final "order", whatever its nature might be. He doesn't proceed like a computer program (= order) that generates a final product (computation = work = new order). The human creative process takes place in a mysterious way that has been often called intuition, inspiration or *illumination*. In the previous section we saw the emphasis that has traditionally been given in the "liberating" processes, processes of "loss of rationality" in relation to creativity. We have also reviewed the conception that new ideas come from the unconscious, from the cognitive and emotional magma of the subconscious world, from dreams.

"Dreams and the fantastic open the door to the unconscious. The surrealists Ernst, Masson, Miró, Magritte and Dalí dove into it, while attaching themselves to psychoanalysis. Opposed to any form of order and logical convention they preached the value of impulsions, revolt, dreams, desires, and of a delirious and hallucinated imagination" (Vigouroux, 1992, p. 250).

We can already suggest an outline of the creative process, and we begin at a starting point that we will conventionally situate in the chaos (see Figure 3-4).

make jumps).

Some adventurous neuroscientists soon applied these ideas to the study of the brain, a system that resists being described with linear equations and deterministic paradigms. We already have biochemical theories of schizophrenia (King et al, 1981) based on the French mathematician René Thom's "catastrophe theory" (Thom, 1977). Neurophysiological models of brain functioning based on the idea of the brain stem/limbic system as aleatory/chaotic generators of information have been formulated (Bergtrom, 1967); other researchers (Gray, 1979; La Violette, 1979) have proposed differ-

3-4
The creative process as a chaos/order cycle.

Can we say something more beyond this rather philosophical speculation? Is it possible to formulate it in biophysical, neurophysiological or mathematical terms?

Recent trends in physics and mathematics are approaching the study and analysis of non-linear systems, of chaotic dynamics of fluids, of a new, non-deterministic physics. Newton's universe has become too limited to explain phenomena of high complexity (e.g. the neurobiological phenomena), and modern science denies the old Leibniz maxim, "Natura non facit saltum" (Nature does not

ent hypotheses about memory and brain functioning based on non-linear models.

The "*attractor*" concept has been defined by chaos scientists as a phenomenon that relates the worlds of order and chaos. The attractor is a phase space basin that exerts a "magnetic" attraction upon a system. Therefore, it is a kind of magnet that attracts a system from chaos towards order. When we analyze the phenomenon of turbulence, we will describe it specifically as a "strange attractor" (Briggs & Peat, 1989). This way of thinking about the biological universe seems promising and it allows us to approach psychological phenomena such as *creativity* in a totally novel way. Creativity, as a process of conversion from chaotic to ordered states, can be analyzed as a *self-organization* process.

The brain may be understood as having a spontaneous drive to self-organization, as clouds, air and water have. It forms undulations and whirlwinds. The world of self-organization constitutes a "new dialogue with nature", according to the Nobel prize physicist Ilya Prigogine (1979):

"I think we are beginning to perceive nature in a completely opposite way to the way we perceived classical physics. We will stop thinking of nature as a passive object. In front of a cloud of dots the mind plays spontaneously, connecting them together in lines. The internal attractor in our brain creates an ordered universe for us" (Prigogine & Stengers, 1979).

We find again, thus, the above mentioned pareidolia understood now under the light of a radically contemporary conception.

"La vie est ondoyante" (life is wavy), said Montaigne, and it is so because the brain, the instrument that allows us to observe and verify it, is also "wavy". The brain is plastic, ever changing, and even if highly structured, it generates a flux of variable and oscillating activity. Brain activity fluctuates throughout the day (circadian rhythm). Other internal oscillators probably cause brain activity swings throughout longer periods (a month, a year). There are also oscillations between hemispheric activation and we know that the different parts within them also go through variations of state and functioning. Changing,

oscillations, swings are therefore a fundamental characteristic of brain activity.

We can imagine the mind as a system where experiences/memories/ideas are registered and accumulated. These units establish among themselves certain links, probably by activation patterns of concrete neuronal networks that are, in a certain way, unstable and alterable. The nexus among units are fluid and changing such that the units can establish multiple if not infinite connections and configurations (Edelman, 1992).

Now, does this fluidity have any relationship with the concrete oscillations of the brain? Can we think of the brain as a system oscillating between more structured states (order) and less structured ones (chaos)? What would creativity be in this context?

I would like here to propose a tentative model to answer those questions. This model relates well known facts (i.e. central nervous system activation levels) with a speculative association of mental states and chaos theory: on the linear scale of central nervous system general activation, there are low activation states (sleep, unconsciousness) and states of alertness and hyperactivation (normal, drug-induced, psychopathological) (see Figure 3-5). In another dimension, mental states would be distributed in a biphasic space, following a vertical axis that we might call "cognitive order" indicating the degree of mental structuring (Figure 3-5).

Low levels of the reticular activating system (RAS) activation (sleep, unconsciousness) would bring mental states to the "chaotic zone". An example of unstructured mental activity would be night dreaming. High levels of RAS activation (excitement, manic states, drug-induced states, maybe some kinds of epileptic activity) can also

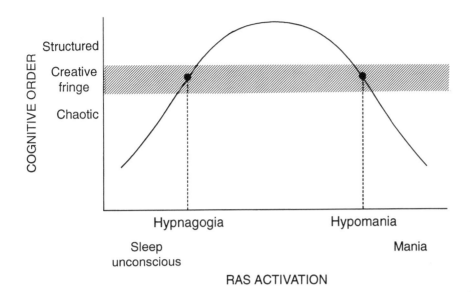

3-5
Relationship between cognitive order and activation of the reticular activating system (RAS).

cause cognitive destructuring, and therefore they would also provoke mental states to fall into the chaotic zone.

States of *hypnagogia* have been traditionally associated to creativity and problem-solving (Mavromatis, 1987). Classical examples of brilliant discoveries, like Kekulé's benzene ring, remind us of Novalis' statement: ". . . to dream and at the same moment, not to dream. This synthesis is the genius' operation . . ." (quoted in Mavromatis, 1987). And this takes place in the subtle transition of hypnagogia.

"The period that precedes illumination often implies . . . a drop in vigilance activities. These states allow a free association of mental objects and favour thus the comparison processes of internal representations. One can understand, therefore, how periods of drowsiness, close to falling asleep, can constitute propitious moments for inspiration" (Vigouroux, 1992, p. 271).

Transition states are, thus, the most interesting, since they are the ones that would facilitate the surge of cre-

ative moments or states. In the transition from alertness to tiredness (hypnagogia) as well as in the transition from normality to mania (hypomania, euphoria) the phenomenon of creation (sometimes so ephemeral) might be produced. The brain "strange attractor" would be acting in these transitions, i.e. the "creative fringe", generating "new orders".

REFERENCES

Alajouanine, Th. (1968). *L'Aphasie et le Langage Pathologique.* J.B. Baillière, Paris.

Andreasen, N.C. (1986). *Can Schizophrenia be Localized in the Brain?* American Psychiatric Press, Washington, D.C.

Arnheim, R. (1980). *Hacia una Psicología del Arte. Arte y Entropía*, Alianza Forma, Madrid, p. 207.

Bear, D.M. (1991). The neurology of art: artistic creativity in patients with temporal lobe epilepsy. In *Symposium on Neurology of Art.* University of Chicago (in press).

Benson, D.F. (1991). The geschwind syndrome. *Advances in Neurology*, **55**, 411–21.

Bergtrom, R.M. (1967). An analysis of the information-carrying system of the brain. *Synthese*, **17**, 425.

Briggs, J. & Peat, D. (1989). *Turbulent Mirror.* Harper & Row, New York.

Critchley, M. (1962). Speech and speech cross in relation to the duality of the brain. In *Interhemispheric Relations and Cerebral Dominance*, Ed. V.B. Mountcastle. Johns Hopkins University Press, Baltimore.

Cutting, J. (1990). *The Right Cerebral Hemisphere and Psychiatric Disorders.* Oxford Medical publications, Oxford.

Diggs, C.C. & Basili A.G. (1987). Verbal expressions of right cerebrovascular accident patients: convergent and divergent language. *Brain and Language*, **30**, 130–46.

Dubuffet, J. (1967). *Prospectus et tous Ecrits Suivants.* Gallimard, Pons.

Edelman, G.M. (1992). *Biologie de la Conscience*, O. Jacob, Paris.

Gainotti, G. (1972). Emotional behavior and hemisphere side of lesions. *Cortex*, **8**, 41–55.

Gajdusek, D.C. (1970). Physiological and psychological characteristics of Stone Age Man. In *Symposium on Biological Bases of Human Behavior, Eng. Sci.*, **33**, 26–33, pp. 58–59.

Gardner, H. (1982). *Art, Mind, and Brain. A Cognitive Approach to Creativity.* Basic Books, New York.

Gastaut, H. (1984). New comments on the epilepsy of Fyodor Dostoiesvky. *Epilepsia*, **25**, 408–411.

Gazzaniga, M. & LeDoux, J.E. (1978). *The Integrated Mind.* Plenum, New York.

Gray, W. (1979). Understanding creative thought process: an early formulation of the emotional-cognitive structural theory. *Man–Environment Systems*, **9**, 1.

Habib, M. (1986). Visual hypoemotionality and prosopagnosia associated with right temporal lobe isolation. *Neuropsychologia*, **24**, 577–582.

James, W. (1985). *Les Varietats de l'Experiència Religiosa.* Edicions 62, Barcelona.

Jones, S. (1991). A message from our ancestors. *The Independent*, London, November 14.

King, R., Raese, J.D. & Barchas, J. (1981). Catastrophe theory of dopaminergic transmission: a revised dopamine hypothesis of schizophrenia. *J. Theor. Biol.*, **92**, 373.

Kosslyn, S.M. & Koenig, O. (1992). *Wet Mind: The New Cognitive Neuroscience.* The Free Press, New York.

La Violette, P.A. (1979). Thoughts about thoughts about thoughts: the emotional perceptive cycle theory. *Man–Environment Systems*, **9**, 1.

Lenain, T. (1990). *La Peinture des Singes*, Edit. Syros Alternatives, Paris.

Lévi-Strauss, C. (1962). *La Pensée Sauvage*. Plon, Paris.

MacLean, P.D. (1990). *The Triune Brain in Evolution. Role in Paleocerebral Function*. Plenum, New York.

Mandell, A.J. (1980). Toward a psychobiology of transcendence: God in the brain. In *The Psychobiology of Consciousness*, Eds J.M. Davidson & R.J. Davidson. Plenum, New York.

Mavromatis, A. (1987). *Hypnagogia. The Unique State of Consciousness Between Wakefulness and Sleep*. Routledge and Kegan Paul, London.

Miró, J. (1959). Je travaille comme un jardinier. Paris, *XXème Siècle*, **1**, 11.

Miró, J. (1977). *Ceci Est la Couleur de mes Rêves. Entretiens avec Georges Raillard*. Editions du Seuil, Paris, p. 108.

Penfield, W. (1975). *The Mystery of the Mind*. Princeton University Press, Princeton.

Prigogine, I. & Stengers, I. (1979). *La Nouvelle Alliance*. Gallimard, Paris.

Stuss, D.T. & Benson, D.F. (1986). *The Frontal Lobes*. Raven Press, New York.

Thévoz, M. (1981). *L'Art Brut*. Skira, Genève.

Thom, R. (1977). *Stabilité Structurelle et Morphogénèse*, 2nd Edn., Inter Editions, Paris.

Tisher, P.W., Holzer, J.C., Greenberg, M., Benjamin, S., Devinsky, O. & Bear, D.M. (1993). Psychiatric presentations of epilepsy. *Harvard Rev. Psychiat.*, **1**(4), 219–228.

Trimble, M.R. (1988). *Biological Psychiatry*. Wiley, Chichester, pp. 307–308.

Vigouroux, R. (1992). *La Fabrique du Beau*. O. Jacob, Paris.

Weinberger, D.R. (1991). Anteromedial temporal–prefrontal connectivity: a functional neuroanatomical system implicated in schizophrenia. In *Psychopathology and the Brain*, Eds. B.J. Carroll & S.E. Barrett. Raven Press, New York.

Winner, E. & Gardner, H. (1977). The comprehension of metaphor in brain-damaged patients. *Brain*, **100**, 717–29.

CHAPTER 4

THE EXPRESSION OF MELANCHOLY IN THE WORK OF J.M. DE SUCRE: A CASE STUDY

CRISTÓBAL GASTÓ

INTRODUCTION

Melancholy occupied a prominent place in Europe in the seventeenth and eighteenth centuries (Jackson, 1989; Berrios, 1988). The term was used in various senses, referring to the mood, the behavior and even the social status of certain people (McDonald, 1981). Taken from the standard medical vocabulary, it became an almost aristocratic and intellectual term. Melancholy, particularly in the European Romantic period, was considered a prelude to either madness or genius. In medicine the term was used as an attempt to specify a clinical condition which could be differentiated from others such as mania or paranoia. Melancholy is described in the classic texts as a state involving both mental and physical symptoms, caused by an alteration in the balance of two fluids. This bipolar theory of moods was to dominate medical thinking for centuries and still underlies current biochemical hypotheses (e.g. Schildkraut, 1965), which maintain that one of the causes of major depression is an alteration in the balance of chemical substances, recognizable through the analyses of the blood, urine and other body fluids. The early theory on moods is thus very similar to its present-day counterpart, which has only changed in accordance with the technological progress in biology and medicine.

Given that medical terms have more than one meaning (even for the doctors themselves), among them their poetic and philosophical meanings (Simon, 1978), the idea of the melancholic artist may be accepted as a historical reality. If we deny this, we are denying the existence of a generic and deeply meaningful symbol (Wittkower & Wittkower, 1963). We must ask ourselves what purpose will be served by analyzing this idea in terms of a single artist. The reply might be that in order to pinpoint the small areas of relative certainty in medicine and art it is helpful to know not only the corruptible matter of man, but also his symbols.

The person and symbols of Josep María De Sucre reveal a space where the creative achievements give way to dark facets of the human soul. Facets glimpsed in his obsessive masks which, like imaginary and reiterative self-portraits, attempt to transcend man or perhaps his "pathological" fate: desperation, anguish and guilt (Figure 4-1). Today, De Sucre's work may be seen as the starting point of *art informel* in Catalonia. And it currently serves as a point of reference for all Catalan artists and art critics.

THE MAN AND HIS BACKGROUND

Josep María De Sucre was born in 1886 in the district of Gràcia in Barcelona and died in 1969 in the family home. It

4-1
JOSEP MARIA DE SUCRE
MASK, 1964
Painting
© Photographs of the
Museu Nacional d'Art de
Catalunya (Barcelona).
Photographs by MNAC
Photographic Service
(Calveras/Sagristà)

is said, or De Sucre at least believed, that through his father's side of the family he was connected with the oldest French nobility and through his mother's side he had deep roots in Catalonia and particularly close ties with artistic and literary circles. In his memoirs (De Sucre, 1963) it is stated that in his youth he was a friend of Rubén Darío, Leopoldo Lugones, Paul

Valery, Paul Claudel and Remy Gourmont. As a young man he published three poems in Catalan, *Apól noi* (1910), *Ocell Daurat* (1920), and *Poema Barbar d'en Serrallonga* (1921), and one in Spanish, *Poemas de Abril y Mayo* (1922). (See Perucho, 1964.)

His republican father, who was a solicitor and deputy mayor of Gràcia, advised him not to pursue a higher education but to be alert to everything that happened in the world around him (Ibarz, 1982). He worked as a civil servant until he was dismissed for incompetence at the age of 37. De Sucre was ill-at-ease in an official environment, working set hours for a regular salary, and preferred to frequent intellectual gatherings or the city's cultural associations for the working class. The critic Manzano (1983) describes him as follows: "De Sucre was a pilgrim-like man, not very tall, dressed in a tight-fitting blue overcoat that was worn thin; around his neck the inevitable lead grey home-knitted scarf. His thinning hair must have originally been blond; his pale eyes were worn out from reading. He walked with the erect posture of those who are unaccustomed to servility". In 1922 he had his first exhibition at the Galeries Dalmau in Barcelona, showing unsigned works. He exhibited again in 1928 without arousing the slightest public interest. In 1929 he exhibited once more at the Galeries Dalmau. Although this time De Sucre's paintings were signed, the result was still the same.

De Sucre was intensely involved in Barcelona's cultural movements, particularly *modernisme* and the most closely-knit group of the time, *Els 4 gats* (1897–1903), which had been an idea of Ramón Casas and Miquel Utrillo and was inspired by the Chat Noir in Paris. This group, among whose members were Nonell, Rusiñol, Utrillo and the young Picasso, shook up the Barcelona art world of the early twentieth century. In De Sucre's "memoirs" there is a long list of shady figures who were part of the group, some of whom met with tragic fates: both Gerbal, a hairdresser and writer, and Carlos Costas, who brought European theater to Barcelona, hanged themselves (De Sucre, 1963). Another friend of De Sucre's, Soler de las Borjas, also committed suicide (Manzano, 1983).

During World War I, a number of French artists were exiled in Barcelona, among them Arthur Cravan, a former boxing champion and painter who, together with the French-Cuban Picabia, published the journal *391*, inspired by such New York publications as *Camera Work* and *291*. This Barcelona journal encouraged the art dealer Dalmau to start promoting avant-garde art. His gallery held the first Picabia exhibition, which was the embryo of the future surrealist movement. De Sucre began his creative endeavours around this time, producing poetry that was more surrealist than his visual art (Garrut, 1974). Nevertheless, it was following the Spanish Civil War that he became a symbol in Barcelona. After having miraculously avoided being shot by Franco supporters, who confused him with *el noi del Sucre*, a Catalan anarchist who had already been dead for years, De Sucre embarked on a personal crusade to promote avant-garde art (Vila-San Juan, 1982).

During the period after the Civil War and during World War II the Cercle Maillol was formed under the auspices of the French Institute. De Sucre was the President and mainly devoted himself to sponsoring the "escape" of young avant-garde artists to France, by making certain they were awarded grants (the only way to acquire an official passport). Many young artists benefited from the Cercle Maillol, among them Tàpies, Tharrats, Subirachs, Todó, María Girona and Ràfols Casamada (Vila-San Juan, 1982).

At the beginning of the 1960s De Sucre slowly began to withdraw from the art scene, partly because of his extreme financial circumstances and partly because of his misanthropic personality. He hid at home with his only sister and tirelessly painted his *Masks*. As Manzano (1983) described it: a terrible illness progressively "furrowed his flesh" as he painted the *Masks*, using the wax technique to make furrows in the cardboard he sometimes retrieved from the trash bins of Barcelona. In 1969 De Sucre died in utter poverty, unknown by the public.

DE SUCRE AND EUROPEAN EXPRESSIONISM

The German neologism *Expressionismus*, which literally means to "extrude" or "twist" rather than to express shapes or images (González Rodríguez, 1990), alludes to the stark drama of mankind's emergence from the ruins of nineteenth-century European culture. The term "Expressionism" soon became the vanguard of European culture, thanks to the painters (Ensor, Kirchner, Nolde, Macke, Munch, Dix, Viani, Soutine among others); the writers (Sternheim, Kaiser, Meyrinks, Kafka); the poets (Heym and Trakl) and filmmakers (Wiene, Wegener, Lang). This new vision of the world echoed man's futile struggle to escape from the trap of a society empty of content and with obsolete values. Without being "committed" art, Expressionism was a reaction against art for art's sake, a personal reaction of the individual artist. The conceptual elements of this movement also differed greatly from those of the turn of the century's impressionist movement and of the emerging abstract art. To the standard working materials (oil and acrylic paints) the Expressionists added whatever other material was available (earth, gesso, etc.), enhancing the possibilities of visual art. The search for an effect of the work was secondary to the expression of the artist's most primitive or immediate emotions. Thus expressionist artists would appreciate an *unfinished quality* in a work because it reflected their incomplete and anguished concept of man; in short, *Schwermut* as opposed to the bucolic euthymia of nineteenth-century art.

The expressionist attitude therefore corresponded to a mysticism of the *corruptible matter* and a negation of form as a receptacle *per se* of the spirit. This school of *art informel* had few followers in Catalonia. Worth recalling are Ajeo Clapes (1850–1920) and Mariano Pidelaserra (1877–1947). Only De Sucre remained true to the purest form of northern Expressionism. In France, Jean Fautrier, Maurice Estève, Edouard Pignon and Jean Bazaine (the so-called "middle generation") kept this movement alive (Lucie-Smith, 1969).

The series of paintings called *Rehén* by Jean Fautrier, whose subject was ostensibly the mass deportations of Jews during the Nazi occupation of France, was to have special influence. The earthy tactile quality of Fautrier's materials was to recur in De Sucre's *Masks*, and later in the work of Tàpies—who was directly influenced by these "matter painters," the precursors of *art informel* (Lucie-Smith, 1969).

Although De Sucre was bound stylistically to the expressionism of Munch, Ensor, Kokoschka and Kirchner, as President he was to open the Cercle

Maillol to all the artistic styles of his time. De Sucre alleged: The Cercle Maillol is an open group of artists, especially young artists, of different styles; they meet together every Tuesday night, at the French Institute in Barcelona, for a friendly interchange of ideas and their personal appraisal on the evolution of art, with the aim of improving their artistic creations (Torres, 1994). Nevertheless, the forceful expressionism of De Sucre greatly influenced an immediate generation of young painters, who in 1949 created the "Grupo Lais" (Rogent, Hurtuna, Capdevilla, Suros, among others). This group signed "El Manifiesto Negro" (The Black Manifesto), which was undoubtedly the exaltation of Catalan expressionism (Calvo Serraller, 1985). Some of the points in this "Manifiesto Negro" clearly reflect De Sucre's work:

1. Painting is intellectual.
2. A picture is a surface completely covered with colours arranged according to a certain order. When the "black light" is added to a painting, all the other colours are intensified by simultaneous contrast. From this it follows that in a painting black means "light".
3. A colour can be impossible, or contrary to reality, but it will always be justified if it is suggestive and expresses an intense feeling.
4. A painting must contain an element of mystery—if it does not it is not a painting.
5. Drawing is not shape, it is the way of seeing shape.
6. An exact imitation of reality will never be art.
7. Art only begins with interior reality.

The different concepts represented in this "manifesto", particularly that of "visible darkness" and "internal reality", recur throughout the whole of De Sucre's work, especially in his disturbing *Masks*.

THE IMAGINARY AND REITERATIVE SELF-PORTRAIT

De Sucre can be said to have painted only himself and an alleged ancestor, *The Field Marshal* in a style reminiscent of the expressionist Goya. In De Sucre's work the symbol of man and his passions needs no additional support from allegorical elements as it does in other artistic movements (such as Surrealism) where objects take on a meaning in accordance with the artist's troubled imagination. The only symbol here is the mask, multi-expressive and threatening. It is a purely human symbol and at the same time primitive, or what amounts to the same thing, irreducible. For years De Sucre shut himself up in his tiny studio obsessively drawing and painting masks, living off small donations from some of his friends. Some critics have pointed out the possible sacred or religious nature of his work, wishing to see in these pictures a distant influence of primitive Romanesque painting.

Yet another possible interpretation would be that De Sucre was obsessed by his identity, his past, which was perhaps the stuff of fantasy, his anguished present and his increasingly impossible future as a man and an artist. Although in public he appeared as arrogant, reserved and mysterious all at the same time, he never managed to convince himself of his artistic talent, either as a painter or a writer, or of the respect and recognition of his art by artists and art critics. Puig (1963), in his prologue to *Memorias*, says that De Sucre was an individual that everyone knew when it suited them, but easily forgot when they had got what they wanted from him. This dichotomy of sociability and misanthropy, social activity and voluntary silent reclusion is extremely reminiscent of a melancholic personality. The anguished feeling of uncertainty, traditional in expressionist art, is reflected in De Sucre's observation that ". . . art will never attain total expressiveness. The day that art is perfect, the artist will no longer have the personal stimulus of his own creative search" (De Sucre, 1963).

Not only did De Sucre feel that art should remain unfinished, he also believed that man too is incomplete and therefore tormented by an obsessive search for his identity. Through the memory of his imagined lineage, he transferred himself to a distant place where there was no room for pain and sadness. In contrast, his *Masks* reveal the dramatic dregs of his identity, a man doomed to sadness and death. As Christian Delacampagne, former director of the French Institute in Barcelona, pointed out, De Sucre's work resembles the *Art Brut* that Jean Dubuffet was producing at the end of the 1940s, with his pitiful figures of the ill and the mad (Delacampagne, 1982). However, the dramatic, alienated expression of the *Masks* and their dark coloring bear an even stronger resemblance to an earlier predecessor, the group of tormented figures in Goya's *La Romería de San Juan* (1820–22; Museo del Prado, Madrid) than to the smooth lines of Dubuffet (Nordstrom, 1962).

The melancholic atmosphere in almost all of De Sucre's *Masks* was a harbinger of what might be called the "disturbing qualities" seen years later in the work of Balthus and Bacon, while modern European painting quickly evolved along very different lines (Lucie-Smith, 1969). In De Sucre, this atmosphere mirrors a dark interior space that abruptly reveals its moods, as opposed to the luminous, gentle and apparently incorrupt exterior space found in the Catalan new-impressionist paintings of the 1950s and 1960s.

De Sucre's thoughts were obsessed with his mother, his father, his ancestors, his city and his breeding or lineage. These themes call to mind the great Expressionist poet Georg Trakl, who submitted to the dreadful destiny of his family and his city, expressed in this poem: "Where that rotting lineage lives cold and malign/preparing a somber future for its grandchildren so pale" (Georg Trakl, *Cantos de Muerte*; see Becker, 1972). During the last five years of his life, De Sucre, who was then almost blind, lived in seclusion, cared for by his sister and only protector, while his mind continued obsessively churning out self-portraits. De Sucre appears to have personally experienced that combination of melancholy and brilliant vision of a man reduced to his fatal reality: hopelessness, solitude and death.

THE LIMITS OF PSYCHOPATHOLOGICAL INTERPRETATION

Psychopathological reasoning has always been fascinated by symbolic manifestations of health and illness in man. However, there are few systematic studies on the subject. For many critics and art historians the concepts of *creativity* and *genius* cannot be reduced to elements beyond the laws, if any, of art. However, it does not seem reasonable to ignore the personality traits of many artists, without which their work would never have existed.

As summarized in Chapter One, one of the first systematic studies of creativity and mental illness was carried out by Andreasen & Canter (1974), and was enlarged upon and refined in successive works (Andreasen, 1987; Andreasen & Glick, 1988). These studies concentrated exclusively on writers who were considered by society to be either "successful" or "geniuses" (among them John Cheever, Robert Lowell, John Irving, Robert Coover, Phillip Roth, Kurt Vonnegut, Stanley Elkin and Anthony Burgess). According to these studies there is a close, statistically significant link between the pathology of mood and creativity, both in the writers and in the members of their immediate families compared to control groups. The resurgence of the idea of "depressive temperament" and Akiskal's "subaffective" hypothesis (1989) permits us to assume that among both geniuses and ordinary people there are those who are affected by melancholy that conditions their vision of the world, their identity and their work. In this sense Akiskal's (1989) taxonomy of temperaments is completely in line with the Renaissance humanistic tradition, where the *humors* were not considered simply pathogenic fluids but also traits, identifiable through the styles of individual and social behavior of the genius and the ordinary person (Babb, 1951; Madden, 1966). Indeed the long list of melancholics and suicides in the Renaissance, brilliantly analyzed by the Wittkowers, supports the hypothesis that there is a link between pathology of mood and creative activity (Wittkower and Wittkower, 1963). Nevertheless, although the pathology of mood has been widely studied from various perspectives (biological, psychological and social), the creative act is perhaps a term that is not comprehensible by "psychopathological reasoning". *Janusian thinking* (Rothenberg, 1983) does not appear to be a phenomenon that is unique to or characteristic only of geniuses or certain mentally ill individuals.

The creative act is a complex phenomenon in which the artist's mood unquestionably plays a key role in such diverse matters as selecting subject matter and material, and even his life-style and acceptance or rejection of the socioeconomic means to subsist. Although psychopathological reasoning has certain precise limits, its desire to understand creativity is not new. Attributing to artists the ability to see beyond the material world and embody this vision in their creative work was severely criticized by Edmund Burke, whose *Philosophical Enquiry into the Origin of Our Ideas of the Sublime and the Beautiful*, published in 1756, was the first attempt to establish a psychobiological basis of aesthetics (Gombrich, 1984). However, one day we will learn to truly know these phenomena (for example, the aesthetic brain and its disorders), thanks to the endlessly creative activity of some human minds that work without being restrained by the conceptual trends of their times.

In this sense De Sucre was one of the few examples of Catalan expressionist painters. The description of him by Perucho (1964) is immensely revealing: ". . . thin, angular, emitting a turmoil of decaying memories and brilliant real presences. There is a strange defunct air in his house of noblemen slowly rotting in their family vaults, but there is also something uncommonly alive and loquacious". This disposition, tending towards sadness and probably obsessiveness, fostered in De Sucre a creative activity both solitary and powerful, which had a decisive influence on future Catalan artists. Conclusive studies are needed on De Sucre's work to allow us to approach this enigma of the creative personality in a rational way.

ACKNOWLEDGEMENTS

I thank Mr. Jacques Bover, ex-Secretary of the French Institute in Barcelona, for his cooperation and information on J.M. De Sucre, and the Catalan National Museum of Art for their permission to reproduce the work of J.M. De Sucre.

REFERENCES

Akiskal, H.S. (1989). Validating affective personality types. In *The Validity of Psychiatric Diagnosis*, Eds Lee N. Robius and James E. Barrett, pp. 217–227. Raven Press, New York.

Andreasen, N.C. (1987). Creativity and mental illness: prevalence rates in writers and their first-degree relatives. *Am. J. Psychiatry*, **144**, 1288–1292.

Andreasen, N.C. & Canter, A. (1974). The creative writer: psychiatric symptoms and family history. *Compr. Psychiat.*, **15**, 121–131.

Andreasen, N.C. & Glick, I.D. (1988). Bipolar affective disorder and creativity: implications and chemical management. *Compr. Psychiat.*, **29**, 207–217.

Babb, L. (1951). *The Elizabethan Malady. A Study of Melancholia in English Literature: from 1580 to 1642*. Michigan State College Press, Michigan.

Becker, A. (1972). *Georg Trakl. Cantos de Muerte. Antología de Poemas.* pp. 13–43. Al-Burak, S.A., Madrid.

Berrios G.E. (1988). Melancholia and depression during the 19th century: a conceptual history. *Br. J. Psychiat.*, **153**, 298–304.

Calvo Serraller, F. (1985). *España. Medio siglo de Arte de Vanguardia, 1939–1985*, Vol. I pp. 264–265. Fundación Santillana, Ministerio de Cultura, Madrid.

De Sucre, J.M. (1963). *Memorias Del Romanticismo al Modernismo*. Editorial Barna, Barcelona.

Delacampagne, C. (1982). Josep Maria De Sucre a la recerca de la identitat. *El Mon*, **28**, 5.

Garrut, J.M. (1974). *Dos siglos de Pintura Catalana (XIX–XX)*. Ibérico Europea de Ediciones, S.A., Madrid.

Gombrich, E.H. (1984). *Tributes. Interpreters of our Cultural Tradition*. Phaidon, Oxford.

González Rodríguez, A.M. (1990). *Las claves del Arte Expresionista*. Editorial Planeta, Barcelona.

Ibarz, M. (1982). Primera exposició dels autoretrats de Josep M. De Sucre. Reivindicació d'una artista peculiar. *Avui*, May 7, p. 33, Barcelona.

Jackson, W. (1989). *Melancholia and Depression: from Hippocratic Times to Modern Times*. Yale University Press, New Haven, CT.

Lucie-Smith, E. (1969). *Movements in Arts Since 1945*, Thames and Hudson, London.

Madden, J.S. (1966). Melancholy and literature: some historical considerations. *Br. J. Med. Psychol.*, **39**, 125–130.

Manzano, R. (1983). Aproximación a Josep Maria De Sucre. *El Noticiero Universal*, January, 27, p. 38, Barcelona.

McDonald, M. (1981). *Mystical Bedlam, Madness, Anxiety and Healing in Seventeenth Century England.* Cambridge University Press, Cambridge.

Nordstrom, F. (1962). *Goya, Saturn and Melancholy. Studies in the Art of Goya.* Almquist & Wiksell, Stockholm.

Perucho, J. 1964. *El Arte en las Artes,* Ediciones DANAE, Barcelona.

Puig, A. (1963). La Historia es vida. Prologue, in De Sucre, J.M., *Memorias Del Romanticismo al Modernismo,* pp. 1–3. Editorial Barna, Barcelona.

Rothenberg, A. (1983). Psychopathology and creative cognition. *Arch. Gen. Psychiat.,* **40**, 937–942.

Schildkraut, J.J. (1965). The catecholamine hypothesis of affective disorders: a review of supporting evidence. *Am. J. Psychiat.,* **122**, 509–522.

Simón, B. (1978). *Razon y locura en la Antigua Grecia.* Akal Universitaria, Madrid.

Torres P. (1994). *Le Cercle Maillol. Les avantguardes barcelonines i l'Institut Francés de Barcelona sota el franquisme.* Parisfol Edicions, Barcelona.

Vila-San Juan, S. (1982). Trienta cuadros desconocidos replantean el enigma de Josep Maria De Sucre. *El Correo Catalán,* May 5, p. 41, Barcelona.

Wittkower, R. & Wittkower, M. (1963). *Born under Saturn. The Character and Conduct of Artists: a Documented History from Antiquity to the French Revolution.* Weidenfeld, London.

CHAPTER 5

TREATING THE DEPRESSED ARTIST

CARL SALZMAN

It is now well established that creativity in some people is linked with varying degrees of affective disorders (Andreasen, 1987; Andreasen & Powers, 1975; Andreasen & Canter 1974; Jamison, 1989, 1993; Ludwig, 1994; Schildkraut et al, 1994; Schildkraut & Hirshfeld, 1995;). Both bipolar disorders (manic "highs" and depressive "lows") as well as unipolar disorders (depressive "lows" only) are over-represented among creative people such as visual artists (painters, sculptors), verbal artists (writers, playwrights, poets), and musicians (composers and performers).

Although the relationship between creativity and psychiatric disorders has been known for some time and has been the subject of both popular as well as medical literature, research into the effects of treatment as it may positively or negatively affect the creative individual has only begun with the development of modern psychiatric pharmacotherapy. Serious recurrent depressive illness can now be successfully treated with antidepressant drugs, achieving favorable response rates as high as 80 or 90% (American Psychiatric Association, 1993). The discovery of the mood-stabilizing and therapeutic effects of lithium, and more recently anticonvulsant medication (American Psychiatric Association, 1994), has made it possible for large numbers of patients with bipolar disorder, who experience oscillating and unpredictable moods, to achieve degrees of mood stabilization not previously possible. In order to understand the potential role of treatment in the creative person, it is necessary to consider the effect of dysregulated affect on the creative process.

The relationship between mood disorders and creativity has been increasingly discussed in the psychiatric literature (e.g. Goodwin & Jamison, 1990; Jamison et al, 1980; Jamison, 1993, 1989; Andreasen, 1987; Andreasen & Canter, 1974; Andreasen & Powers, 1975; Marshall et al, 1970; Andreasen & Glick, 1988; Richards et al, 1988; Schildkraut et al, 1994; Schildkraut & Hirshfeld, 1995). Although there is a strong association between creativity and affective illness (Andreasen, 1987), this relationship is complicated. Richards et al (1988) note that creativity may be enhanced in subjects showing milder and perhaps subclinical expressions of mood disturbance (especially those with cyclothymic disorder or potential bipolar disorder). Andreasen & Glick (1988) postulate that controlled hypomania may be a more useful state for painters than for writers, since painting is often more intuitive than analytic. Moreover, writing may demand sustained effort over a number of months, which is less likely to be enhanced by hypomania (although shorter works such as poems might be produced during a hypomanic period).

It is likely, however, that for most individuals truly creative output is diminished by severe disturbance of affect, either manic or depressed. For example, a group of 14 well known writers "... consistently indicated they were unable to work when they were depressed ... the writers who experienced mania also indicated that the work produced during mania was of poor quality" (Andreasen & Glick, 1988). However, even at extremes of affective disturbance, some creativity is possible, and these extreme periods may serve as the inspiration for later creativity (Richards et al, 1988). For example, depression may lead to introspection, empathy and psychological insights that enhance an artist's capacity to create (Schildkraut et al, 1994; Schildkraut & Hirshfeld, 1995). For mania, Andreasen & Glick (1988) comment that the hypomanic period "... may provide an incubation phase during which ideas are developed that can then be explored when the mood is more neutral and the mind is more rational". They further note that such an incubation period may also occur during a period of depression, although actual creative work during a very severe depression is unlikely. Virginia Woolf is offered as an example of a writer who rarely wrote while depressed but considered her depression eventually to enhance her creativity (Andreasen & Glick, 1988). For most creative people, however, Richards has proposed that the relationship between mood disorder and creativity is probably best described as an inverted U-shaped curve (Richards et al, 1988). This curve suggests that at the lowest end of depression and the highest ends of mania, both creative inspiration as well as productivity may be compromised.

The hypothesis of an inverted U-shaped curve relating mood disturbance and creativity is consonant with the clinical experience of non-creative people with mood disorders as well. In severe depression, there is marked psychomotor slowing, i.e. people commonly report their thought processes and mental energy are significantly diminished, along with their physical energy. Thinking, concentrating, or even passive attention to stimuli such as movies or watching television become difficult. Depressed persons commonly report that they are unable to pay bills, write cheques, or even attend to the normal daily mental functions of life. It is not surprising, therefore, that creative individuals suffering the same experience may be unable to find creative inspiration or be creatively productive during the depressive episode. For example, William Styron (1990, p. 46) notes: "I could no longer concentrate during those afternoon hours, which for years had been my working time, and the act of writing itself, becoming more and more difficult and exhausting, stalled, then finally ceased". Jamison (1993, p. 249) cites the poet Robert Lowell: "In depression, one wakes ... and fades into the dread of the day. Nothing will happen, but you know 12 hours will pass before you are back in bed ...".

At the opposite end of the inverted U-shaped curve is very severe mania. In this state, individuals have an impairment of associative thinking, i.e. the ability rationally to link thoughts together is impaired and there is also a marked acceleration in the rate of thinking. At the most extreme manifestation of mania, thinking may become out of control, scattered and non-productive. However, sometimes even these extreme manic states may be occasionally associated with some creativity.

TREATMENT OF THE CREATIVE INDIVIDUAL WITH MOOD DISORDER

In three superb reviews, Jamison (Jamison, 1989, 1993; Goodwin and Jamison, 1990) reviewed past experience of treating affective illness in creative people. In one study of artists and writers, ". . . 38% had been treated for an affective illness; three-fourths of those treated had been given antidepressants, lithium, or had been hospitalized" (Jamison, 1989). One-third of poets had received medication for depression; 17% required hospitalization, ECT or lithium for mania. Among the writers, playwrights had the highest total rate of treatment for depression (63%). Jamison (1989) notes that the prevalence of treatment in this group is "strikingly high" when compared to known prevalence rates for mood disorders in the USA (approximately 1% bipolar; 5% unipolar depression).

Andreasen (1987) surveyed 30 creative writers and reported an incidence of 37% of unipolar major depressive disorder (i.e. non-bipolar depression) and a 43% incidence of bipolar disorder in these writers; taken together they were significantly higher than in a control group who were not writers. She further noted a high incidence of bipolar II affective disorder, which is a disorder of alternating depression and mania in which depression predominates in both frequency of appearance and intensity of symptoms (Andreasen, 1987; Andreasen & Canter, 1974; Andreasen & Glick, 1988). She comments (Andreasen & Canter, 1974) ". . . a tendency toward melancholia may in fact be an occupational hazard of writers . . .".

The high incidence of mood disturbance as well as the high rate of psychiatric treatment suggests that even though mood disturbance may be linked to creativity, at some point the depression or mania becomes too intense and is experienced by the creative individual as unwanted, or as interfering with creative function. Fieve (1989, pp. 48–54) describes a painter of international reputation who suffered from severe bipolar illness. As his moods oscillated, so did his productivity. During mild highs he apparently produced numerous paintings described as "inspired". As his hypomania progressed, however, his paintings became fragmented, as he became restless and easily distracted, and then eventually aggressive, assaultive and dangerous.

Treatment of the creative person with mood disorder has been comprehensively discussed by several writers (Fieve, 1989; Jamison, 1993). Three issues must be addressed when considering the treatment of these patients. First, some creative individuals do not wish to be treated, believing that their illness is an important part of their creativity, or even fuels their creativity. Thus, Jamison (1993, p. 241) quotes the painter Edvard Munch as saying: "They (emotional disorders) are part of me and my art. They are indistinguishable from me and [treatment] would destroy my art. I want to keep those sufferings" (Figure 5-1). Second, there is the question of whether pharmacological treatment interferes with the creative process. Recent research that explores the effect of psychotropic medications on the creative processes is discussed in the next section of this chapter. Third, it is now possible to predict what may happen over time when the creative person, like others with mood disorder, is not treated. This will be discussed in the final section of this chapter.

5-1
EDVARD MUNCH
*EVENING (MELANCHOLIA),
1896*
*Woodcut colored by hand
14⅞ × 17¾ in (37.7 × 45 cm)*
© *The Cleveland Museum
of Art, 1995, Gift of Mrs
Clive Runnells in memory
of Leonard C. Hanna, Jr.,
59.82.* © *1996 The Munch
Museum/The
Munch–Ellingsen
Group/Artists Rights
Society (ARS), NY*

Most discussions of the treatment of bipolar disorder focus on the use of lithium. This compound, in clinical use for over three decades, has been definitively shown to control the mood oscillations of bipolar disorder, and in many cases to prevent their recurrence. For large numbers of young and middle-aged adults, side effects are limited to minor annoyances of increased thirst and urination. Side effects increase in some people as they age, however, and for some lithium use is accompanied by a physical tremor of the hands, which might interfere with the manual arts of painting, drawing and sculpting.

One of the best publicized reports on the therapeutic efficacy of lithium on a creative individual was provided by Fieve (1989) in a description of his patient, the well-known Broadway producer, Joshua Logan. Logan himself discussed his own experiences, confirming Fieve's observations and amplifying them with a first-person account. Although there are many such biographical accounts of bipolar disorder in creative people, Joshua Logan's story is remarkable for its insight into the therapeutic effects of lithium. After years of severe mood oscillations, from profoundly inactive and despairing depressions to exalted, grandiose, elated and irritable highs that required hospitalizations, electro-convulsive therapy and numerous trials of various medications, he was begun on lithium. As quoted by Fieve (1989, p. 34), Logan states, "I have now been taking lithium carbonate for four-and-a-half or five years, and I've not been conscious of the slightest highs or lows out of what would be considered a normal proportion. And yet, I seem to be as productive as I've ever been. I've collaborated this past year on two different musical comedies, and I'm writing my own autobiography. It's been a rewarding and enjoyable experience".

The stabilizing and obviously beneficial effects of lithium as described by Logan, however, sometimes also exact a price. In addition to the side effects already mentioned, concern has been expressed that lithium, either through direct chemical effects on the brain, or indirectly by controlling the hypomanic states that are associated with creativity, may interfere with both creative inspiration and creative productivity. The psychiatrist Mogens Schou took lithium and reported a number of symptoms, including ". . . being separated from environmental stimuli by a glass wall", which might suggest interference with creativity (Schou, 1968). And in a study of non-bipolar individuals who were medical researchers, lithium induced a state of malaise and passivity and apparently interfered with intellectual initiative (Schou, 1968). In another study of non-bipolar volunteers, lithium induced a state of apathy and a decline in motivation, as well as increased boredom, lethargy, confusion and an inability to

concentrate (Judd et al, 1977a,b). However, these investigators, Judd et al (1977b), found that semantic fluency (a measure of creativity) was not inhibited by lithium carbonate in normal people; neither did lithium influence esthetic perception or judgment. These findings by Judd et al (1977a,b), suggest that lithium may inhibit creativity in some individuals but not in others. Gitlin et al (1989) have reviewed the side effects of lithium and reported that lithium produced poor memory and mental slowness. Bech et al (1976) also noted that patients taking lithium reported "difficulties with concentrating and remembering". Shaw et al (1986) found that lithium use was associated with a decrease in the number of word associations to verbal stimuli, and Christodolou et al (1981) reported that lithium decreased visual retention.

There may be a diversity of responses to lithium, possibly due to differences in patient populations, severity of illness, age, and serum levels of lithium; and some creative individuals may not experience lithium as interfering with their creative processes. For example, Andreasen & Glick (1988) cite novelist Richard Stern's description of Robert Lowell's experience of lithium.

"He showed me the bottle of lithium capsules. Another medical gift from Copenhagen. Had I heard what his trouble was? 'Salt deficiency'. This had been the first year in eighteen he hadn't had an attack. There'd been fourteen or fifteen of them over the past eighteen years. Frightful humiliation and waste. He'd been all set to taxi up to Riverdale five times a week at $50 a session, plus (of course) taxi fare. Now it was a capsule a day and once-a-week therapy. His face seemed smoother, the weight of dis-

tress-attacks and anticipation both gone."

Schou (1979) interviewed 24 manic-depressive artists who had received lithium and were successfully treated. Twelve reported increased artistic productivity while taking lithium, six unaltered productivity, and six lowered productivity. Schou offers his views of some of his subjects, illustrating these effects:

"Although during treatment he missed the manic periods of excessive joy and initiative, he was in no doubt that the treatment raised his productivity. Not only did it prevent the unproductive depressions, but it also saved him from manic, valueless over-production, which later had to be sifted carefully in order to retrieve the few pieces of some merit."

"Before lithium treatment the patient had his best creative periods at the start of manic and depressive episodes. (With lithium) the patient feels that his net productivity is the same as before lithium treatment."

"The patient asserts that depressions do not interfere with her artistic productivity. While she took lithium, however, she found her creative power diminished and she regarded this as a direct drug effect."

Schou (1979) concludes, therefore, that in creative bipolar patients the effects of lithium may be variable, sometimes enhancing creativity, sometimes having no effect on creativity, and sometimes decreasing creativity. He comments further, however, that when artistic productivity decreases, it may only be temporary.

It would be useful to extend Schou's observations of the relative frequency of these three possible effects of lithium on creativity to a larger sample of artists and writers. This is particularly important since it may be difficult to disentangle drug effects from illness effects (Andreasen & Glick, 1988; Gitlin et al, 1989). For example, impaired cognitive processes that are noticed by the artist or writer after lithium treatment has begun, may be due to the lithium, to the residual effects of partially treated mania or depression, or to a combination of both. There is, in addition, the possible change in the style of the individual's creativity that develops after lithium treatment which may not be as acceptable or as valued by others. The international painter described by Fieve, for example, developed a new style during his lithium treatment which he called his "lithium period" (Fieve, 1989, p. 53). Schou also cites a painter described by Villeneuve (1973) whose style became modified on lithium treatment, becoming more figurative, with colors of softer tone. Robert Lowell's literary biographer, Ian Hamilton (cited by Andreasen & Glick, 1988), commented that Lowell's poems were different after lithium therapy, showing a "low-key agreeableness". Andreasen & Glick note that Lowell's improved productivity and stability may have come at some expense in "poetic power", although Lowell himself "apparently felt an improvement rather than a decline in his ability as a poet" (Andreasen & Glick, 1988).

Clinical experience suggests that the effects of lithium on the subjective experience of mental function and creativity not only vary from person to person, but may be very subtle and escape detection by normal psychological tests. Small but perceptible changes in associative fluency, image production, flights of fantasy, or unorthodox thinking that occur in some people as a result of treatment may assume great importance for the creative individual. The terms used by creative people to describe this experience vary among individuals, and also among different creative artists. A painter may describe this experience as a loss of a sense of the subtle relationships between colors. A writer might comment that his or her thinking is too linear and organized. A composer might experience a diminution of musical variations in his or her mind. It is important to note, however, that despite these descriptions of lithium's effect on creativity, not all creative individuals will experience lithium in the same way. Furthermore, not all creative individuals depend on hypomania for their inspiration (Schou, 1979).

Recent data have suggested that drugs used to control seizure disorders (anticonvulsants) may also have a significant therapeutic mood-stabilizing effect in bipolar disorder. There are no studies that examine the effect of anti-seizure medications on creative persons, or on the creative process. However, the use of anticonvulsants alone, or in conjunction with lithium, may provide mood stabilization with a diminished degree of side effects and possibly less interference with creativity.

There are also no research studies that specifically focus on the treatment of the depressed creative individual. Clinical experience, anecdotal reports and the biographies and autobiographies of creative individuals themselves, attest to the return of creative powers when depression is adequately and successfully treated. Unlike studies of lithium and other mood stabilizers, there are no studies that specifically investigate the effects of antidepressant drugs on creative inspiration or productivity. At usual therapeutic doses, antidepressants do not interfere with cognitive processes such as abstract thinking, synthetic creativity or concentration.

What of the creative patients who do not choose to receive treatment for their mood disorder or who discontinue treatment? Studies of the longitudinal course of these illnesses clearly demonstrate that, in most untreated patients, they progress over time so that both frequency and intensity of manic or depressive episodes increase with age. The long-term effect on creativity is not known, but it is reasonable to assume that creative inspiration and productivity would become progressively impaired as the disease worsens over time.

Untreated mood disorder, particularly depression, also carries with it a significant risk of suicide. It is estimated that 15% of depressed patients will successfully commit suicide (Winokur, 1981); and estimates of unsuccessful but serious attempts may be considerably higher. Loss of a creative person through suicide is not only an individual tragedy, but is tragic for society as well. As Jamison comments (1993, p. 249): "We will never know what Thomas Chatterton and Virginia Woolf might have written or Vincent van Gogh painted had they lived rather than committing suicide".

The decision whether or not to treat the creative individual with modern pharmacotherapy should be jointly made between patient and physician. Clinical experience of the author and others (Fieve, personal communication, 1994; Grinspoon, personal communication, 1994) and research data (Schou, 1979) suggest that, for many creative individuals, therapeutic mood stabilization and prevention of uncontrolled mood swings does not interfere with creativity. Indeed, the mood stabilization may actually help the individual achieve stability to proceed through a project requiring

MOOD DISORDERS AND ARTISTIC CREATIVITY

time and concentration. For the most severely afflicted individual, treatment may be life-saving, especially during the depressive periods. For creative individuals with less severe mood dysregulation, the decision to treat, not to treat, or to interrupt successful treatment may be based on a variety of factors. Careful evaluation of the life-course history of the patient, family history of affective disorder (which often provides a clue into the potential severity of an individual's own disorder), past experience with drug side effects, and the individual's own personal philosophy regarding life, art, and creativity must be weighed. For creative individuals who choose not to receive or maintain treatment, continued association with a trusted and valued clinician who can evaluate changes in mood status of the patient may avert catastrophic exacerbation of illness.

What of the creative individuals who, once having been successfully treated, discontinue their treatment. Fieve (personal communication, 1994) notes that lithium discontinuation is not uncommon. Schou (1979) indicates that six of the artists in his survey (as well as artists who are described in earlier reports) discontinued lithium after treatment had begun. The most common reason among these artists was the experience of decreased creativity and productivity, consonant with the report of Gitlin et al (1989) citing cognitive impairment as a major reason for interruption of lithium treatment. A successful painter with bipolar disorder illustrates this pattern of treatment discontinuation (Grinspoon, personal communication, 1994). When not depressed, he stated that his mind was always filled with colorful visual images and symbolism. When depressed, however, he was unable to work, and was placed on lithium. On lithium, he commented

that although no longer depressed, "painting has gone out of my head". He discontinued lithium, and was rapidly plunged into a severe recurrent depression requiring hospitalization.

Recent data (Suppes et al, 1991; Goodwin, 1994) have indicated that even after years of mood stabilization with lithium, discontinuation of the drug may result in a reappearance of dysregulated mood which may be quite severe. Jamison (1993, p. 248) comments that some creative individuals may discontinue drugs or choose a low dosage level "in the hopes of achieving a kind of controlled cyclothymia". Some apparently do well; those with more severe and psychotic forms of the disorder, however, frequently relapse and cease to function creatively until mood stability is regained (Fieve, personal communication, 1994). Indeed, as noted by Fieve (1989), it is the depression that often stimulates creative people to seek treatment, for it is at these times that they truly understand that their functioning is impaired.

Clinical experience suggests that depressed patients may also discontinue antidepressant treatment when no longer depressed. Whether or not creative individuals are more or less likely to inappropriately discontinue medication is not known.

CONCLUSION

Although mood disorder and creativity are often linked together, it is not necessary to have a mood disorder in order to be creative, neither is one necessarily creative just because one experiences disordered mood. Severe disturbances of mood in creative individuals, however, most likely interfere with the creative process at least at some points in the individual's life. It is likely that as the illness progresses, interference with creative inspiration as well as productivity will result. Under such circumstances, treatment of the individual may actually facilitate a restoration of creative function, although the artistic products may differ in form from those prior to treatment.

Not all unhappiness is depression, and not all exuberance or energy is mania. There is a wide spectrum of alternating moods that exists between the severe degrees of serious depression and serious mania. Normal or even mild fluctuations of mood in creative individuals do not necessarily require treatment. It is possible that, for creative individuals with mild bipolar illness, treatment with lithium carbonate may subtly interfere with cognitive processes linked to creativity. However, the treatment of depression in non-bipolar creative individuals often results in an enhanced sense of well-being and increased capacity for creative output.

New medications for the treatment of mood disorder are regularly introduced into clinical practice. Pharmacologic advances have begun to produce therapeutically effective drugs with significantly fewer side effects. If drug side effects are the primary cause of impaired creativity, then the development of these newer compounds may promise effective treatment without creative impairment. If, however, control of dysregulated mood itself interferes with creativity in some individuals, then the decision to treat or not treat the current illness with psychopharmacology is a matter of concern for the artist, the clinician and society. Continued studies of the relationship between mood, creativity and pharmacologic treatment may offer additional insights.

REFERENCES

American Psychiatric Association (1993). Practice guidelines for major depressive disorders in adults. *Am. J. Psychiat.*, **150**(4) (suppl), 1–26.

American Psychiatric Association (1994). Practice guideline for the treatment of patients with bipolar disorder. *Am. J. Psychiat.*, **151**(12) (suppl), 1–36.

Andreasen, N.C. (1987). Creativity and mental illness: prevalence rates in writers and their first-degree relatives. *Am. J. Psychiat.*, **144**, 1288–1292.

Andreasen, N.C. & Glick, I.D. (1988). Bipolar affective disorder and creativity: implications and clinical management. *Compr. Psychiat.*, **29**, 207–217.

Andreasen, N.C. & Powers, P.S. (1975). Creativity and psychosis. *Arch. Gen. Psychiat.*, **32**, 70–73.

Andreasen, N.C. & Canter, A. (1974). The creative writer: psychiatric symptoms and family history. *Compr. Psychiat.*, **15**, 123–131.

Bech, P., Vendsborg, P.B. & Rafaelson, O.J. (1976). Lithium maintenance treatment of manic-melancholic patients: its role in the daily routine. *Acta Psychiatr. Scand.*, **53**, 70–81.

Christodolou, G.N., Kokkevi, A., Lykouras, C., Stephanis, C.N. & Papadimitriou, G.N. (1981). Effects of lithium on memory. *Am. J. Psychiat.*, **138**, 847–848.

Fieve, R.R. (1989). *Moodswing.* Bantam Books, New York.

Gitlin, M.J., Cochran, S.D. & Jamison, K.R. (1989). Maintenance lithium treatment: side effects and compliance. *J. Clin. Psychiat.*, **50**, 127–131.

Goodwin, G.M. (1994). Recurrence of mania after lithium withdrawal: implications for the use of lithium in the treatment of bipolar affective disorder (editorial). *Br. J. Psychiat.*, **164**, 149–152.

Goodwin, F.K. & Jamison, K.R. (1990). *Manic-Depressive Illness*, pp. 332–367. Oxford University Press, New York.

Jamison, K.R. (1993). *Touched With Fire: Manic-depressive Illness and the Artistic Temperament*. Free Press, New York.

Jamison, K.R. (1989). Mood disorders and patterns of creativity in British writers and artists. *Psychiatry*, **52**, 125–134.

Jamison, K.R., Gerner, R.H., Hammen, C. & Padesky, C. (1980). Clouds and silver linings: positive experiences associated with primary affective disorders. *Am. J. Psychiat.*, **137**, 198–202.

Judd, L.J., Hubbard B., Janowsky, D.S., Huey, L.Y. & Attewell, P.A. (1977a). The effect of lithium carbonate on affect, mood, and personality of normal subjects. *Arch. Gen. Psychiat.*, **34**, 346–351.

Judd, L.J., Hubbard B., Janowsky, D.S., Huey, L.Y. & Takahashi, K.I. (1977b). The effect of lithium carbonate on the cognitive functions of normal subjects. *Arch. Gen. Psychiat.*, **34**, 355–357.

Ludwig, A.M. (1994). Mental illness and creative activity in female writers. *Am. J. Psychiat.*, **151**, 1650–1656.

Marshall, M.H., Neumann, C.P. & Robinson, M. (1970). Lithium, creativity, and manic-depressive illness: review and prospectus. *Psychosomatics*, **XI**, 406–408.

Richards, R., Kinney, D.K., Lunde. I., Benet, M. & Merzel, A.P.C. (1988). Creativity in manic-depressives, cyclothymes, their normal relatives, and control subjects. *J. Abnormal Psychol.*, **97**, 281–288.

Schildkraut, J.J., Hirshfeld, A.J. & Murphy, J.M. (1994). Mind and mood in modern art II: Depressive disorders, spirituality and early deaths in the abstract expressionist artists of the New York School. *Am. J. Psychiat.*, **151**, 482–488.

Schildkraut, J.J. & Hirshfeld, A.J. (1995). Mind and mood in Modern Art I: Miró and "Mélancolie". *Creativity Res. J.*, **8**, 1089–1102.

Schou, M. (1979). Artistic productivity and lithium prophylaxis in manic-depressive illness. *Br. J. Psychiat.*, **135**, 97–103.

Schou, M. (1968). Lithium in psychiatric therapy and prophylaxis. *J. Psychiatr. Res.*, **6**, 67–95.

Shaw, E.D., Mann, J.J., Stokes, P.E. & Manevitz, A.Z.A. (1986). Effects of lithium carbonate on associative productivity and idiosyncracy in bipolar outpatients. *Am. J. Psychiat.*, **143**, 1166–1169.

Styron, W. (1990). *Darkness Visible*. Random House, New York.

Suppes, T., Baldessarini, R.J., Faedda, G.L. & Tohen, M. (1991). Risk of recurrence following discontinuation of lithium treatment in bipolar disorder. *Arch. Gen. Psychiat.*, **48**, 1082–1088.

Villeneuve, A. (1973). Psychological and clinical problems in the treatment with lithium. In *Lithium and Psychiatry. A Synopsis*, Ed. A. Villeneuve. University Laval, Quebec.

Winokur, G. (1981). *Depression: The facts*. Oxford University Press, Oxford.

PART II
THE SPIRITUAL IN MODERN ART

INTRODUCTION

JOSEPH J. SCHILDKRAUT

Part II opens with an essay by the eminent Catalan artist Antoni Tàpies. In his chapter, entitled "Psychological Truths In Present-day Aesthetics", Tàpies writes that the "new vision of the world" revealed by modern physics has pervaded the thought and culture of the twentieth century; and he notes that the epistemological problems encountered by the new physics have focused attention on "the subjective, spiritual and even moral aspects of human nature". Referring to the works of Jung, Tàpies calls for us to "once again listen to 'the trends set by the gods'—which might ultimately prove to be the ancestral voices of Nature itself. . . ."

In his brief essay, "Tàpies, Between Spirit and Matter", Daniel Giralt-Miracle reminds us that Tàpies' art cannot be read "as if we were deciphering an alphabet of ideograms, but rather [that] we must look in all his work for the profound coherence of an active contemplation, based on an ever-open *meditation*". He writes, "Transmitting the spirit to matter and/or extracting from matter its spirit is the vital proposal which Tàpies achieves with his work".

The next chapter in Part II is "Inner Content, Outer Expression: A Brief Note on Kandinsky and the Spiritual in Modern Art" by Patricia C. Ballard. Konrad Oberhuber then provides us with his observations on "Artistic Form and Spiritual Experience". In this chapter he summarizes his thoughts on the differences in the artistic products of Eastern religions, the Americas, and the Christian works created in Europe. He goes on to show the evolving stages of spirituality in certain artists and he emphasizes the importance of the teachings of Rudolf Steiner for Kandinsky, Mondrian, and other early twentieth-century artists.

José Corredor-Matheos, in an evocative essay, "Spirituality in the Work of Eduardo Chillida", describes how Chillida's art "metamorphoses before our eyes". And Corredor-Matheos writes, "We can contemplate it as an object of meditation and, as such, it opens our spirit to an adventure without end", allowing us to see the dimension of reality we call the "spiritual".

Without having prepared anything in advance of the symposium, Eduardo Chillida, the renowned Spanish artist, generously agreed to share with us some personal reflections concerning his thoughts and work, spirituality and matter. His "Reflections on the Theme of this Symposium" concludes Part II.

CHAPTER 6

"PSYCHOLOGICAL TRUTHS" IN PRESENT-DAY AESTHETICS

Antoni Tàpies

"Every speck of dust has a marvelous soul, but before you can understand that you have to rediscover the magical and religious meaning of things" (Joan Miró, 1936).

Do not expect these lines to propose a set of aesthetic rules. I am simply questioning myself once again about some cultural truths that are right before our very eyes. The major changes that have taken place in this century's art were provoked by many different factors, among which there are surely some aesthetic theories that are by no means negligible. But, according to critics and historians, one of the things that has done most to produce these changes is the evolution of science, which has also taken place in the past 100 years. They particularly mention the influence of the new vision of the world revealed by physics. The truth is that this branch of science, with its revolutionary ideas about matter, space and time, cause and effect, pervades all twentieth-century human activities: the world of thought, our entire culture, modern technology.

THE TEACHINGS OF THE NEW SCIENCE

Attributing the changes in art to science, and particularly to physics, might flatter the unconditional champions of materialism, rationality and objectivity, many of whom might think that this means that the misty world of the spirit has now been displaced. But nothing could be further from the truth. To begin with, it is important constantly to remember that it is precisely since encountering epistemological problems that physics, which was previously dedicated only to the "materialness" of things—their physis—and utterly convinced about objective reality, has begun stressing the need to pay more attention to the subjective, spiritual and even moral aspects of human nature.

This is a subject that has been widely discussed for some time now, especially in terms of the new physics' interest in the spirituality of certain oriental wisdom and religions. Years ago Niels Bohr, the celebrated physicist, said, "Nowadays we have to turn towards the epistemological problems encountered by thinkers like Buddha or Laotzu when they attempted to reconcile our roles as both spectators and actors in the great drama of existence" (quoted in Capra, 1979, p. 18). Many other scientists have also pointed out that the new approaches to physics are closely related to all the mystically-oriented Western schools of thought. And now science itself is cautioning us not to forget that the role of the new physics in today's culture is inseparable from the role of research in the world of spirituality and religion, where changes are likewise taking place. This is a world that is being modernized as quickly as science, although in the West it is frequently dogged by ancient institutions that want to monopolize it and sometimes even immobilize it. Consequently, art that is related to the new science cannot keep from also relating to subjects involved with what many scientists now accept, if only as the "psychological truths" of religions and particularly mysticism. And by extension they accept many of religion's moral values—although religions do not have the monopoly on such values—despite the fact that all this business of religions and their moral authority strikes many "materialists" as something from another age.

ART AND THE APOPHATIC APPROACH (VIA APOFÁTICA)*

As has often been observed, it would be ridiculous to ignore the fact that art has always had a magic–religious purpose. But a lesser known fact is that, starting with the modern movements that established "creative individualism, cornerstone of the artist's emancipation" (Argullol, 1989), the purpose of art has taken on a new dimension that parallels the evolution of science. I am obviously referring to the movements that span the periods from Romanticism to Expressionism, from Cubism to the pioneers of abstract art, from Dada to Surrealism—and, generally speaking, to all those movements that have recaptured the original meaning of art and have proved able once again to enter into the great symbolist tradition. All these movements were aware that their psychic, religious or moral content did not necessarily have to be expressed through the positive dogmatic–theological thought and language of institutionalized religions, but could also be

expressed more spontaneously, indirectly, through other mechanisms of our psyches that sometimes operate on the basis of negation, the mystics' famous *apophatic approach* ("via apofática"). These are mechanisms that even quite orthodox authors sometimes find more appropriate than those of positivism. Moreover, these mechanisms often include (but are by no means diminished by) many traditional religious attitudes. To put it more precisely, these are the mechanisms that make up the generic framework of what some scholars have labeled "anthropological mysticism" in order to distinguish it from the more specific theological mysticism. (Remember that, as C.G. Jung observed, even a ceremony as singular as the Mass can be included among the general repertoire of rites of *sacrifice* and *transformation* found in various civilizations.)

Interdisciplinary studies of depth psychology, ethnology and comparative religion agree that this apophatic way embraces the impressive processes by which our unconscious minds create symbols, the important messages received from the world of the imagination, mythic creations, divine figurations, our attraction to mysteries, the ecstasies of certain believers, prophetic intuitions, the fantasies of some children, the hallucinations of certain people who are ill or even mad, the language of dreams, numerous impulses of desire, affection, hate. All of these are things that often give works of art that magical religious aura I mentioned earlier, without there necessarily being any liturgical framework for it and sometimes without the artists themselves even being aware of it.

Do we have to be reminded how important the interrelation of science and religion has been in the post-Freudian era in order to understand all this more clearly? The discovery of the

---

*Recognition of the limits of human rational understanding in relation to the transcendent or spiritual.

world of the unconscious has been compared to the geographic discoveries made during the Renaissance and the astronomical discoveries made when the telescope was invented. Likewise, it may be only since the studies of C.G. Jung, and others of his disciples, such as J.L. Henderson, M-L. von Franz, A. Jaffé and J. Jacobi (see Jung et al, 1964.), revealed the wealth of this unconscious world that the unconscious began to be understood as a function of the human spirit that has important positive effects on the cognitive and ethical evolution of nations and their cultures and which has contributed a great deal to their progress. Scientists have, therefore, begun studying it ever more closely and their study has also revived the old controversy about the role of art in society, giving it a really modern and progressive twist that is far different from the many misguided attempts to socialize culture.

It is not for nothing that in the past 60 years there has been such a proliferation of studies about the way our unconscious minds work and the images and symbols they produce. It is not for nothing that, in culture in particular, many beliefs borrowed from the symbolic world of different religions, innumerable rites and sacred celebrations have begun moving into a new category (although even for non-believers they continue to play a leading role as the depositories and producers of a large part of these symbols) just as are some of the so-called "alternative beliefs", certain esoteric doctrines, the world of the Mysteries, gnosis and cabala.

These are subjects in which psychologists, ethnologists, philosophers, theologians, orientalists and, as I mentioned before, a number of prominent representatives of the physical sciences, have been passionately inter-

ested since the late 1920s and early 1930s. They are subjects which are an essential component of what could be termed "the spirit of our times" and which are continually being examined in workshops, symposia, colloquia and congresses. These studies have proliferated in the past few years and have even been the basis of major international exhibitions which included the work of the most renowned artists. To mention just a few of them: there were the exhibitions held at the Los Angeles County Museum in 1986 and at the Gemmente Museum in The Hague in 1987, both of which were significantly titled *The Spiritual in Art: Abstract Painting 1890–1986*. There was also *Gegenwart Ewigkeit. Spuren des Transzendenten in der Kunst unserer Zeit*, which was held at Berlin's Martin Gropius Bau in 1990. The 1988 Venice Biennial, whose theme was the links between art and science, dedicated a major section of the exhibition to possible parallels between art and alchemy. This section was organized by A. Schwarz, a specialist in the work of Marcel Duchamp, who is in fact considered to have been "the alchemist of the avant-garde".

THE ALCHEMIC MODEL

Obviously, there is a danger that casual observers will regard these studies as a sort of return to non-scientific credulity, and even attribute them to the fondness for occult sciences and paranormal phenomena that is so fashionable in today's entertainment culture. This danger is particularly great at present when, after all Eastern Europe's problems with anything that even vaguely hinted at spirituality, many people throughout the continent have reacted by accepting the belief that religion is the answer and that it may well be the Vatican that will provide the formulae for solving the world's social and economic problems. (Indeed, it would not be surprising were the oscillating trends of fashion to lead us from today's materialistic and rationalistic excesses to an exaggerated wave of spirituality and religiousness, a bandwagon on which many people would of course immediately jump to promote their own interests.) But no matter what they may seem to be, these studies have a certain scientific and cultural weight that cannot be overlooked, no matter how trivialized or misunderstood they might be.

Let us take the parallels between art and alchemy as an example. The idea of a parallel is obviously outrageous if we view alchemy as no more than a set of superstitions, errors and pseudo-scientific ideas that gradually developed into the most "serious" studies of modern chemistry. As Mircea Eliade so clearly saw, it is a mistake to view alchemy as nothing more than a sort of pre-chemistry (Eliade, 1990). Many alchemists actually performed ritual symbolic "operations", that were essentially very similar to those required by some spiritual exercises, certain sacramental forms, Zen-assisted meditation, yoga—all of which serve as catalysts that are necessary to stimulate our imaginations and bring us nearer to inner knowledge. This is confirmed by Henry Corbin, an expert in Islamic alchemy: basically, "... it is our true imagination that makes alchemical operations synonymous with inner transmutation", that illuminating transmutation sought by all wisdom (Corbin, 1986).

It is true, then, that without forgetting the different aims and the numerous branches that make up (and have often discredited) this huge conglomerate known as alchemy, some of its relations to art explain why it is no wonder that alchemy has stimulated the imagination of some artists. Perhaps the most notable relation is between art and the "hermetic branch" of alchemy, with its more universal aspirations of discovering and intimately experiencing the *ultimate causes* and the *essential elements* of reality. Here we actually find an attitude that is similar to that of many artists and poets, like Rimbaud for instance, with his idea about "the alchemy of the verb". This poetic metaphor expressed a genuine desire, shared with some of those ancient alchemists, to delve deeply into the occult, into the "final mysteries" that illuminate our arcane selves at the level of their deepest roots in nature.

Another good way to study the relationship between art and alchemy is by exploring the wealth of iconography that has illustrated alchemistic treatises throughout time. Nowadays we know that we are not simply attracted to this iconography for purely aesthetic reasons or because of the intellectual effort involved in delving into ancient beliefs and rituals. The attraction is much more immediate because this iconography is an example of the symbols traditionally produced by all human spirits. It is what Jung labeled the "archetype of the collective unconscious" and similar images have been used by all races throughout time. And what holds true for these images of alchemy also holds true for the "imagery" of all religions.

SURREALISM: ITS SUCCESSES AND FAILURES

For many people in the world of art what I am saying here is nothing new. The entire spectrum of symbols produced by the human unconscious, ranging from the most sublime to the most scatalogical, was already a subject of discussion among the international avant-garde as far back as the first decades of the twentieth century, and particularly among the artists and theorists of the Dada and Surrealist movements. But it is worth mentioning again in order to demonstrate that the declarations of these groups on the aforementioned subjects did not always hit the mark. The 1930s surrealist defense of irrationality, paranoia, the absurd, demoralization, confusion, and its systematic discrediting of all other functions of the psyche, strike us nowadays as demogogic rhetoric based on a misunderstanding of certain concepts of psychoanalysis, a childish radicalism that actually played into the hands of the conservatives when not surrendering to them completely. It is no wonder then that many of the leading artists and poets soon abandoned the movement. (This was the case of Catalonia's two leading artistic and literary figures—Joan Miró and J.V. Foix—who, for these and a number of other related reasons, promptly distanced themselves from Dalí's clique (Molas, 1983).) There is no need, of course, to even mention some of their antics, which were designed to *shock* polite society but which overuse eventually robbed of all impact. Just consider the difference between the "convulsive beauty" of a sewing machine and an umbrella atop a dissecting table in Lautremont's time and the banality of the subsequent combinations of so many objects.

In contrast, the original surrealist group's mode of expression, based on the total liberation of the invididual spirit, psychic automatism and the independence of the artist, definitely remains valid today. This is particularly true in the case of the surrealists, who were more interested in ethnology and delving into the history of tribal and Asiatic arts (e.g. Bataille, Leiris), as well as those who felt themselves to be the heirs of other aesthetic trends that were more universal and also closer to the new brand of science, all of whom have obviously continued blazing their own trails.

THE NEW SITUATION OF MODERN ART

It is clear that all of this has gradually changed the situation of modern art. It is not that those who still give free reign to expressing their unconscious impulses—and indeed this movement continues to be the best—should be rejected. Rejecting a method from which the art world has truly gained would be every bit as ridiculous as the reaction, in just the opposite sense, of George Mathieu, the informalist painter whose studio was filled with portraits of the encyclopedists, all turned face to the wall. Nowadays some artists are more aware that all kinds of things emerge from the unconscious, from the most creative to the most destructive, from the most divine to the most satanic, and that making good use of this interplay of contradictions is much more difficult, risky and dangerous than it first appears. It is no wonder, then, that artists have recently been urged to be more severely critical, better prepared and sometimes even to adopt a certain discipline, as all wisdom recommends, before letting themselves be "carried away" by the unconscious. Unfortunately, there are still many who do not realize that no unconscious is worth anything, just as there is no imagination, intuition, vision, art, mysticism (as theologists well know) that is worth anything unless it is accompanied by a vigilant "spirit" and a "doctrine" that gives them meaning; in other words (and to put it in lay terms) unless they are counterbalanced by all the achievements of our conscious minds and the rational side of us that is preserved by humanity. But, nevertheless, the artistic climate—obviously under pressure from other factors as well—is unquestionably changing.

As Jung himself said, "The study of symbolism, both individual and collective, is an enormous task that is not yet under control. But it has finally begun. The first findings are encouraging and hint at responses to many problems of contemporary mankind". In any case, there are a good number of people who are already convinced that many symbols and values of the ancient and modern spiritual and religious worlds, the great religions and what strike us as primitive folk beliefs, must be revised and given greater respect. We do not know what shape all this will take but in line with the recommendations of analytical psychology, it certainly appears that it would be a good thing to once again listen to "the trends sent by the gods"—which might ultimately prove to be the ancestral voices of Nature itself—if they can really "cure us of the disassociation" that is an inherent part of the famous Western schizophrenia that separates spirit from matter, and thereby bring our knowledge and our behavior into better balance.

Recent physiological studies of the brain appear to confirm this need to strike a balance between the two "cognitive" approaches and allow them to complement one another, because neither the one nor the other alone can develop its full potential or lead us to that global knowledge so badly needed by contemporary mankind. Part of this century's art has done a great deal in this direction, but it goes without saying that there are still a number of amazing paths open to us, and especially to the new generations of artists (despite those who maintain that art is on the decline), paths that will inspire us to follow them further and further inward, not only in the work of the artist alone but also in revising the context in which this work must be presented so that all of society can truly benefit from its influence.

REFERENCES

Argullol, R. (1989) *Tres Miradas Sobre el Arte*. Destinolibro, Barcelona.

Capra, F. (1979). *Le Tao de la Physique*. Tchou, Paris.

Corbin, H. (1986). *Alchimie comme Art Hiératique*. L'Herne, Paris.

Eliade, M. (1990). *Alchimie Asiatique*. L'Herne, Paris.

Jung, C.G., von Franz, M.-L., Henderson, J.L., Jacobi, J. & Jaffé, A. (1964). *L'Homme et ses Symboles*. Pont Royal, Paris.

Jung, C.G. (1990). Transformation symbolism in the Mass. In *The Mysteries. Papers from the Eranos Yearbooks*, Vol. 2, 5th Edn, Princeton University Press, Princeton, NJ.

Miró, J. (1936). Ou allez-vous Miró? Interview with Joan Miró by Georges Duthuit. *Cahiers D'Art*, **XI** (8–10), 262.

Molas, J. (1983). *La Literatura Catalana d'Avantguarda, 1916–1938*, Ed. Antoni Bosch, Barcelona. (Recounts the brief history of Dali's local Surrealist clan.)

6-1
ANTONI TÀPIES
ZOOM, 1946
Mixed media on canvas. 25⅝ × 21¼ in (65 × 54 cm)
Photograph courtesy of Fundació Antoni Tàpies, Barcelona. © 1996 Artists Rights Society (ARS), NY/ADAGP, Paris

6-2
ANTONI TÀPIES
NEWSPRINT CROSS, 1946–1947
Watercolor and collage on paper, 15¾ × 12¼ in (40 × 31 cm)
Photograph courtesy of Fundació Antoni Tàpies, Barcelona. © 1996 Artists Rights Society (ARS), NY/ADAGP, Paris

CHAPTER 7

TÀPIES, BETWEEN SPIRIT
AND MATTER*

DANIEL GIRALT-MIRACLE

"L'experiència íntima de la realitat profunda desvetllada per certes analogies, imatges i símbols tradicionals és un fet comú a la naturalesa humana, al cervell humà, a moltes cultures ... i ve de molt lluny" ("The intimate experience of profound reality awakened through certain analogies, images and traditional symbols is a fact common to human nature, to the human brain, to many cultures ... and it has been with us since very long ago") (A. Tàpies, 1990a).

The most striking element in Tàpies' work is its coherency. Those of us who, over the last 40 years, have been able to follow the affirmation of his personality (parallel to his internationalization), observe that the coherency factor is that which agglutinates all his creative work's points of departure and manifestations.

The life and work of an artist run in parallel; they are two faces of the same being, two aspects of a single personality. In the final assessment, what really matters is not art, even if it is an essential manifestation, but

*Translated by Henrietta J. Fielden

rather that which art manifests, reveals and manages to communicate to us.

For the profound exploration of reality which Tàpies sets before us, at an epistemological, existential, material, sociological and plastic level, he is an artist who surprises us intensely. From this perspective, he has never dissociated ethics and aesthetics, he has been demanding and critical with himself, with others and with his circumstances. At bottom his work is the reflection of this intellectual and moral process that, with a radical and unmistakable personality, expresses itself through the tools peculiar to art.

In order to understand Tàpies one cannot linger at an initial analytical level, one has to penetrate and share the aesthetic and intellectual proposal that he makes us, because what is reflected in a painting, a print, a sculpture . . . are certain ideas, thoughts full of passion and energy, overwhelming in their construction, their treatment and morphology, a philosophy of existence.

It is as though all his work were a calligraphy of the spirit, the direct transmission of certain impulses, certain reflections, certain feelings that, little by little, are transformed into matter, form, plastic thought. A rich symbolic repertory, profoundly codified, which finds the mastery of a language which has developed, through different moments and periods in space, the signs, matter and color, and which, in spite of showing differential traits, always displays a unifying conceptual coherency.

It is probably for this reason that Tàpies has laid special emphasis on art's spiritual values, on the contemplative meaning of the artistic experience, on the inherent energy of the spiritual states that finally lead him to a philosophy of action.

From Western metaphysics or oriental philosophies such as *tao* or *zen*,

7-1
ANTONI TÀPIES
TRIPTYCH, 1948
Oil on canvas,
38¼ × 25⅝ in/38¼ × 51⅛ in/
38¼ × 25⅝ in (97 × 65 cm/
97 × 130 cm/97 × 65 cm)
Photograph courtesy of
Fundació Antoni Tàpies,
Barcelona. © 1996 Artists
Rights Society (ARS),
NY/ADAGP, Paris

7-2
ANTONI TÀPIES
KAKEMONO, 1977
Ink on paper, 78 × 15¾ in
(198 × 40 cm)
Photograph courtesy of
Fundació Antoni Tàpies,
Barcelona. © 1996 Artists
Rights Society (ARS),
NY/ADAGP, Paris

Tàpies has understood this deepening of being as something more than an interiorizing speculation: as a philosophy of action, as an active meditation that uses all the elements at its command to discover the most profound dimensions of being, directly related to reality, to nature, to our fellow man. Tàpies had the courage to reflect publicly on this dimension of being at the beginning of the seventies, when both the *materialist* and the *spiritualist* contexts manipulated like a puppet, and in opposite directions, the intrinsic meaning of what Tàpies calls the "hunger of the absolute".

He has since defined it in a more precise way in two speeches: *Art i espiritualitat* (Tàpies, 1988), given at the University of Barcelona on the occasion of his investiture as Doctor Honoris Causa (June, 1988) and, more recently, *L'Art i la contemplació interior* (Tàpies, 1990a), his introductory speech to the Real Academia de Bellas Artes de San Fernando (Royal Fine Arts Academy of San Fernando) (December, 1990).

Clearly, it comes down to a meaning of the sacred which goes further than the sectarianizing confessions of the spirit's values and which has its base in that exceptional approximation made by Rudolf Otto, at the beginning of the century, when he analyzed these values as a fundamental part of man's cognitive faculties and of his behavior (Otto, 1980). Not for nothing does Tàpies coincide in these conclusions with many scientists in the fields of physics and biology.

What might seem to be an obsolete mysticism, self-absorbed, removed from circumstantial reality, dangerously close to the monastic ivory tower, is, in Tàpies' case, transformed into an alliance between contemplation and praxis, between creative action and thought. "The mystic phe-nomenon"—says Tàpies—"also serves to set the artist's creative process in motion" (Tàpies, 1990b).

For this reason he was one of the first to revindicate the character of Ramon Llull* (Doctor Illuminatus) as a man of thought, as a man of action, and as a man of spirit, a dimension which later can be found in the surrealists' proposals or in Bertrand Russell's philosophy, with the deliberate desire to connect globally with material mysticism, in a permanent interrelation between the exterior world and the interior (Lewis, 1972).

This unity between that which is thought, as an intellectual manifestation, and that which is art, as a plastic manifestation, is displayed in his work without fissures. The cohesion between what is theory and concept, and what is practice and execution, is total. Austerity, subtlety, the commands of composition, economy of means, severity of color, poverty of materials, dialog between the full and the empty, chance factors, instinct, naturalness, serenity, liberty; all these are not only present in his painting, but in all his plastic work, because they are the conclusion of the philosophy of life which inspires the Japanese to say that "real beauty can only be discovered by one who mentally completes the incomplete".

We should not lapse into a facile determinism which makes us read into his production the keys of his thinking, as if we were deciphering an alphabet of ideograms, but rather we must look in all his work for the profound coherence of an active contemplation, based on an ever-open *meditation*.

Tàpies continues to exercise that

---

*Ramon Llull (c. 1232–1316); philosopher, theologian and writer of Palma de Mallorca who studied contemplation, mystic thought and the science of the time.

7-3
ANTONI TÀPIES
LOVE, TO DEATH, 1980
Acrylic painting on cloth mounted on canvas, 78¾ × 148 in (200 × 376 cm)
Photograph courtesy of Fundació Antoni Tàpies, Barcelona. © 1996 Artists Rights Society (ARS), NY/ADAGP, Paris

7-4
ANTONI TÀPIES
DRAGON, 1980
Acrylic painting, pencil and varnish on wood, 35 × 57⅝ in (89 × 146.5 cm)
Photograph courtesy of Fundació Antoni Tàpies, Barcelona. © 1996 Artists Rights Society (ARS), NY/ADAGP, Paris

knowledge he acquired very young in the *Tea Book* of Okakura Kakuzo (1989), of not wanting to say everything in one single piece, to leave the spectator with the opportunity of completing it with his own thoughts, of integrating them into the piece, just as when the experience of artistic communication occurs.

His attitude towards the work of art, thus, has always been radical, because he has not understood it as an object of consumption, but as something more, as a penetration into the form and foundation of things in order to show the extensions of reality, "to transport the spectator's mind and take it to other levels of consciousness, even as far as a level of interiorization which makes the consciousness one with the cosmos" (Tàpies, 1989) so that the spectator can become the active protagonist of his reflection.

7-5
ANTONI TÀPIES
RED SIGNS, 1985
Oil and collage on wood,
51⅛ × 76¾ in
(130 × 195 cm)
Photograph courtesy of
Fundació Antoni Tàpies,
Barcelona. © 1996 Artists
Rights Society (ARS),
NY/ADAGP, Paris

In view of these positions we understand that there is no real difference between what we traditionally call *material* and what we know as *spiritual*; transmitting the spirit to matter and/or extracting from matter its spirit is the vital proposal which Tàpies achieves with his work.

REFERENCES

Kakuzo, O. (1989). *El Llibre del te* [*The Tea Book*] (Trans. Carles Soldevila). Editorial Altafulla, Barcelona.

Lewis, J. (1972). Misticismo y lógica. *Bertrand Russell: Filósofo y humanista*, Chapter IX. Editorial Ayuso, Madrid.

Otto, R. (1980). *Lo santo, lo racional y lo irracional en la idea de Dios*. Alianza Editorial, Madrid.

Tàpies A. (1988). Art i espiritualitat. Dissertation in the Investment Doctor Honoris Causa by the University of Barcelona, Barcelona, June 22, 1988. Published in *Nous Horitzons*, Barcelona, **110**, November 1988. Published in *Valor de l'Art*, Fundació Antoni Tàpies-Editorial Empúries, Barcelona, 1993.

Tàpies, A. (1989). *El arte como energía*. Interview with Antoni Tàpies by J.J. Navarro-Arisa, El Pais, Barcelona, April 1.

Tàpies, A. (1990a). Arte y contemplación interior. Dissertation by the Honorary Academician, M Antoni Tàpies. Madrid. Royal Academy of Fine Arts of San Fernando, December 2. Published under the title *Art i Contemplació Interior*, in *Valor de l'Art*, Fundació Antoni Tàpies-Editorial Empúries, Barcelona, 1993.

Tàpies, A. (1990b). *El pintor que creó una nube* (The painter who created a cloud). Interview with Antoni Tàpies by Lluís Permanyer, *La Vanguardia*, Barcelona, May 27.

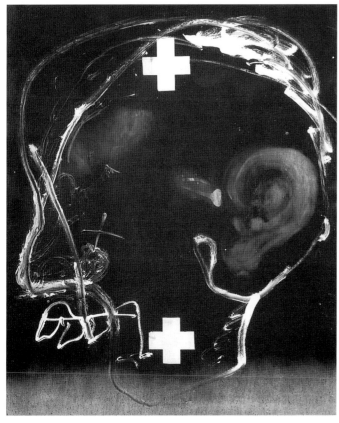

7-6 (left)
ANTONI TÀPIES
OVAL ON WHITE, 1985
Oil on wood, 31⅞ × 39⅜ in (81 × 100 cm). Photograph courtesy of Fundació Antoni Tàpies, Barcelona. © 1996 Artists Rights Society (ARS), NY/ADAGP, Paris

7-7 (below left)
ANTONI TÀPIES
HEAD WITH TWO CROSSES, 1985. Oil on wood, 51⅛ × 38¼ in (130 × 97 cm). Photograph courtesy of Fundació Antoni Tàpies, Barcelona. © 1996 Artists Rights Society (ARS), NY/ADAGP, Paris

7-8 (below)
ANTONI TÀPIES
FOOT AND CROSSES, 1991
Painting on synthetic textile, 59 × 48 in (150 × 122 cm). Photograph courtesy of Fundació Antoni Tàpies, Barcelona. © 1996 Artists Rights Society (ARS), NY/ADAGP, Paris

INNER CONTENT, OUTER EXPRESSION: A BRIEF NOTE ON KANDINSKY AND THE SPIRITUAL IN MODERN ART

PATRICIA C. BALLARD

"The spiritual life, to which art belongs and of which she is one of the mightiest elements, is a complicated but definite and easily definable movement forwards and upwards. This movement is the movement of experience. It may take different forms, but it holds at bottom to the same inner thought and purpose (Kandinsky, 1912/1977, p. 4).

Although the twentieth-century Russian painter and theorist Wassily Kandinsky was by no means the first to extol art as a crucial contributing element in the betterment of humanity, early works from his literary legacy have provided the most impassioned and distinguished visions linking spirituality to artistic creativity in this century. His first major text, *Concerning the Spiritual in Art* (Kandinsky, 1912/1977), is a pint-sized but powerful blend of spiritual primer, social critique and aesthetic manifesto that has obtained a prominence rivaled by few other artist–authors since its publication in 1912. In it, Kandinsky proclaimed the need for a "spiritual revolution", a rebellion against the social ills of materialism and what he perceived to be a general absence of "soul" in his time. According to Kandinsky's idealistic text, artists would play key roles in this development towards an "Epoch of the Great Spiritual," utilizing their creativity to reveal mystic "inner" expressions leading to "the improvement and refinement of the human soul" (Kandinsky, 1912/1977 p. 54).

The concept of the artist as mystic visionary has a long and complex history. But unique to this century is the fact that so many spiritually-inspired artists and their works are well documented and recognized by scholars (Tuchman & Freeman, 1986). Unlike past centuries, where art informed by occult mysteries and spiritual ideas outside of mainstream Christianity was known only to select groups of dedicated admirers, artists throughout this century who have embraced the arcane and esoteric themes of spiritual disciplines have garnered significant critical support and widespread attention. Certainly, Kandinsky's *Concerning the Spiritual in Art* (1912/1977) has played a crucial role in promoting such interest.

In the years preceding the First World War, Kandinsky was deemed the standard-bearer of avant-garde artistic theory and abstraction as it related to mysticism. Kandinsky scholars Rose-Carol Washton Long and Sixten Ringbom have scrupulously docu-

8-1
WASSILY KANDINSKY
SKETCH FOR "COMPOSITION II",
1909–10
Oil on canvas, 38⅜ × 51⅝ in
(97.5 × 131.2 cm)
The Solomon R.
Guggenheim Museum,
New York. Photograph by
David Heald © The
Solomon R. Guggenheim
Foundation, New York (FN
45.961). © 1996 Artists
Rights Society (ARS),
NY/ADAGP, Paris

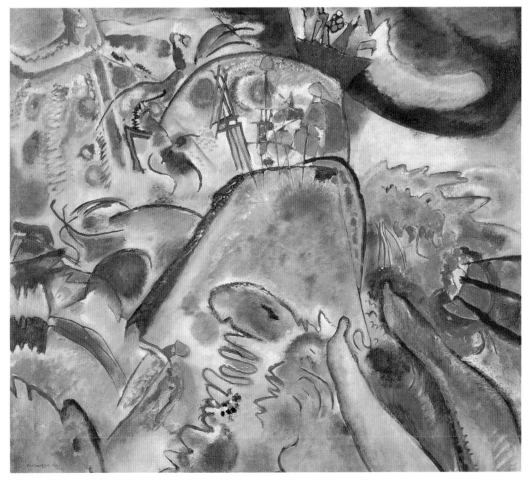

8-2
WASSILY KANDINSKY
SMALL PLEASURES, 1913
Oil on canvas, 43¼ × 47⅛ in
(109.8 × 119.7 cm)
The Solomon R.
Guggenheim Museum,
New York. Photograph by
David Heald © The
Solomon R. Guggenheim
Foundation, New York (FN
43.921). © 1996 Artists
Rights Society (ARS),
NY/ADAGP, Paris

mented the resounding effect of the artist's tome and oeuvre upon other European artists (Washton Long, 1986; Ringbom, 1970). Artists such as Paul Klee, Kazimir Malevich and numerous others began to transform their art towards non-objectivity in the wake of Kandinsky's revelations. When Kandinsky read sections of his book to a congress of his fellow countrymen in the year prior to its original publication in Germany, one critic declared him "the preacher of the newest art" (see Bowlt & Washton Long, 1980, p. 13). In the same year, Kandinsky influenced several other disenchanted artists in the "Neue Künstler-vereinigung" group, such as August Macke, Franz Marc and Gabriele Münter, to secede and form the "Blaue Reiter".* Along with Marc, Kandinsky edited and contributed to the *Blaue Reiter Almanac* (published late 1912), which served to further reinforce and expand Kandinsky's vision of spiritual freedom and theories for the "outer expression" of "inner content" in art.

Despite the rebellious tone expressed in *Concerning the Spiritual in Art*, Kandinsky's mystical ideas were dramatically shaped by the age in which he was born. The late nineteenth century had produced a thriving and diverse undercurrent of occult organizations throughout Europe. Already in his mid-40s by the time of the publication of his book in 1912, Kandinsky had successfully distilled and adapted several established occult philosophies into his personalized discourse regarding spirituality (see

Ringbom, 1966). Specifically, it is the doctrines of the Theosophical Society that emerge most clearly in Kandinsky's text.

With chapters in numerous countries and possessing a significant following, the Theosophical Society was the most widespread occult group. Begun in 1875 by the charismatic Helena P. Blavatsky, a Russian émigré, and Henry Steel Olcott, the Society defined its aim as the establishment of a transcultural study of science, philosophy, religion and inner spiritual truths. Although Blavatsky culled many of the original theosophical principles from Hinduism and Buddhism, elements of Christianity were subsequently added by other spiritual theorists, most notably Rudolf Steiner, a German theosophist-turned-anthroposophist.** Steiner's numerous writings and lectures were largely responsible for the immense success of the Theosophical Society within Germany.

Kandinsky proclaimed his admiration for the Theosophical Society in the early pages of *Concerning the Spiritual in Art*. Mentioning Blavatsky directly, the artist praised the organization's visionary search for the "eternal truth" (Kandinsky, 1912/1977, p. 13). Besides his obvious familiarity with Blavatsky's literature, Kandinsky is known to have owned copies of Steiner's lectures and books, some of which were annotated by the artist or his companion Gabriele Münter, in his private library (Tuchman & Freeman, 1986).

---

*Although Otto Fischer, the primary theorist of the Neue Künstlervereinigung, and Kandinsky agreed in their dislike of "art for art's sake" (as in the case of the decorative style of the Jugendstil), Fischer did not support Kandinsky's forays into the realm of non-objectivity. Fischer stated that "a picture without an object is meaningless."

**Steiner left the Theosophical Society in 1913. Heavily influenced by Goethe, Rosicrucianism and the Revelation of St John, Steiner developed Anthroposophy as a "spiritual science", in which humanity would experience the mystical through the physical body instead of the ethereal experience of the divine sought by the Theosophical Society.

Quoting Madame Blavatsky in his book, Kandinsky wrote, "the earth will be a heaven in the twenty-first century in comparison with what it is now" (Kandinsky, 1912/1977, p. 14). At this point in time, only brief years away from the dawn of the new millennium and a little over 80 years after Kandinsky's first call for spiritual revolution, it is now possible for us to reflect upon the spiritually influenced art of the past century created in the wake of Kandinsky's visionary text.

REFERENCES

Bowlt, J.E. & Washton Long, R.C. (1980). *The Life of Vasilii Kandinsky in Russian Art: a Study of the Spiritual in Art*. Newtonville, MA: Oriental Research Partners, citing Khudozhestvennye besti s zapada. Germaniia, *Apollon* (St. Petersburg) (1912), **3**, 9, p. 56.

Kandinsky, W., (1912/1977). *Concerning the Spiritual in Art* (Trans. M.T.H. Sadler). Dover, New York.

Kandinsky, W. & Marc F. (1912/1974). *The Blaue Reiter Almanac*. Thames and Hudson, London.

Lindsay, K.C. & Vergo, P. (1994). *Kandinsky: Complete Writings on Art*. Da Capo Press, New York.

Ringbom, S. (1970). *The Sounding Cosmos: a Study in the Spiritualism of Kandinsky and the Genesis of Abstract Painting*. Åbo Akademi, Åbo.

Ringbom, S. (1966). Art in the Epoch of the Great Spiritual, Occult Elements in the Early Theory of Abstract Painting. *Journal of the Warburg and Courtauld Institutes*, **29**, 386–418.

Tuchman, M. & Freeman, J. (1986). *The Spiritual in Art: Abstract Painting 1890–1985*. Los Angeles County Museum of Art and Abbeville Press, New York.

Washton Long, R.C. (1986). Expressionism, abstraction, and the search for Utopia in Germany. In *The Spiritual in Art: Abstract Painting 1890–1985*, M. Tuchman & J. Freeman, pp. 201–217. Los Angeles County Museum of Art and Abbeville Press, New York.

CHAPTER 9

ARTISTIC FORM AND SPIRITUAL EXPERIENCE: SOME OBSERVATIONS

KONRAD OBERHUBER

The insights presented in this lecture in very concise form presuppose a method of looking at art and of thinking about it which has been developed by this author in many years of teaching at Harvard University and the University of Vienna. It is based on the so-called Vienna School of Art History and its founder Alois Riegl on the one hand (Riegl, 1992), and on the other hand on the teachings of Rudolf Steiner, a philosopher, writer, spiritual teacher and artist who, contemporarily with Riegl, developed further the thoroughly artistic method of scientific observation practised by Johann Wolfgang Goethe (Steiner, 1963).

Riegl searched for the underlying principles uniting the various phenomena of art and sought to find the laws of development that govern them. He did this by thoroughly acquainting himself with all products of a period and seeking for the formal element that unites the various manifestations of a culture. He linked these to major psychological elements in human nature, as when he distinguished between "haptic" and "optic" phenomena, a predominantly tactile or predominantly visual perception of the world. Goethe similarly departed strictly from sense observation and looked for archetypes like the famous "archetypal plant" (Urpflanze), which contained in essence all the possible manifestations resulting from trans-formation in time and place according to guiding laws or principles. Rudolf Steiner not only reconstructed the implied but never explicitly stated philosophy of Goethe's scientific work but also showed the central place of this method in the exploration of all phenomena of life. He called the center of his movement in Dornach, Switzerland, the "Goetheanum" (Biesantz, 1978). Steiner has recently been recognized as a thinker who was of great importance for the new artistic impulses at the beginning of our century which have led to the formation of abstract art. Steiner, like Goethe, experienced the profound unity of all cultural manifestations of man. It results from his teachings, but also from those of Alois Riegl, that each formal property of art must be related to the cultural and spiritual background of the artist. While this background was for a long time the common source for all masters working in a specific culture, today individual artists can hold specific religions or spiritual ideas and thus modify the general art forms typical for their region and time according to their beliefs. The kind of observations here presented are still very new, but become increasingly important as research is more and more interested in the influence of spiritual and religious tendencies on art, where recognizable subject matter no longer holds the primary importance for the onlooker (Tuchman & Freeman, 1986, 1988; Loers, 1995). In a lecture given at the occasion of a symposium held at the end of the exhibition "The Spiritual in Art: Abstract Painting, 1890–1985" of 1986 in Los Angeles, I presented for the first time some observations on the relationship between artistic form and spiritual experience (Oberhuber, 1987, 1988). For this purpose I compared artistic products of Eastern religions with those of the Americas and finally with Christian works created in Europe. I came to the conclusion that products of Eastern thinking and feeling, e.g. sculptures of a meditating Buddha or a dancing Shiva, tend to be light and mobile and totally coherent as a whole, while American, Western ones such as Aztec sculptures were heavy, static and composed of many equal and exchangeable parts. Eastern works are filled with inner life and rest in themselves; Western ones tend to show the lifeless structures of the mineral world and can extend equally in all directions. Parallel to this formal difference, Eastern religions tend to flee the world for more perfect realms aloft, where the individual merges into one with all creation, while Western religious thinking prefers the brave and courageous behavior of the individual who faces pain and death with equanimity. The beyond seems like an extension of the physical world and does not promise relief from its challenges but rather greater strength to face them. Between the dead, heavy and analytically clear structure of the West and the alive, light, synthetic and mysterious structure of the East is the place of the structure created by the European mind, whose religious desires finally found their expression in Christianity. European form struggles to create a balance between weight and lightness, between life and death,

between the analytical and the synthetic, the rational and the mysterious. It is born out of the experience of polarities and strives towards the trinity. Love, as the medium through which the spiritual can be made manifest within the material, is at the center of this art.

It is in Europe, therefore, that artists have clearly distinguished between depictions of the spiritual and the material. While these distinctions tend to be close to our characteristics of Eastern and Western structure they are not the same. The main difference between the two poles lies in the experience of space. *Spiritual* experiences are described as taking place in a spaceless, flat environment, where size is given according to the importance of the figure, not according to its distance from the beholder. Colors are light and transparent, and there is a tendency towards geometric clarity in the arrangement of figures and forms which informs the beholder immediately of their relationship to each other. This can ultimately even lead to the diagramatic or schematic. The *material* world, on the other hand, is organized by the rules of perspective and relates to the beholder's point of view. Colors are dense and opaque and the composition can be free and chaotic, as if governed by chance. This distinction can be best experienced in Raphael's *Transfiguration* (Oberhuber, 1982). The representation of spiritual things thus reflects the way in which ideas appear in man's mind, while that of the material world is created according to its appearance to the senses. This distinction, which most clearly manifests in European art since the Renaissance, is the result of the dualistic thinking developed there during the Middle Ages and of the opposition of soul and body as developed by the Catholic Church. It stands in contrast to the monistic thinking of both Asia and America, where the material world can be seen as Maya, i.e. as an illusion, behind which the spiritual world reigns supreme on the one hand, or as the true reality filled with spiritual content on the other. Europeans have experienced America as the place where the material and the spiritual seem to be one, while the Orient is often described as a spiritual dream that is never fully real (Oberhuber, 1993).

Into this already complex situation distinguishing between three very basic spiritual attitudes, each of which can again be varied, a further historically determined distinction has to be introduced with regard to the experience of space in art. All three streams described so far, whether they depict the spiritual or the material world, have done this since the dawn of history out of an experience of the three-dimensional world in the center of man's being. The center of gravity was and still is experienced within man himself and projected by analogy into the center of the earth. In Asia this three-dimensionality, as it manifests in the vertical, horizontal and depth dimensions according to which sculptures and paintings but of course also architecture are created, is a product of the constructive mind. It is the knowledge or wisdom that the world is made in this way, that one experiences as a beholder. The three dimensions do not manifest in terms of weight or force, but rather as inner directives and organizing principles. In China each dimension leads even to the creation of a specific painting form: the hanging scroll for height, the horizontal scroll for horizontality and the album leaf for depth. In the Americas, on the other hand, the spatial structure is totally and overtly manifest as the organizational form of weight in the outer world. Things stretch out in

all directions until they are brought to an end. This is not only evident in early American sculpture and architecture but even more clearly in the city structures of our modern time, where the grid extends in all directions and the height is only restricted by the daring and finances of the builder. Each lot seems exchangeable and one feels free to build there according to one's wishes. This is totally different from the structures of both European and Asian cities, with their much more hierarchically or organically determined plans. In Europe three-dimensionality is experienced as a problem of dynamic balance. One feels the qualities of each dimension: weight and lightness determine the vertical; order and chaos as manifestations of right and left are balanced in the horizontal; the experience of movement and rest dominate the dimension of depth. These artistic problems become for the first time fully conscious in Greek art, but have not been articulated in all their complexity until modern times. The European mind with its experience of the polarity of the inner and outer world articulates the pictorial space according to the inner body feeling. The European mind has also created the geometric and scientific tools with which to come to grips with this feeling of space: Euclid's geometry, with its construction from one central point on the one hand, and Newton's theory of gravity on the other.

Early prehistoric manifestations of art were not yet determined by the three dimensions of space. Cave painters and the engravers of bones or rocks at the dawn of mankind do this out of a prespatial experience of the world. Moreover, in our time some painters, particularly Wassily Kandinsky, managed to create paintings from non-Euclidian experiences of space. It was Rudolf Steiner who at the beginning of this century expressly instructed artists to liberate themselves from the traditional experience of three-dimensionality as manifested in the body. Steiner devised spiritual exercises through which he hoped to help mankind to experience thinking as an activity free from bodily influence. He also created art forms, particularly the art of artistic movement called "Eurythmy", but also certain forms of painting, that should help man to overcome the feeling of gravity in the center of his body and thus to subdue egocentricity (Figure 9-1). Steiner believed that the time had now come in which man had to reverse the direction of earth's evolution and to develop such altruistic spiritual forces within himself to literally turn things inside out. As a true European he proposed that this could only be done if the Western experience of matter and materiality were enlivened and lightened through the lightness and the organic life so manifest in the streams of Eastern thought. In his works as architect he sought to demonstrate this by bringing the heaviest matter, pure exposed concrete, to life by the principles of organic growth and metamorphosis (see Biesantz & Klingborg, 1978; Steiner, 1994; Kugler, 1995; Oberhuber, 1995).

Steiner states that in our time the spiritual can no longer rightly be experienced in a centralized, i.e. Euclidian, way as earlier art tended to represent it, nor through diagramatic schemes and linear abstractions as was so often the case in the past. These correspond, according to him, to the dying forces of the created world and to that of our conceptual thinking. In order to overcome the forces of death, the spirit has to be found in the living forces of color and light that can be experienced when man looks at himself and at the world from the outside, i.e. from the periph-

ery, and thus experiences those spiritual and creative forces which radiate out from within himself and from the inside of the world. Christ's word, that the kingdom of heaven is within you, had to be taken literally. Steiner, moreover, did not want man to impose the dead contours of his concepts onto the living creative forces. The new art had to start from an experience of mobile and dynamic forces of color and the images had to arise slowly from their

9-1
RUDOLF STEINER
EASTER (THREE CROSSES),
1924
Watercolor, 39 × 26⅜ in
(99.3 × 67 cm)
Rudolf Steiner
Nachlassverwaltung,
Dornach (cat. no. K.553)

interaction. This reversal of the traditional space, but also that of the traditional approach to the subject matter of painting, has been independently arrived at by a number of artists and artistic movements. Cubism, for example, tends to define form with the help of tangents coming from the periphery, rather than to determine it from the center, and thus follows non-Euclidian geometries as developed in the nineteenth century. German expressionism tended to give predominance to color over form in its search for a renewal of life. Artists like Paul Klee recommended to their students that they should start from purely artistic problems and find their subject matter within the creative process. Max Weiler, the Austrian colorist, starts, as Steiner recommended, from color juxtapositions and develops his pictures from there, stating that in this he follows the creative principles of nature (Breicha, 1995; Weiler, 1995). He is in this procedure also close to Kandinsky, who in his early abstract work clearly adopts a peripheral vision and gives predominance to the problems of color over those of linear form.

In my previous work (Oberhuber, 1987, 1988) I have tried to demonstrate that spiritual disciplines can have an impact on an artist's form and that differences between the art of various masters active at the same time and place can in part be accounted for by their religious or philosophical inclinations. I contrasted the work of Mark Tobey and Jackson Pollock, for example, showing that the spirit of dematerialization in the first had to do with his Oriental religion, the Bahai faith, while Pollock's grasp for the materiality and the surface of his pictures as well as his manifest power of structure were in harmony with his admiration for the indigenous

American spirituality of the Indians. It has also been demonstrated that the abstraction which Piet Mondrian found for himself from indications in theosophy, differed from that of Kandinsky's because the two artists worked with the same premises in a completely different way. In contrast to Kandinsky, Mondrian did not do the exercises devised by Steiner but rather rationalized what he found in the writings to create his own concepts of the world. These allowed him to create an abstract sign language with which he could express a great variety of moods and situations in the world, but did not lead him into the cosmos of alive creative forces which Kandinsky found on his meditative spiritual path. Mondrian's thinking penetrated to where he could experience the cross of verticality and horizontality in the material world. Kandinsky went beyond it into the forces of the resurrection.

In addition to summing up what I have already said in different words in the publications just quoted, I want to show here how some artists with spiritual inclinations go through various stages of spirituality. This is evident in Mondrian and Kandinsky themselves. Yet this time I would like to focus on two relatively little known artists. One of them is the Swedish painter Hilma af Klint (1862–1944), who has at least received some attention recently in the context of spiritual art and was presented for the first time in the exhibition in Los Angeles for which I developed the thoughts here presented (Fant, 1988; Fant, 1991–1992; Klint, 1995). Hilma af Klint came from an upper class Swedish family and was trained as a painter in the traditional late nineteenth-century style. In the years 1879–1882 she participated in spiritualistic séances. For some time she belonged to the "Edelweissförbundet" (Edelweiss Club) with other ladies of similar spiritualist inclinations. She then became interested in theosophy. In the late 1890s she gathered around herself a group of women of her own to practise spiritualist séances. In this context Hilma functioned occasionally as a medium producing small drawings and got in contact with certain spirits that guided her actions. From 1904 she was asked to do paintings and in the summer of 1905 these spirits told her to prepare herself for a very special task. She was then commanded to paint with the help of spirits that guided her hand on grounds of specific sizes that were again indicated to her by her spirit guides. Some of these were pictures of extraordinary size (3.28–2.40 m). They were called "paintings for the temple". The results are astonishing, partly abstract, partly figurative paintings, some of unusual shape and size (Figure 9-2). The non-figurative ones are among the earliest works of its kind. Some of them are reminiscent of tantric art, others seem to prefigure Miró. Most pictures contain strange words in ornamentalized writing whose meaning was in part interpreted in Hilma's diaries and notebooks. They also contain spiral forms and other shapes that recur throughout the rest of her work and can be interpreted as symbols. The same is true for her colors. Much of the subject matter has to do with the polarity of male and female as well as with the evolution of man. A major cycle, known as the "Ten largest", has to do with the life stages of man (Figure 9-3). Important for our investigation is the fact that these paintings seem to be entirely free of spatial experience. The signs float free in the colorfields without reference to body experience or three-dimensionality. It is evident from this that they were created in a state of trance without participation of the feelings of weight and body balance in their creation on the part of the artist. She did indeed claim that her hands were guided. The consciousness seems to be prespatial, as in works before the dawn of history. Under the impact of mediumistic practice this artist seems to have fallen back into an early primitive type of artistic practice. Something similar can be experienced in other works of mediumistic artists as collected in the Musée de l'Art Brut in Lausanne.

In 1908 Hilma af Klint encountered Rudolf Steiner, who seems to have told her that her work could not be immediately understood by her contemporaries. He might also have told her about the dangers of mediumistic practice. Steiner's teaching strove for a new kind of clairvoyance with the conscious participation of the self. He regarded all elimination of consciousness in order to experience spiritual things as no longer timely for modern man. Whether Steiner talked to her

9-2
HILMA AF KLINT
ORIGINAL CHAOS No. 1, 1906
Oil on canvas, 19⅝ × 15 in
(50 × 38 cm)
Hilma af Klint
Foundation, Järma (no. 1)

9-3
HILMA AF KLINT
THE TEN BIGGEST, NO. 1,
1907
Oil and tempera on paper
on canvas, 129¼ × 94½ in
(328 × 240 cm)
Hilma af Klint
Foundation, Järma
(no. 102)

which Steiner favored, others relate in a very original way to theosophical writings that Hilma studied. Again the polarity of male and female and the question of evolution and transformation stand in the center of her interest. Hilma now was able to develop a kind of abstract language of colors and forms with which she could work similarly to Mondrian, even though her art is perhaps more conscious and less intuitive than his. At the end of the decade she was able to make visual comments on various religions and their spiritual content (Figure 9-5) and even more astonishingly on the quality of plants in the various regions of Scandinavia. All these works show Hilma in a fully conscious relationship to the three dimensions of space and also fully aware of the traditional differences in the depiction of the physical and the spiritual world as we described them above. Hilma paints in the style of a conscious modern person in full conformity with the most avant-garde productions in Holland and even Russia.

Yet her work was again interrupted by an encounter with her spiritual teacher Rudolf Steiner. Between 1920 and 1930 she went several times to his center, the Goetheanum in Dornach. There she encountered the new way of painting which Steiner had devised and which is described above. Hilma now changed style again. From the 1920s onwards she struggled with the same male–female polarities, but also with the expression of specific plants and with many other problems in a dynamic painterly style in which the colors have primacy over form (Figure 9-6). In these pictures she was able to free herself from the three dimensions of outer space in order to create a kind of quality space determined purely by the spatial properties of color itself. This part of her work still has been little explored, but presents an

about this or not, Hilma could have gathered this also from his writings. As a result Hilma ceased to create new works for several years. When she then painted again from 1912 onwards it is not clear whether she continued to receive the physical guidance from her spirits as before or whether she was given concepts in words or inner visions for which she had to find artistic expression. The new products look now like geometrical schemes and diagrams presented with great clarity of proportion and sensitivity to color (Figure 9-4). Many of them are strongly related to Goethe's color theories, extraordinary body of material produced by a woman who certainly now was in possession of the kind of clairvoyant faculties Steiner wanted to develop for mankind through his teaching. From this point in her life onwards we hear no longer of spirit guides but of Hilma's own spiritual striving. From this we can conclude that it is possible for an artist in our time to go through three stages of spatial experience, prehistoric space, modern conscious space and Steinerian body-free space, within the development of one lifetime. Hilma af Klint's early mediumistic clairvoyance was transformed in the process into a modern conscious one.

A similar, even though somewhat different transformation can be experienced in the work of the Austrian artist Hans Strigl (1897–1956) (Strigl, 1968). Strigl did not become an artist right away. In the early 1920s Strigl felt a

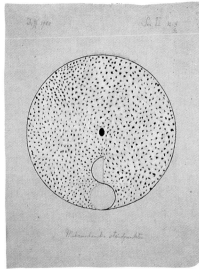

9-4 (far left)
HILMA AF KLINT
THE SWAN, NO. 23, 1915
61 × 59⅞ in (155 × 152 cm)
Hilma af Klint
Foundation, Järma
(no. 171)

9-5 (left)
HILMA AF KLINT
THE MOHAMMEDAN POINT OF
VIEW, 1920
14⅛ × 10⅝ in (36 × 27 cm)
Hilma af Klint
Foundation, Järma
(no. 473)

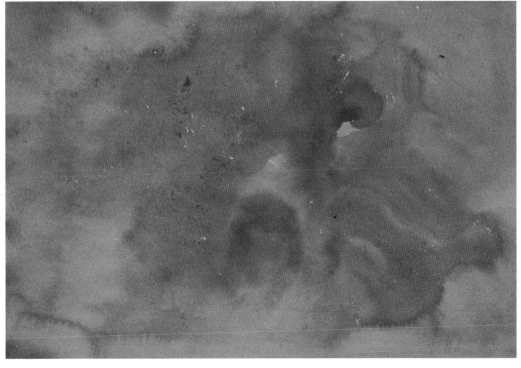

9-6 (below)
HILMA AF KLINT
LOOKING AT THE DOG-ROSE,
1922
Watercolor, 10¼ × 13¾ in
(26 × 35 cm)
Hilma af Klint
Foundation, Järma
(no. 635)

9-7
HANS STRIGL
ROSE PEARL ON BLUE SHELL-
BOWL, c. 1945
Watercolor, 19⅝ × 15¾ in
(50 × 40 cm)
Ursula Frisch, Linz

spiritual calling and began to paint. He took classes with a local painter who taught him the traditional landscape and portrait art of his time. Soon Strigl incorporated notions of astrology and reincarnation in symbolic form into his paintings without giving up the traditional European space in his work. In March 1938 he was suspended from his work as a teacher and from then on devoted all his energy to painting, even after he was reinstated in 1945. In 1944 he painted his first abstract painting, followed by a large number of watercolors and oil paintings. While some were fully abstract, he also painted many pictures of flowers and people in which the visible world was depicted in a realistic way while the aura which he experienced around it was painted in an abstract style. For our purposes I want to look at his early abstractions first created around 1945 (Figure 9-7). Strigl followed in them some of the principles outlined above for the depiction of the supernatural in European art. The colors are transparent and forms overlap and interpenetrate. Moreover, in Strigl's work the suggested movement of the forms is so carefully balanced that it appears ambiguous. One can experience it as coming towards the beholder, but also as fleeing from him. Sometimes round forms can be read as hollow funnels, sometimes as full spheres. There is a lightness that pervades the whole work and keeps it floating. Strigl furthermore always stressed the musical content of his compositions. He wanted one to hear the forms as producing sounds. The ideal of this early work is then clearly one inspired by the Eastern principles of weightlessness and organic movement in a unified totally spiritual space, even though one always feels even here a breathing rhythm that betrays the European and Christian artist.

The Christian Duality is more obvious in a somewhat later work, where a magic sun appears above a landscape apparently crossed by a river and a bridge (Figure 9-8). Themes like this were common in early theosophical painting, even though Strigl knew nothing about them. Strigl now attempts to face the European conflict of spirit and matter by creating a new unity where one mirrors the other. The light of the sky is reflected on the earth and both parts are pervaded by the same dynamic forces. The colors are more substantial but still luminous. Strigl is clearly no longer painting in an oriental spiritual mode but in a fully European one.

Towards the very end of his life, however, he changed his style once more. Instead of watercolors he now often used colored crayons which produced a much heavier and solid but at the same time very intense color (Figure 9-9). Strigl had now given up all indications of space and shading and worked with pure color contrasts in the plane. The result was a very tensely integrated whole in which colors and forms balance each other

9-8
HANS STRIGL
IDEAL LANDSCAPE WITH
TURNPIKE
Watercolor, 16⅞ × 23¾ in
(43 × 60.3 cm)
Ursula Frisch, Linz

9-9
HANS STRIGL
COMPOSITION "CABBAGES"
Colored Stabilo crayons,
washed, 23¾ × 15⅞ in
(60.5 × 40.5 cm)
Private collection, Vienna

and linear structures are largely suppressed. While not fully following Steiner's prescriptions Strigl expressed at that time his conviction that he had now given priority to color in his work. Strigl knew of Steiner's recommendations and often talked about them with the knowledge that his previous work did not conform to them.

In Strigl's, just as in af Klint's, work we can follow a transformation of spiritual attitude by means of the study of their paintings. In our times spiritually-minded artists often start with earlier spiritual attitudes and slowly transform these in the course of their development into ones which are in conformity with contemporary necessities, unless they hold fast to the once held beliefs. The reason for this can not be explained beyond the general laws of evolution, which clearly demand a repetition of earlier evolutionary stages every time a completely new stage in the process develops. Modern man can undergo this process even in a fairly conscious way since he has access to spiritual teachings from all periods of time since the dawn of human culture and from all parts of the globe.

Spiritually inclined people today are often first attracted by older modes of communicating with the universe and only slowly develop a more modern attitude in conformity with the demands of the contemporary cultural and spiritual climate. The two artists here discussed, just like Kandinsky before them, were, moreover, attracted at the end of their lives to the new spirituality taught by Rudolf Steiner and created an art that followed his principles, which according to his beliefs will be prevailing in the spiritual art of the future, replacing the still predominating principle of line with that of color. Many phenomena in most recent art seem to point to the truth of Steiner's prediction.

References

Biesantz, H. & Klingborg, A. (1978). *Das Erste Goetheanum, Der Bauimpuls Rudolf Steiners*. Dornach.

Breicha, O. (1995). *Max Weiler, "Wie eine Landschaft", Bilder von 1961–1967*.

Österreichische Galerie, Belvedere, Vienna.

Fant, Å. (1988). Hilma af Klints hemliga bilder, *Nordiskt Konstcentrums utställningskatalog*, No. 3, Stockholm.

Fant, Å. (1991–1992). *Okkultismus und Abstraktion, Die Malerin Hilma af Klint (1862–1944)*. Graphische Sammlung Albertina, Wien.

Klint, G. af (1995). Hilma af Klint. In *Okkultismus und Avantgarde, von Munch bis Mondrian*. V. Loers & P. Witzmann, pp. 114–116. Shirn Kunsthalle, Frankfurt.

Kugler, W. (1995). Wenn der Labortisch zum Altar wird—Die Erweiterung des Kunstbegriffs durch Rudolf Steiner. In *Okkultismus und Avantgarde, von Munch bis Mondrian*. V. Loers & P. Witzmann, pp. 46–57. Shirn Kunsthalle, Frankfurt.

Loers, V. & Witzmann, P. (1995). *Okkultismus und Avantgarde, von Munch bis Mondrian*. Schirn Kunsthalle, Frankfurt.

Oberhuber, K. (1982). *Raphaels "Transfiguration", Stil und Bedeutung*. Urachhaus, Stuttgart.

Oberhuber, K. (1987). *Newsletter of the American Society for Anthroposophy*, **Spring**.

Oberhuber, K. (1988). Das Geistige in der Kunst und das Wirken Rudolf Steiners. In *The Spiritual in Art: Abstract Painting 1890–1985*. M. Tuchman & J. Freeman, pp. 7–15. Los Angeles County Museum of Art and Abbeville Press, New York.

Oberhuber, K. (1993). Anmerkungen zu einer Psychologie des Museums. In

Kunst Psychologie Heute, Kunst und Psychologie 2, Ed. W. Schurian, pp. 197–207, especially p. 201. Göttingen, Stuttgart.

Oberhuber, K. (1995). Rudolf Steiner— Das Erste Goetheanum. In *Okkultismus und Avantgarde, von Munch bis Mondrian*. V. Loers & P. Witzmann, pp. 713–729. Shirn Kunsthalle, Frankfurt.

Riegl, A. (1992). Introduction by D. Castriota. Preface by H. Zerner. *Problems of Style, Foundations for a History of Ornament* (Trans. E. Kain). Princeton University Press, Princeton, NJ.

Steiner, R. (1963). Goethes Weltanschauung. *Rudolf Steiner Gesamtausgabe 6*, 5th Edn., Dornach.

Steiner, R. (1985). Kunst und Kunsterkenntnis. *Rudolf Steiner Gesamtausgabe 271*. Dornach.

Steiner, R. (1994). *Tafelzeichnungen, Entwürfe, Architektur*, Ed. M. Hentschel. Württembergischer Kunstverein, Stuttgart.

Strigl, H. (1968). *Hans Strigl 1897–1956 zum 70. Geburtstag. Aus seinem abstrakten Werk*. Wolfgang Gurlitt-Museum, Neue Galerie der Stadt Linz.

Tuchman, M. & Freeman, J. (1986). *The Spiritual in Art: Abstract Painting 1890–1985*. Los Angeles County Museum of Art and Abbeville Press, New York.

Tuchman, M. & Freeman, J. (1988). *Das Geistige in der Kunst, Abstrakte Malerei 1890–1985*. Urachhaus, Stuttgart.

Weiler, M. (1995). *Zeichnungen von 1961–1967*. Graphische Sammlung Albertina, Vienna.

CHAPTER 10

SPIRITUALITY IN THE WORK OF EDUARDO CHILLIDA

JOSÉ CORREDOR-MATHEOS

Art has been gradually losing its spirituality, particularly since Renaissance times. Transcendental references have become fewer and fewer, producing an impoverishment that is now approaching its penultimate stage. Nevertheless, the most meaningful contemporary art still reveals a spiritual concern, although it is not usually explicitly expressed. Nowadays the work of artists who venture into *terra ignota* (unknown and mysterious territory) reflects the serious failures of our society; its breakdown, the attempts to reconstruct it and the anguish caused by the widespread lack of spirituality and even of meaning are somehow apparent in their work.

How is all of this expressed in the art of Eduardo Chillida? A close examination of his sculptures reveals silence. In fact, one of them is entitled *Música Callada* (Silent Music). The silence of this work emerges from the void or, as Kosme Maria Barañano put it, "... the modulation of different spaces, the orchestration of what is not said, the emptiness". It is a void shaped by non-created spaces, just as, Barañano continues, quoting Marguerite Yourcenar, "the silence that follows the chords doesn't have anything to do with ordinary silence, which lives" (Barañano, 1992).

The opposite of this silence is the noise of most contemporary art, a noise that attempts to drown out the voices of silence, to avoid hearing or sensing the emptiness that lies at the very heart of art and life. Because if, to use an Oriental simile, art is like an onion or an artichoke, when we gradually peel away its outer layers—everything that appears to be art and yet veils it (subject matter; form; composition; sociological, psychological and historical references; etc.)—we end up revealing only its profound emptiness, an emptiness that penetrates the core of its first and last meaning. And this, which can be perceived as an aroma or a vibration as delicate as the flutter of wings, is what remains and truly enriches us.

Eduardo Chillida has on occasion spoken of this aroma: "I sense something which, for lack of a better word, I have to call incarnation of the form. I sense it; I would say that I inhale it. It's like an aroma ... Space can be as much an obsession as fragrance" (Chillida, 1967 p. 23). This concept of aroma is also revealed at the end of the process, in the completed work. It emanates from the void that is revealed, signifying that a spiritual objective has been met. This point marks a limit: the limit of what is real. Many lesser works resign themselves to staying within more or less familiar spaces: only art reaches—and reaching implies surpassing—the limit. I am not speaking only of beauty, "this quality which", according to Rainer María Rilke in his first *Duino Elegy*, "we can still endure".

As Bernard Noël so clearly stated in his observations on the work of Chillida, "The limit is the present". We are rarely able to live on its edge, which consists not only of time but also of that fragile and pervasive quality that Noël labelled "presentness" (Noël, 1980). A present which, I would venture to add, also embraces space, is inseparable from time, and constitutes the sculptor's very material. If we accept that the material he works with might be solid iron, steel, marble, bronze, wood or alabaster, we can make the mental adjustment and accept that space too is a material because it is from space and simultaneous with space that matter is born. Chillida himself confirms this when he writes, "Limit is the true protagonist of space, just as the present, another limit, is the true protagonist of time" (Chillida, 1970 p. 20), and the present can only be perceived when we abstract the notion of time itself. The act of creation takes place in an extended present, which is tantamount to saying that time, in passing, disappears.

Rationality as a paradigm, intelligibility as something immediate, a belief that the real and the artistic belong exclusively to the visible world: all these things prevent us from getting truly close to works of art and this includes the work of Eduardo Chillida. His work is not immediately accessible. Like the sacred art of other eras, it is an object of contemplation. In addition to producing aesthetic pleasure, Chillida's sculpture, drawings and all his other work are first and foremost a source of learning. And because of this they can be said to have a spiritual dimension. The spiritual leaders of all traditional cultures, including our own, speak to us of learning: "Learning is what makes a work beautiful". These are the words of

10-1
EDUARDO CHILLIDA
MONUMENT TO FLEMING, 1951
Granite

10-2
EDUARDO CHILLIDA
GNOMON, 1965
Steel, 14 × 15 × 16½ in
(35.5 × 38 × 42 cm)
Private collection, Spain.
Photograph by Claude Gaspari © Galerie Maeght, Paris

Saint Bonaventure, as Coomaraswamy (1980) reminds us. Eduardo Chillida also referred to learning when he said, "We can never learn enough. As a result, in everything we know well we also find and are attracted by something we don't know" (Chillida, 1970 p. 22). This plunges us into the true meaning/non-meaning of learning: a situation without end. All works of art are intended somehow to bewilder us. They issue a challenge to which we, the viewers, must respond. They are not an end, but a beginning. The words of Chillida continue to echo not just in our ears, but in our entire beings: "In everything we know well we also find and are attracted to something we don't know".

All the anxieties and efforts of this great artist are tangibly expressed in certain of his works. In the beginning of this chapter, I pointed out that ours is an age of fragmentation in both what we call the "real" world and in art. Some artists strive, with greater or lesser degrees of success, to rebuild this world, while others console themselves by adding to its confusion, by shattering still further the already splintered mirror. As Burckhardt (1976 p. 135) has said, "Man ceases to be truly a man when he no longer has God

as his centre; from then on, his image begins to decompose . . . it is gradually destroyed, and modern art aims to conclude the process by systematically negating and disfiguring it". In my opinion, this does not necessarily imply that one must accept the idea of divinity: it is perhaps enough to believe in the inscrutable, inaccessible nature of what is real and, consequently, in the mystical condition of art.

In the most radical modernity and the most subjective art—and I wish to stress this here—the spiritual, the transcendent, is glimpsed in the void left by its absence, which produces anguish. The tortured nature of the work of Van Gogh, Munch, Wols, Pollock and Beuys reveals the spiritual in negative form. Marcel Duchamp's lucid, though ultimately negative, annihilation has the same meaning. I do not believe this is true of Chillida's work because spirituality is its true goal. Some critics have mentioned this

10-3
EDUARDO CHILLIDA
DÜSSELDORF MONUMENT,
1971
Steel, 11 ft 10 in × 14 ft 1 in × 16ft 5 in (360 × 430 × 500 cm)

explicitly. I am thinking of Pierre Volvoudt (1967) in particular. When referring to the interplay of volumes and hollows and to what he calls the "vault" that lies at the heart of Chillida's sculpture, Volvoudt says that "This non-space, a finite and infinite void, is where the Sacred One dwells. A presence retreats into the void, only to subsequently light up from within, explode into powerful lines, abrupt outcroppings, abundant rifts". He then goes on to draw an "...analogy between this hidden part of the soul that is stripped of all outward appearance, this great void produced when the power of the soul overflows from the deepest reaches mentioned by St John of the Cross, and this withdrawal from form into the innermost core, which is produced by and prone to this very withdrawal". According to Volvoudt, "It is here that one encounters a great and singular, and undoubtedly not fortuitous, correspondence between art and mysticism".

It is when all the layers of a work of art have been stripped away, revealing this final void, that the Spirit, the Enigma, appears. "The Sacred One", Volvoudt continues, "hides from our gaze". (God, if he exists, can only be a hidden God.) Although Volvoudt also refers to "the empty vessel of Tao", we must not forget that this is manifested in infinite transformations. Burckhardt reminds us of this, precisely in relation to the Taoist vision. "The art of reality", he writes, "is essentially the art of transformation: nature is endlessly transformed". This explains why Chillida's work, like all true art, metamorphoses before our eyes. The Basque artist's bars and blocks, their innermost spaces, are not immobile. They move in time to a certain rhythm. "The object of art", and here I again quote Burckhardt, "is to adapt to this cosmic rhythm" (Burckhardt,

1976 p. 6).

Chillida's sculpture, like his work in general, produces feelings of both tranquility and unrest. We can contemplate it as an object of meditation and, as such, it opens our spirit to an adventure without end. And it does this with solid materials, whose rhythm and movement oppose and initiate contrasting dialogues—simultaneously conversing and clashing—that constitute a game, an imago of the cosmic interplay. The fact that a work of art opens its outer, visible skin to another dimension does not imply that the materials used should not be immediate. Indeed, only they, properly handled, can do this. Marble, stone, iron and steel, alabaster, wood and even paper must affirm their immediacy as materials. Chillida confirms this by stripping them of everything that could possibly be adornment. His works are always naked. By letting us see their strict materialness, their inaccessibility, he affirms the world and its contingency. This makes the contrast with what is sought, the final

10-4
EDUARDO CHILLIDA
HOMAGE TO ARCHITECTURE,
1973
Alabaster, 9⅞ × 5⅞ × 7½ in
(25 × 15 × 19 cm)
Photograph © F. Catalá-Roca, Barcelona

101

void, even more evident. And these works are washed clean of sentiment. Because art—as was the case with the sacred art of the past—introduces our most pressing concerns into its subject matter, albeit unconsciously. Art should not transmit emotions but instead become a symbol, recalling too the symbolic nature of reality itself.

The simplicity with which great artists appear to achieve this lofty aim makes us think that the goal is at our fingertips, just as their works are but a glance away. As Reinhold Hohl (1986 p. 9) put it, "Chillida reveals what we would always have seen had we shared his lucidity. He causes us to see fundamental facts of our existence, isolating them as formal themes and articulating them as artistic figures". These facts of existence are so transparent that they allow us to see another dimension of reality which, for the sake of understanding, we refer to as spiritual. Chillida lives in this world, takes part in it, but his final objective is beyond it or, if you prefer, deep within it. The ways to approach this objective are infinite, although few artists do so with the determination, the plenitude, the skill and the stature of Eduardo Chillida.

10-5
EDUARDO CHILLIDA
PRAISE OF WATER, 1987
Concrete, 15 ft 1 in × 21 ft 8 in × 13 ft 1 in (460 × 660 × 400 cm)
Photograph © F. Catalá-Roca, Barcelona

REFERENCES

Barañano, K.M. de (1992). Chillida en Venezuela. In *Chillida escala humana* (exhibition catalogue). Centro Cultural consolidado, Caracas.

Burckhardt, T. (1976). *Principes et Méthodes de l'Art Sacré*. Dervy-Livres, Paris. (Spanish version, 1982), Ediciones Lidiun, Buenos Aires.)

Chillida, E. (1967). Quoted by Pierre Volvoudt. In *Chillida*, p. 23. Verlag Gerd Hatje, Stuttgart and Editorial Gustavo Gili, S.A., Barcelona.

Chillida, E. (1970). Notes extraites des carnets d'Eduardo Chillida. *Derrière le Miroir* (Paris), **183** (February).

Coomaraswamy, A.K. (1980). *Christian and Oriental Philosophy of Art*. Taurus Ediciones, S.A., Madrid. (Spanish version of book previously published in English by Munshiram Manoharlal Publishers, New Delhi.)

Hohl, R. (1986). *Chillida o la Descoberta Permanent* (exhibition catalogue), p. 9. Fundació Joan Miró, Barcelona.

Noël, P. (1980). Ajours de terre. *Derrière le Miroir* (Paris), **242** (November).

Volvoudt, P. (1967). *Chillida*, p. 16. Verlag Gerd Hatje, Stuttgart and Editorial Gustavo Gili, S.A., Barcelona.

10-6
EDUARDO CHILLIDA
PRAISE OF THE HORIZON, 1989
Concrete, 32 ft 10 in × 41 ft × 50 ft 10 in (10 × 12.5 × 15.5 m)

CHAPTER 11

REFLECTIONS ON THE THEME OF THIS SYMPOSIUM

EDUARDO CHILLIDA

On my way here today I was wondering what I was going to say, not having written down or prepared anything in advance. After listening to what has been said so far, I can say a few words that might help some of you to understand something about what has happened to me during my life, in terms of my work, in terms of spirituality, in terms of matter and many other things that are all related to one another.

Like time, for instance. Very few people realize that I have learned as much from time—probably through music and by thinking about time—as I have learned from space. I have reached a point where I have the feeling that time and space always behave very similarly, no matter what the circumstances. As an example: a long time ago, when I was very young, I wrote something intuitive, where I said I believe that "limit is the protagonist of space, just as the present, another limit, is the protagonist of time". I've been turning this idea over and over in my mind since then, without ever developing it completely, but every day my feeling about this is stronger.

A few days ago I was talking about this with René Thom, the French mathematician, who is an admirable person with an exceptional intellectual capacity. Anyway, we were talking about this and the things that came out were very curious. For instance, one of the things that surprises me most is that never in the history of philosophy has anyone ever dared try to solve a problem about time like the one I'm going to describe now. And even he was surprised because it is such an absolutely basic problem: "The present is a dimensionless place. Everything happens in this dimensionless place, but if we add up all the presents, we get dimension; how is this possible?" I asked René Thom, and it is an almost childish question, but curiously enough it suggests many possible answers and many further questions.

This same type of problem also comes up in relation to limits in space (he wrote something about the problem of limit). In the Theory of Catastrophes he talks about "the edge" and I remember asking him: What do you consider the edge? What is the edge in relation to the limit? Are the limit and the edge the same thing? He said they weren't and he was absolutely right. Obviously, the edge is the end of something and the limit is the point where one thing turns into another. It's what separates two things that touch, but remain different.

We were talking about the problem in relation to the Theory of Catastrophes, which I wasn't familiar with. I knew he'd written a book about it but I haven't read it because to read a book like this you need more than the two years of pure mathematics I did when I studied architecture. That's not enough for talking to a mathematician like René Thom.

11-1
EDUARDO CHILLIDA
RUMOUR OF LIMITS IV, 1960
Forged iron, 40½ × 37 × 30 in
(102.9 × 94 × 76.2 cm)
Washington University
Gallery of Art, St. Louis.
Gift of Mr and Mrs Richard
K. Weil, 1962

11-2
EDUARDO CHILLIDA
On BOARD, 1957 or '58
Wrought iron, 22 × 59 ×
31½ in (56 × 150 × 80 cm)
Kunsthaus, Zürich (inv.
no. 1962/12)

Later on I discovered how he has taken this Theory of Catastrophes and followed a path that involves folds, applying them to problems of higher mathematics and winning the most important medals, which are the equivalent of a Nobel Prize in mathematics. I didn't know about this.

11-3
EDUARDO CHILLIDA
PENCIL DRAWING, 1961
*Drawing, 4⅛ × 5 in
(10.5 × 12.9 cm)*
*Photograph courtesy of
the artist*

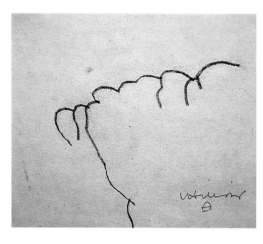

Several years ago—this is something I think will be published soon—a really strange thing happened to me and I described it yesterday in Valencia too. I was looking at a painting in the Prado—the *Crucifixion* by van der Weyden, a painting I have known forever; it was just an ordinary day and I was practically not seeing the painting when I suddenly asked myself: how can 50% of the surface of a painting like this consist of folds? There is only 50% of the painting where there are no folds. There is the body of Christ, the hands, the head, the cross and a few other things. Everything else is folds. What is the reason an artist does this?

I know that art history is full of folds, but I had never really thought about it until that day. What's the reason for this? I didn't understand what it could be. There must have been a very important reason for this to be the way it was in this painting. I went on to look at other paintings in a lot of museums and I analyzed art history through this question: why have folds been so important throughout art history?

I didn't draw any really extraordinary conclusions, but one day I read a scene in Aldous Huxley's book *The Doors of Perception*, where some young men are drinking coffee and they offer him a drug, mescaline. And after he tries it and is sitting in an armchair with his legs crossed, the boys ask him: "Do you notice anything?" And he replies "No, I don't notice anything". After a while they asked him again and he said, "Yes, I'm seeing the folds in my trousers as though I were van Eyck".

Then I realized that perception, artifically produced in this case, allowed him to see the folds in his trousers with a marvellous intensity. He himself, a very cultured man, realized that he was seeing the folds as he had never before seen them in his life.

This got me thinking and I've been working on something (that I might publish) which I believe occurs throughout the history of art because this doesn't just happen with van der Weyden; it also happens with Dürer, in Roman art, Greek art, Flemish art. You

11-4
EDUARDO CHILLIDA
PENCIL DRAWING, 1961
*Drawing, 3¾ × 7⅛ in
(9.5 × 18.1 cm)*
*Photograph courtesy of
the artist*

11-5
EDUARDO CHILLIDA
LINE DRAWING, 1994
*Drawing, 5¾ × 8¼ in
(14.6 × 21 cm)*
*Photograph courtesy of
the artist*

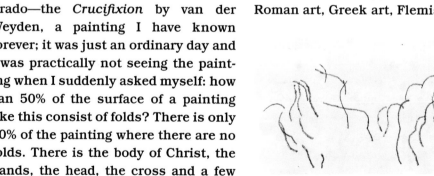

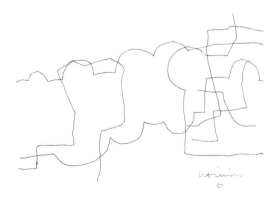

can't ignore the importance of folds in art history and I wonder if they are not a kind of code language.

Folds throughout art history are a kind of art. I wouldn't call it non-figurative, but I would say it is an art that is aimed solely at the people who are capable of perceiving it, without it having to be a motif that is easy to resort to the way other kinds of things could be.

I am asking these kinds of questions now in terms of space. All of us who are interested in art can recognize an artist by the way he paints. You can show any one of us here a corner of a painting, not even the whole canvas, just a corner where there is a fold and we will say that's a Dürer, that one's a Zurbarán; we can all do it. In other words, every artist has his specific code language.

This is a subject that is probably extremely coherent and very closely related to these great artists in particular and to all the major schools. But it is not a directly figurative relation, it is not an analysis by a figurative artist, although there have obviously been those as well, but they don't create a language with folds.

The person who creates this language might be Dürer, for example, where everything he does looks as though it is made of wood, from those medieval German woodcarvings. On the other hand, Grünewald's folds look like they come from water, from observing creeks. In the Isenheim altar, the Virgin is a creek, she's the analysis of water.

Dürer's folds are, therefore, more related to space (and now I'm going to connect what I said before to space) because of the wood and the volume, whereas Grünewald's are related to time and almost to music.

It was things like this I was talking about with Thom and he was surprised that we had been touching on such similar themes, because he uses folds to support his Theory of Catastrophes, to reach his latest and most advanced theories about higher mathematics. Some very curious things have happened to me lately and I'm describing them because, in my opinion, they are very interesting.

All that we've been talking about here also brings to mind something about Gaston Bachelard, a curious thing that reveals how sensitive he was. He was a poet and a philosopher. He was a tremendous poet and says in his *Poetry of Space* something I think is marvelous, spiritual, and magnificent, expressed in terms of a more pedestrian, more ordinary world. He explains that the average house should have three stories: the ground floor, the cellar and the attic. And he says that the stairs that connect the ground floor with the attic are different than the stairs that link the ground floor to the cellar. The stairs that lead to the attic always go up and the stairs that lead to the cellar always go down. In other words, they work on your imagination so that you think the stairs that lead to the attic go up and that the ones that lead to the cellar go down.

This is the analysis of a poet, a philosopher, who knows perfectly well that staircases go both up and down, but they still mark the imagination of a man like this, and anyone who thinks about this will realize that this happens in a lot of life's situations. This kind of thing has surprised me. I was fortunate enough to meet him, but aside from this, I was surprised because all my life I've encountered situations like this.

I don't know if this is good or bad, if it's due to a special sensitivity or perception. I believe that it is perception that makes these kinds of unexpected associations possible, but I don't think that there is anything abnormal about it because I know perfectly well that these stairs Bachelard talks about go both up and down. In short they are subjects that, curiously enough, are much broader than they seem.

I haven't talked about spirituality so far, but I have experimented with it in order to move closer to a subject that is as fundamental for me as spirituality. Now, I can't talk about my own spirituality. What I can do is tell you some curious things that I have observed in the world of art, and particularly in poetry, in mysticism. For example, and most particularly, in St John of the Cross, with whom I have been involved for a long time. He says surprising things in this sense. I know it by heart, so I am going to recite something concrete that is very moving if you analyze it from the standpoint of this seminar. You probably all know it: the spiritual canticle:

"Y todos cuantos vagan
de ti me van mil gracias refiriendo
y todos más me llagan
y déjame muriendo
un no sé qué quedan balbuciendo".

There is no translation for this. I apologize to those of you who don't understand Spanish, but I don't think it could have been translated into any language. Poetry of this level is untranslatable, but this man wants to touch on certain points, and for all of us who want to do likewise a simple analysis of this says all there is to say.

Who are those who wander? All those who wander, might not they be everyone who is trying to reach the unreachable, who wants to know the unknown, and wouldn't artists, some of them more or less unbalanced, others balanced, belong to this group that St John of the Cross called "all those who wander"?

Obviously, St John of the Cross was speaking generally, but there are a lot of examples, for instance Mozart (I can't speak for anyone but myself, I can't do anything more than talk about my personal vision of the problem I am describing). As we all know, Mozart was a wonderful and fantastic musician, but knowing his music, it's my impression that he knew that the best things he did were his adagios, his slow movements: but I am nevertheless convinced that he sensed that he didn't have time to write slow movements, that he had to write fast movements because he wasn't going to live very long.

I have the feeling that he knew it. Otherwise, I can't understand why he didn't write more slow music, because Mozart's music, when it is slow, has a power that it seems to me no other music has. Mozart's music gives the present, which is dimensionless, a dimension, more than any other music I know. And this is a power that he, who was a most gifted man, must have been aware of, but at the same time he must have known or sensed that he would not live many years and said "I have to hurry because I can't go slowly".

PART III
JOAN MIRÓ

INTRODUCTION

JOSEPH J. SCHILDKRAUT

Part III begins with a chapter by Joseph J. Schildkraut and Alissa J. Hirshfeld entitled "'Rain of Lyres, Circuses of Melancholy': Homage to Miró". The title of this chapter comes from the poetic phrases Miró inscribed on the engraving, *Portrait of Miró* (see Figure 12-2, p. 114), that he created in 1938 during his midlife period while working in collaboration with Louis Marcoussis. Focusing on Miró's self-portraits, starting with those from his midlife period, and on the escape ladder as a symbol of transcendence, this chapter examines the interrelatedness of Miró's tragic temperament, his depression, his spiritual beliefs, and his artistic creativity (see Note 1, p. 110).

The following chapter is a scholarly and evocative essay by David Lomas entitled "The Black Border: Joan Miró's Self-portraits, 1937–1942". Noting that Miró created more self-portraits between 1937 and 1942 than at any other time in his career, Lomas asserts that, for Miró, ". . . the act of self-portrayal was imbued with such urgency because his identity as an artist could no longer be taken for granted". Lomas goes on to say, "Miró not only reinvents the nearly moribund genre of self-portraiture, he also reinvents himself". In the concluding paragraph, discussing Miró's *Self-Portrait on an Envelope* (1942), Lomas writes, ". . . his own self-portrait is addressed to him, bizarrely, in the form of a death notice", and he perceptively comments, "Miró mourns for an identity lost, a concern at the heart of this tiny image, just as it was seen to be in the majestic *Self-Portrait I*". Lomas' aim in this chapter is, ". . . to examine . . . the cultural and political factors" that impinged on Miró's self-portraiture from 1937 to 1942, and his focus in this final paragraph is on the death of a Catalan identity, rather than on Miró's confrontation with his own mortality. Nonetheless, Lomas provides us with compelling psychological insights concerning Miró's passage through his midlife identity crisis, although he does not label it as such (see Note 2, p. 110).

In the next chapter, entitled "Chaos as a Stimulus", Rosa Maria Malet puts forth the thesis that ". . . the problems that either affected . . . [Miró] . . . personally or affected the world around him . . ." gave Miró ". . . strength to confront adversity". She writes, "Miró's work and the development of his artistic personality can . . . be seen as a parallel to the conflicts he was forced to confront throughout his lifetime".

In a widely quoted statement of the late 1920s Miró said, "I want to assassinate painting". An analysis of the roots and meaning of this statement is provided in the chapter by William Jeffett entitled "Assassinating Painting: Collage and Sculpture as a

Crisis of Identity?". Based on his analysis, Jeffett concludes that "Miró's call for the murder of painting was a strategy with ramifications which reached far beyond the limited confines of art . . . [and] called for a radical rethinking of our understanding of subjectivity and artistic identity".

The final chapter of Part III is an essay by Barbara Rose entitled "Miró Finds his Vocation as an Artist". Drawing on her extensive knowledge and experience, Rose examines the psychological and cultural forces that shaped Miró's development. She notes: "In this context, we may understand the resolution of Miró's adolescent identity crisis as the acceptance of his mission or his vocation as an artist–shaman–priest. He is 'called' to serve divine purposes in the sense that the saint is 'called'".

NOTES

1. In his article for *The New York Review of Books* on the centenary celebration of Joan Miró's birth, John Golding, the painter and art historian, wrote: "Although the literature on Miró persists in calling his illness in 1911 'a minor nervous breakdown', it was clearly not minor at all, and at various points in his career Miró's work shows marked signs of mental anguish . . ." (Golding, 1993, p. 46). In contrast to much of the literature and confirming Golding's assertion, David Fernández Miró, the artist's grandson, described this episode as a "serious physical and mental breakdown, from which he [Miró] recovered at the Mas Miró in Montroig . . ." He went on to comment on Miró's ". . . tragic and taciturn nature that was beset with moments of profound sadness, doubt and loneliness" (D.F. Miró, 1989, p. 240).

Miró himself described this episode as a "serious depression" and

spoke openly of his tragic temperament. "My nature is tragic and taciturn . . ." Miró said at the start of his 1959 interview with Yvon Taillandier, in which he affords us richly detailed glimpses into his sources of inspiration, his methods of working, and his poetic, spiritually infused, animistic thinking (Miró, 1959, cited in Rowell, pp. 247–253). Echoing his opening statement, he concludes this lengthy interview by telling us once again ". . . I am tragic". Some might suggest that these statements were mere posturing on Miró's part; but if we take them seriously, and I think we should, Miró seems to be saying that we must not forget that his art had a tragic core and that he did as well.

2. In his paper on "Death and the Mid-Life Crisis" Jaques (1965) asserts that the painful awareness of one's own mortality and coming to terms with "one's own eventual personal death . . . is the central and crucial feature of the mid-life phase" (Jaques, 1965, p. 506). He saw this as a "depressive crisis" (Jaques, 1965, p. 505) that is reflected in the lives and works of creative artists by an increase in the death rate and the emergence of tragic and philosophical (spiritual) themes in their art. Even for artists with depression who may have pondered the ultimate existential question, whether to live or to die, and thus confronted the possibility of death long before the midlife period, the awareness of growing old and the inevitability of dying remain to be worked through at midlife.

REFERENCES

Golding, J. (1993). Sophisticated peasant. *New York Review of Books*, **XL**(21) (December 16), 45–51.

Jaques, E. (1965). Death and the mid-life crisis. *International Journal of Psychoanalysis*, **46**, 502–514.

Miró, D.F. (1989). Jottings: literature as a constant factor in the life of Joan Miró. In *109 Ilibres amb Joan Miró*. Fundació Joan Miró, Barcelona.

Miró, J. (1959). In Yvon Taillandier (1959). I work like a gardener. *XXe Siecle* (Paris), February 15. Cited in Rowell, M. (1986). *Joan Miró— Selected Writings and Interviews*, pp. 247–253. G.K. Hall, Boston, MA.

CHAPTER 12

"RAIN OF LYRES CIRCUSES OF MELANCHOLY": HOMAGE TO MIRÓ

JOSEPH J. SCHILDKRAUT AND
ALISSA J. HIRSHFELD

"The artistic expression of the primordial mystery of creation, and man's place on earth and in the cosmos . . . [were] recurrent themes in the magical, mystical art of Joan Miró" (Schildkraut, 1982), the pre-eminent Catalan artist who lived from 1893 to 1983. Throughout his life, in his art, writings and interviews, Miró acknowledged and explored the interrelatedness of his tragic temperament, his depressions (Schildkraut, 1993; Schildkraut & Hirshfeld, 1995), his spirituality (Stich, 1980; Schildkraut, 1982; Rowell, 1986) and his artistic creation (see Note 1, p. 127).

Exemplifying his transcendent spiritual beliefs, in 1936 Miró noted: "Every grain of dust has a wonderful soul, but to understand it one needs to regain the religious, magic sense of things, the spirit of primitive people" (Miró, 1936, cited in Stich, 1980, p. 10); and in 1959, Miró summarized his temperament in the following way:

"My nature is tragic and taciturn. . . . When I was young, I went through periods of profound sadness. . . . I'm a pessimist. I always think that everything is going to turn out badly. If

there is something humorous in my painting. . . . [p]erhaps this humor comes from a need to escape the tragic side of my temperament" (Miró, 1959a, cited in Rowell, 1986, p. 247).

Commenting on Miró's moods, Roland Penrose, his friend and biographer, noted:

"Behind the cheerful, innocent, even tranquil look in his face (see Figure 12-1), Miró has never been immune to attacks of violent anguish and depression. . . . He has occasionally expressed this precarious condition in self-portraits, which . . . are metaphoric confessions of his inner life" (Penrose, 1971, p. 96).

PORTRAIT OF MIRÓ AND "MELANCOLIE"

While going through the midlife period, in his 45th year (1937–38), at a time of both international chaos and profound personal introspection, Miró created a series of spiritual or psychological self-portraits, for example, *Portrait of Miró* (1938) shown in Figure 12-2. Since Miró attached a superstitious

12-1 *(right)*
ARNOLD NEWMAN
PHOTOGRAPH OF JOAN MIRÓ, 1979
Copyright © 1980 Arnold Newman

12-2
JOAN MIRÓ AND
LOUIS MARCOUSSIS
PORTRAIT OF MIRÓ, 1938
Engraving and drypoint,
13⅜ × 11 in (33.9 × 28 cm)
Lee M. Friedman Fund.
Courtesy Museum of Fine
Arts, Boston. © 1996
Artists Rights
Society (ARS),
NY/ADAGP/SPADEM, Paris

significance to numbers (see Rowell, 1986, pp. 44, 101, 164; Miró, 1977), turning 45 may have had special meaning for him. From 1921 to 1926, during the crucial period of Miró's development as a mature artist, his studio in Paris was located at 45 rue Blomet, and from 1924 until 1926 Miró also lived at this address (Rowell, 1986, p. 24). Moreover, in 1918 when Miró was 25, he wrote: "I am firmly convinced that no man . . . in modern times . . . will begin to know how to paint until he is 45. . . ." (Miró, 1918, cited in Rowell, 1986, pp. 54–55).

As shown in Figure 12-3, the number 45 is featured prominently in *The Circus*, a painting on celotex, which Miró executed in 1937. Painted sideways, this number appears in the lower right segment of the painting, while the number 5 fills the upper left corner, and the numbers 10 and 30 are painted along the bottom. In the light of what we know of Miró's fascination with numbers, it would seem more than mere coincidence that these last three numbers (5, 10 & 30) add up to 45—particularly since summing a string of numbers is the subject of an earlier (1925) painting by Miró, *L'Addition* (*The Check*).

This raises the possibility that *The Circus* of 1937, as well as many other works that Miró completed around this time (cf. Lomas, Chapter 13, this volume) may constitute psychological self-portraits of a sort, i.e. personal reminiscences and a summing up, characteristic of the midlife stage of psychological development. Lending credence to the notion that Miró is the true subject of *The Circus* is the appearance of his signature (in tiny letters) situated directly above the center of this work. Compatible with this notion is the prominence of the figure with a large oval sitting on its head, boxed in by numbers from below, a black sun on the right (situated above the number 45), and a vertical line on the left intersected by two horizontal lines (Figure 12-3).

A similar configuration of a vertical line on the left intersected by horizontal lines with a central figure and a black sun on the right may be seen in *Portrait of Miró* (1938), an engraving and drypoint created by Miró in collaboration with Louis Marcoussis (Figure 12-2). A surrealistic mental landscape, in effect a psychological self-portrait of Miró, this engraving contains the inscribed phrases "pluie de lyres," translated as "rain of lyres" (or, more freely rendered, "outpourings of artistic creativity") and "cirques de melancolie," translated as "circuses of melancholy" (cf. *The Circus*, 1937). Inscribed as they are on this self-portrait, created by Miró in midlife, one must wonder whether these words were meant to allude to a cyclothymic temperament in the artist.

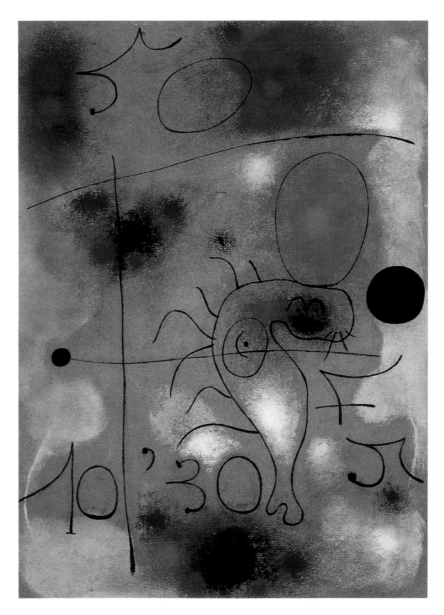

12-3
JOAN MIRÓ
LE CIRQUE (THE CIRCUS), 1937
Tempera and oil on Celotex, 47½ × 35¾ in (120.7 × 90.8 cm)
Algur H. Meadows Collection, Meadows Museum, Southern Methodist University, Dallas, Texas. © 1996 Artists Rights Society (ARS), NY/ADAGP, Paris

The face and hands of Miró, which were drawn by Marcoussis, have been overlaid by a fantastic outpouring of the signs and symbols inhabiting Miró's inner world: stars, a black sun, flames, primordial creatures, astral bodies, and a primitive ladder symbol. Annular forms on the left bring to mind the rings of Saturn, the planet associated with melancholy (Klibansky, Saxl & Panofsky, 1964; Panofsky, 1955; Wittkower & Wittkower, 1963). The artist's head has been set aflame, one eye transformed into a star, the other an empty circle—perhaps a blind eye socket. Miró seems to have depicted himself as a tormented, impassioned visionary, with heightened consciousness of both cosmic and inner reality, poetically suggested by the words "pluie de lyres" and "cirques de melancolie".

Rowell (1986, pp. 4–5) spoke of Miró's entire *oeuvre* as marked by recurrent alternating styles: works "based on a study and transformation of the so-called real world" alternate with paintings in which "Miró appears to have lost touch with outer reality and to refer solely to the inner 'real' of the mind, the spirit, the imagination". Rowell went on to conclude: "In a sense, these two styles correspond to two aspects of the artist's personality: the extroverted or active and the introspective or meditative, in which he claimed to be moved by forces greater than himself" (Rowell, 1986, pp. 4–5).

The phrase "cirques de melancolie" in this midlife engraving by Miró, brings to mind one of Albrecht Dürer's great midlife engravings, *Melencolia I* of 1514 (Figure 0-1, p. xi), probably the most famous portrayal of melancholia in the history of art (cf. Schildkraut, Foreword, this volume). And many of the themes found in Miró's art—isolation, loneliness, despair, dissatisfaction with earthbound limitations, and the yearning to ascend to celestial heights—are all to be found in this master engraving (Schildkraut & Hirshfeld, 1995), that Erwin Panofsky, the great Dürer scholar, called "a spiritual self-portrait of Albrecht Dürer" (Panofsky, 1955, p. 171).

Deep feelings of sorrow, isolation and loneliness were rooted in Miró's childhood. Teased by his classmates because he was quiet and prone to daydream, Miró did not have many friends as a boy. He recounted, "I was very much alone. Nobody paid any attention to me. . . . I felt that loneliness in a very painful, violent way when I was very

young. . . ." (Serra, 1986, p. 29). Miró's father especially did not understand his dreamer son. Of Miró's strained relationship with his father, Dupin (1962, p. 40) wrote, "Miró's love of solitude and his taciturnity doubtless have no other origin".

Miró recalled that when he was young he began drawing in order to escape from his unhappiness. In 1957, he explained: "To escape from the daily drudgery, I took drawing lessons. . . . That class was like a religious ceremony for me; I washed my hands carefully before touching the paper and pencils. The implements were like sacred objects, and I worked as though I were performing a religious rite. This state of mind," he noted, "has persisted, even more pronounced" (Miró, 1957, cited in Rowell, 1986, p. 44).

There is good evidence from his own descriptions, as well as those of his friends and biographers, that Miró experienced periodic episodes of depression. His first known episode occurred in 1911 when he was 18 years old. Opposed to his artistic aspirations, Miró's father forced him to attend business school and subsequently procured a job for him in a large hardware (and chemical) store. Miró recalled, "I was demoralized and suffered a serious depression. I fell really ill, and stayed three months in bed" (Miró, cited in Gibson, 1980, pp. 52–56). Commenting on this period, Penrose (1971, p. 12) noted:

"This was the first major crisis in a life which . . . [was] . . . punctuated with periodic upheavals, each bringing with it marked changes in Miró's work. Their frequency and violence [were] all the more remarkable because of his apparent calm and the gentleness of his nature" (cf. Figure 12-1).

There is no clear-cut evidence that

Miró experienced manic episodes. However, his descriptions of cycles governing his life and work, coupled with the marked variations in his style and productivity, provide reason to speculate about cyclothymia in the artist (Rowell, 1986, pp. 4–5, 279–280; Miró, 1931, cited in Rowell, 1986, p. 117; Miró, 1970, cited in Rowell, 1986, p. 280).

For example, between 1925 and 1927, there was a dramatic increase in Miró's productivity. During this period Miró painted a series of highly poetic canvases that Dupin (1962) termed "dream paintings," works that may have been stimulated by hunger-induced hallucinations, as Miró asser-

ted (Dupin, 1962, p. 157). One of these paintings, *Birth of the World* of 1925, is shown in Figure 12-4. Whereas Dupin (1962) cataloged over 130 paintings completed during the three-year period 1925–27, only 35 were completed during the following three years (1928–30) and only 25 were completed during the preceding three years (1922–24). Although periods of intense inspiration, perhaps occurring during hypomanic states, allowed Miró to work prolifically at times, his nostalgic yearnings and depressed feelings underlay the content of many of his finest paintings, such as *The Farm*, of 1921–22 (Figure 12-5), and *The*

12-4
JOAN MIRÓ
THE BIRTH OF THE WORLD,
1925
Oil on canvas, 8 ft 2¾ × 6 ft
6¾ in (250.8 × 200 cm)
The Museum of Modern Art, New York. Acquired through an anonymous fund, the Mr and Mrs Joseph Slifka and Armand G. Erpf Funds, and by gift of the artist. Photograph © 1996 The Museum of Modern Art, New York. © 1996 Artists Rights Society (ARS), NY/ADAGP, Paris

117

Carnival of Harlequin of 1924–25 (Figure 12-6). The ladder, a symbol of transcendence for Miró, appears for the first time in *The Farm* (Figure 12-5); and perched upon the ladder is a bird capable of flight, one of Miró's mediators between earth and the heavens.

THE ESCAPE LADDER

The ladder is also seen in *The Carnival of Harlequin* (Figure 12-6), one of Miró's first departures from the hyper-realistic style of earlier works, such as *The Farm* (1921–1922), to a more fantastic style which fused a variety of surrealistic images. In *The Carnival of Harlequin*, Miró expressed the mad chaos he felt around him and his longing to escape from the suffering he felt within. The harlequin, with a hole in its abdomen, has been read as a portrait of the artist, hungry and hallucinating as he described himself at that time. A sharp rod or nail pierces into the side of the harlequin's head, perhaps symbolizing Miró's psychological torment.

Miró described this painting in stream-of-consciousness prose (Miró, 1939, cited in Rowell, 1986, p. 164):

"The ball of yarn unraveled by cats dressed up as smoky Harlequins twisting around inside me and stabbing my gut during the period of my great hunger that gave birth to the hallucinations recorded in this painting . . . coming back in the evening to my place at 45 rue Blomet a number that to my knowledge has nothing to do with 13 which has always exerted a tremendous influence over my life . . . I had pulled out a nail from the pedestrian crossing and put it in my eye like a monocle a gentleman whose fasting ears are fascinated by the grace of a flight of butterflies musical rainbow eyes falling like a rain of lyres a ladder to escape the disgust of life."

The "rain of lyres" (cf. Figure 12-2) signifying the ladder seen on the left of *The Carnival of Harlequin* (Figure 12-6) offers an escape from "the disgust of life" into higher realms.

The ladder, in fact, was an important symbol throughout Miró's *oeuvre* (Schildkraut, 1982). In 1948, he explained:

"In the first years it [the ladder] was a plastic form frequently appearing because it was so close to me—a familiar shape in The Farm. In later years, particularly during the war, while I was on Majorca, it came to symbolize "escape": an essentially plastic form at first—it became poetic later. Or plastic, first; then nostalgic at the time of painting The Farm; finally, symbolic" (Miró, 1948, cited in Rowell, 1986, p. 208).

A ladder also appears in *The Dog Barking at the Moon* of 1926 (Figure 12-7) in which Miró addresses the theme of the isolation and loneliness of earthbound creatures. In this painting, the dog longs to climb up the ladder on the left to the realm of the moon and the heavens.

In a group of paintings from 1939 to 1940, Miró graphically portrayed the successive steps of ascent to the firmament. In *The Escape Ladder* of 1939 (Figure 12-8), the creatures are still embedded in their earthly existence, but the ladder, firmly planted on the horizon line, offers a path towards transcendence.

In *The Ladder of Escape* of 1940 (Figure 12-9), the ladder ascends further into the heavens, and the viewer is projected into a celestial realm. However, one has the feeling that one could go higher; the figure on the right reaches upwards beyond the world she shares with the snake-like creature on the left.

And in his painting, *On the 13th the Ladder Brushed the Firmament*

12-5
JOAN MIRÓ
THE FARM, 1921–22
Oil on canvas, 48¾ × 55⅝ in
(123.8 × 141.3 cm)
Gift of Mary Hemingway,
National Gallery of Art,
Washington. © 1995
Board of Trustees,
National Gallery of Art,
Washington. © 1996
Artists Rights Society
(ARS), NY/ADAGP, Paris

12-6
JOAN MIRÓ
CARNIVAL OF HARLEQUIN,
1924–25
Oil on canvas, 26 × 36⅝ in
(66 × 93 cm)
Albright–Knox Art Gallery,
Buffalo, New York. Room
of Contemporary Art
Fund, 1940. © 1996 Artists
Rights Society (ARS),
NY/ADAGP, Paris

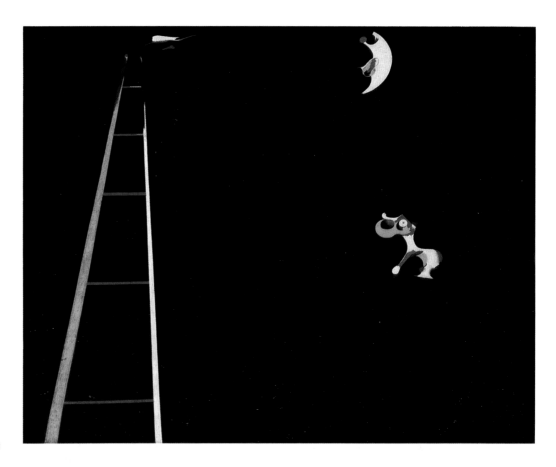

12-7
JOAN MIRÓ
DOG BARKING AT THE MOON,
1926
Oil on canvas, 28⅞ ×
36½ in (73.3 × 92.7 cm)
Philadelphia Museum of
Art: A.E. Gallatin
Collection. © 1996 Artists
Rights Society (ARS),
NY/ADAGP, Paris

(1940), Miró finally reaches the heavens (Figure 12-10). Unlike the other two paintings, here a myriad of astral bodies covers the picture, and we are beyond the realm of creatures.

The Ladder of Escape (1940) and *On the 13th the Ladder Brushed the Firmament* (1940) belong to the series of 23 gouache paintings, known as the *Constellations*, that Miró created from 1940 to 1941, working in the shadow of the Spanish Civil War and World War II. His comments on his state of mind at that time shed light on how Miró was able to transform his depressed feelings into energy for painting:

"... I was going through a very hard period. I was living in Palma, and living almost on the charity of my wife's family. . . . But who was I in those days? Practically nobody, just a poor man who was perhaps a little mad, and who liked to paint things in

a way of his own which nobody here understood. . . . I found myself very much alone, as though forsaken. But I had a great inner strength which made me paint more furiously than ever. With rage, with sorrow, with desperation, because I could see how a civilization in which I had been brought up . . . was being crushed and destroyed. . . . Looking back, I cannot understand how I managed to endure all that. Perhaps it was my very suffering, when I realized my impotence and my insignificance, that gave me new strength to go on painting" (Serra, 1986, pp. 58–62).

And on the theme of man's suffering, in a letter of 1915, Miró wrote:

"Mortals cannot aspire to complete happiness. That would be rebelling against God who was a man and suffered for us. . . . Pain is the insepar-

able brother of pleasure; the one cannot exist without the other. . . . 'La souffrance, c'est le sacrement de la vie'" (Miró, 1915, cited in Rowell, 1986, p. 49).

Moreover, Dupin (1962, p. 156) noted that Miró's "own standard for creative work is the torment necessary to bring it to birth", and in 1917 Miró wrote of the suffering self-critical artist:

"[This] sort of man sees a different problem in every tree and in every bit of sky: this is the man who suffers, the man who is always moving and can

12-9
JOAN MIRÓ
THE LADDER OF ESCAPE,
1940
Gouache, watercolor, and
brush and ink on paper,
15¾ × 18¾ in (40 × 47.6 cm)
The Museum of Modern
Art, New York. Helen
Acheson Bequest.
Photograph © 1996 The
Museum of Modern Art,
New York. © 1996 Artists
Rights Society (ARS),
NY/ADAGP, Paris

never sit still, the man who will never do what people call a 'definitive' work. He is the man who always stumbles and gets to his feet again. . . . [This] man is always saying not yet, it is still not ready, and when he is satisfied with his last canvas and starts another one, he destroys the earlier one. His work is always a new beginning, as though today he was just beginning to paint" (Miró, 1917, cited in Rowell, 1986, p. 51).

SELF-PORTRAITS

Returning to the midlife self-portraits Miró created during his 45th year, Self-Portrait I of 1937–38 (Figure 12-11), is a large drawing in black pencil touched up with oil (cf. Lomas, Chapter 13, this volume). Working before a magnifying mirror, Miró carefully recorded what the eye perceived. But as the work proceeded, Miró the observer was transformed into Miró the visionary, with eyes blazing like miniature suns. Dupin (1962, p. 304) described this work as: "the visionary portrait of a visionary painter.... [in which] we are given a glimpse of the tragic Miró . . . at grips with his inner torment. . . . Both the vision and the fire seem to originate in the eyes".

Indeed, the eyes are wide as if obsessed by inner turmoil, and the face reflects his distress. Miró had great hopes for this work, as he expressed to Pierre Matisse: "I have destroyed my portrait several times; I now feel that I am on the right track.... It will be a work that sums up my life, and it will be very representative in the history of painting" (Rowell, 1986, p. 158).

In *Self-Portrait II* of 1938 (Figure 12-12), Miró depicted himself as a mere pair of eyes—conventionally regarded as windows to the soul—that resemble flaming suns, surrounded by stars and fish. Dupin (1962, pp. 304–306) wrote: "What we have [in *Self-Portrait I* and *Self-Portrait II*] is perhaps a single self-portrait in two pictures. . . . If so, the first . . . would express tragedy, the confrontation of death in pure drawing, painstaking, relentless to the point of fury; the second would celebrate the triumph of life. . .".

Self-Portrait I (Figure 12-11), was an unfinished work, an incomplete piece which Miró signed and put into circulation. Even after it had been circulated, Miró kept an exact tracing of this work in his studio. Dupin (1962, p. 303) wrote, "As a rule, unfinished works . . . betray self-doubts, a looking back, or basic dissatisfactions". Thus, it is perhaps noteworthy, in relation to Miró's psychological sense of identity not only as an artist but also as a person going through the midlife period, that this unfinished work was a self-portrait (cf. Lomas, this volume).

When Miró returned to the copy in 1960, as shown in Figure 12-13, he attacked it with bold black strokes, defacing his own image. In this metaphorically self-destructive act, he imposed a bold, Miróesque personage over his earlier work. The eyes are again highlighted, ringed by two black

12-10
JOAN MIRÓ
ON THE 13TH, THE LADDER BRUSHED THE FIRMAMENT, 1940
Gouache and oil wash on paper, 18⅛ × 14¾ in (46 × 37.5 cm)
Private collection. Color transparency: Stuart Waltzer. © Artists Rights Society (ARS), NY/ADAGP, Paris

circles, one accentuated by a circle of red. A patch of yellow seems to flow from the lower phallic regions of the personage.

In a moving tribute to Miró, the abstract expressionist painter Robert Motherwell (1959, pp. 32–33, 65–67) wrote of Miró's work from that period: "Lately, Miró's art has become more brutal, blacker, torn, heavier in substance as though he had moved from the earlier comedies [of Shakespeare] through *Antony and Cleopatra* and *Falstaff* to *King Lear*, harsher, colder, ironic, more ultimate". And Motherwell concluded, "There is one joke of God's that no one can escape—consciousness of death . . .".

A lithograph (Figure 12-14) created

12-11
JOAN MIRÓ
SELF-PORTRAIT I, 1937–38
Pencil, crayon and oil on canvas, 57½ × 38¼ in (146.1 × 97.2 cm)
The Museum of Modern Art, New York. James Thrall Soby Bequest. Photograph © 1996 The Museum of Modern Art, New York. © 1996 Artists Rights Society (ARS), NY/ADAGP, Paris

12-12
JOAN MIRÓ
SELF-PORTRAIT II, 1938
Oil on burlap, 51 × 77 in
(129.5 × 195.5 cm)
Photograph © The Detroit
Institute of Arts, 1995. Gift
of W. Hawkins Ferry.
© 1996 Artists Rights
Society (ARS), NY/ADAGP,
Paris

by Miró for the 1973 exhibition at the Museum of Modern Art in New York on the occasion of his 80th birthday may be seen as a later self-portrait of the aging artist, here depicted with but one eye. Though his hands are disintegrating, he is still capable of participating in the procreation of a new generation of artists, symbolized by the fresh black hand at the top of the picture and the eyes in the tadpole-like forms flanking a phallic organ and its associated triangular yellow patch at the bottom of the print (see Note 2, p. 128). For Miró, the phallus was a symbol of procreation, the source of seeds giving rise to new life. And the theme of procreation, a sustaining force in Miró's life, was fundamental to Miró's conception of the function of art. As Miró said (Miró, 1959b, cited in Rowell, 1986, p. 251):

"Even more important than the painting itself is what it gives off, what it projects. It doesn't matter if the painting is destroyed. Art can die, but what counts are the seeds it has spread over the earth. . . . A painting must be fertile. It must give birth to a world."

CONCLUSION

In 1925, as noted above, Miró had in fact painted a work entitled *The Birth of the World* (Figure 12-4). Dupin (1962, p. 203) says of Miró's works of this year, "the aim had been to create a primeval void—intensely alive, bound up with the mystery of creation, which could contain within itself the seeds of all births and all metamorphoses". The large size of this painting, more than 8 × 6 ft, envelops the viewer; and there is a sense of being drawn into the

12-13
JOAN MIRÓ
SELF-PORTRAIT, 1937–60
Oil and pencil on canvas,
57⅞ × 38¼ in (146.5 × 97 cm)
Fundació Joan Miró,
Barcelona. © 1996 Artists
Rights Society (ARS),
NY/ADAGP, Paris

sense of grandeur and of gestation of the world" (Miró, 1941–42, cited in Rowell, 1986, p. 191).

In an age marked by an absence of both societal myth and spiritual beliefs, Miró's art puts the viewer in touch with the cosmic and mysterious forces at work in the universe. Commenting on modern art, the theologian Paul Tillich (1964, pp. 246–249) noted:

"The arts . . . open up a dimension of reality which is otherwise hidden, and they open up our own being for receiving this reality. Only the arts can do this; science, philosophy, moral action, and religious devotion cannot. The artist brings to our senses, and through them to our whole being, something of the depth of our world and of ourselves, something of the mystery of being. . . . And as a theologian I want to say that this period, in spite of its poverty of religious paintings and sculptures in the traditional sense of the word, is a period in which the religious dimension has appeared with astonishing power in non-religious works."

Jung (1966a, 1966b) also wrote of the artist's role in putting the viewer back in touch with spiritual forces repressed by the culture, in giving shape to the human yearning for transcendence. Moreover, Jung (1966b) recognized that the artist is often forced to sacrifice personal freedom and happiness to become an instrument of his or her art, responding to the challenge of representing the collective psychic symbols of humanity.

Expressing similar ideas, Miró explained, "The artist . . . must go beyond the individualist stage and struggle to reach the collective stage. He must go further than the self—strip himself of his individuality, leave it

pulsating, infinite recesses of the dawn of history and the time of the original creation. The contrast between the luminous wash of the background and the solid opaque forms in the foreground creates what Miró called "an unlimited atmospheric space" (Rubin, 1973, p. 32). In connection with this painting, it is interesting that Miró reminded himself, in his working notes of 1941–1942, to "... always have the Bible open . . . that will give me a behind, reject it—and plunge into anonymity" (Miró, 1951, cited in Rowell, 1986, p. 217). Echoing the Spanish mystics (e.g. St John of the Cross and St Teresa) whose works he read avidly (Rowell, 1986, pp. 202, 210, 227), Miró asserted, "Anonymity allows me to renounce myself, but in renouncing myself I come to affirm myself even more" (Miró, 1959c in Rowell, 1986, p. 253).

Throughout his life, Miró's art continued to be fueled by both his depressions and by his visionary strivings. As he explained in a 1931 interview:

"The only thing that interests me is the spirit itself. . . . The only reason I abide by the rules of pictorial art is because they're essential for expressing what I feel, just as grammar is essential for expressing yourself. . . . I'm only interested in anonymous art, the kind that springs from the collective unconscious" (Miró, 1931, cited in Rowell, 1986, pp. 116–117).

And referring to the depressive side of his temperament, he noted: "If I don't paint, I worry, I become very depressed, I fret and become gloomy and get 'black ideas' and I don't know what to do with myself" (Miró, 1947–48, cited in Rowell, 1986, p. 202). This suggests that Miró's psychological sense of identity as a person (as well as his sense of identity as an artist) was dependent on his artistic productivity, and that art making, in part, may have served a healing function (Arnheim, 1992) for Miró.

Thus, through introspection and meditation, Miró's spiritual beliefs sustained him in his suffering, allowing his depressions to fuel his artistic creativity. Isolation, loneliness, despair, dissatisfaction with earthbound limitations, and the yearning to ascend to celestial heights became

·12-14
JOAN MIRÓ
UNTITLED (HOMAGE TO MIRÓ),
1973
Lithograph, printed in color, 35⅜ × 24 in (89.8 × 61.0 cm)
The Museum of Modern Art, New York. Gift of the Museum Department of Publications. Photograph © 1996 The Museum of Modern Art, New York. © 1996 Artists Rights Society (ARS), NY/ADAGP, Paris

themes for his art—an art that transformed these themes into visual images with the power to probe the deepest recesses of the viewer's psyche. In sum, the art and life of Joan Miró may be seen as the rain of lyres or outpourings of creativity amidst circuses of melancholy, the *pluie de lyres* and *cirques de melancolie*, revealed to us in the 1938 engraving and drypoint, *Portrait of Miró*.

NOTES

1. Although it is clear to us, on the basis of our research, that there is a

connection between feelings of despair and inner torment in Miró and the evolution of his art, we cannot at this point match the depressed state to specific artworks. A further limitation of this article is our inability to pinpoint the particular nature of Miró's affective disorder. Retrospective diagnoses made on the basis of historical sources, in the absence of direct clinical examinations, are often problematic; and the problems and pitfalls of the historical approach have been discussed extensively by Runyan (1984). While there is evidence that Miró experienced cyclicity in his moods, we do not know if Miró had a true cyclothymic or manic-depressive disorder. Moreover, we do not yet understand the exact nature of the relation between Miró's mood swings and his productivity or the relation between his depressions and his creativity.

2. The abstract expressionist artists, who emerged as a group in New York during the 1940s and 1950s, can be seen as a new generation of artists spawned by Miró. They were influenced both by Miró's artistic techniques and by his spirituality. After seeing reproductions of his work in European art magazines, they were exposed to a great number of actual works in a Miró retrospective at The Museum of Modern Art in New York (November 18 1941–January 11 1942). Some years later, many of them then met Miró during the 9 months he lived in New York (February–October, 1947). The show, *Miró in America*, organized by Barbara Rose at the Houston Museum of Fine Arts in 1982, documented the relationship between Miró and the abstract expressionists (Rose, 1982). Also see Schildkraut et al (1994 and Chapter 18, this volume) concerning the high prevalence of depression and depression-spectrum disorders in this group of artists.

ACKNOWLEDGEMENTS

This paper is based on an article by Schildkraut, J.J. & Hirshfeld, A.J. (1995). Mind and mood in modern art I: Miró and "Melancolie", *Creativity Research Journal*, **8**, 139–156. This work was supported in part by the Karen Tucker Fund.

REFERENCES

Arnheim, R. (1992). *To the Rescue of Art: Twenty-six Essays*, pp. 164–171. University of California Press, Berkeley.

Dupin, J. (1962). *Joan Miró—Life and Work*. Harry N. Abrams, New York.

Gibson, M. (1980). Miró: When I see a tree . . . I can feel that tree talking to me. *Artnews*, **79**, 52–56.

Jung, C.G. (1966a). On the relation of analytical psychology to poetry. In *The Collected Works of C.G. Jung*, Vol. 15, Eds H. Read, M. Fordham & G. Adler, second printing (1972), pp. 65–83. Bollingen Series XX, Princeton University Press, Princeton, NJ.

Jung, C.G. (1966b). Psychology and Literature. In *The Collected Works of C.G. Jung*, Vol. 15, Eds H. Read, M. Fordham & G. Adler, second printing (1972), pp. 84–105. Bollingen Series XX, Princeton University Press, Princeton, NJ.

Klibansky, R., Saxl, F. & Panofsky, E. (1964). *Saturn and Melancholy*. Basic Books, New York.

Miró, J. (1915). Letter to E.C. Ricart, 31 January 1915. Cited in Rowell (1986 see below), p. 49.

Miró, J. (1917). Letter to J.F. Rafols, 13 September 1917. Cited in Rowell (1986: see below), p. 51.

Miró, J. (1918). Letter to E.C. Ricart, 16 July 1918. Cited in Rowell (1986: see below), pp. 54–55.

Miró, J. (1931). In *Spanish Artists in Paris: Juan [sic] Miró*, Francisco Melgar. *Ahora* (Madrid), 24 January 1931. Cited in Rowell (1986: see below), pp. 116–117.

Miró, J. (1936). In G. Duthuit, Où allez-vous Miró? *Cahiers d'Art*, **XI** (8–10), 262. Cited in Stich (1980: see below), p. 10.

Miró, J. (1939). Harlequin's Carnival. *Verve* (Paris) **I**(4) (January–March), 85. Cited in Rowell (1986: see below), p. 164.

Miró, J. (1941–42). Sculpture and studio (II). *Working Notes*. Cited in Rowell (1986: see below), p. 191.

Miró, J. (1947–48). In Francis Lee, Interview with Miró. *Possibilities* (New York), **Winter**. Cited in Rowell (1986: see below), p. 202.

Miró, J. (1948). In James Johnson Sweeney, Joan Miró: comment and interview. *Partisan Review* (New York), **February**. Cited in Rowell (1986: see below), p. 208.

Miró, J. (1951). Interview by Georges Charbonnier, French National Radio. Cited in Rowell (1986: see below), p. 217.

Miró, J. (1957). Letter to Jacques Dupin, 9 October 1957. Cited in Rowell (1986: see below), pp. 44–45.

Miró, J. (1959a). In Yvon Taillandier, I work like a gardener. *XXe Siecle* (Paris), February 15. Cited in Rowell (1986: see below), p. 247.

Miró, J. (1959b). In Taillandier. Cited in Rowell (1986: see below), p. 251.

Miró, J. (1959c). In Taillandier. Cited in Rowell (1986: see below), p. 253.

Miró, J. (1970). Interview, April 20 1970. Cited in Rowell (1986: see below), p. 280.

Miró, J. (1977). *Ceci est la couleur de mes rêves; entretiens avec Georges Raillard* (This is the color of my dreams; interview with Georges Raillard), pp. 91–92. Editiens du Seuil, Paris.

Motherwell, R. (1959). The significance of Miró. *Artnews*, **58**, 32–33, 65–67.

Panofsky, E. (1955). *The Life and Art of Albrecht Dürer*. Princeton University Press, Princeton, NJ.

Penrose, R. (1971). *Miró*. Harry N. Abrams, New York.

Rose, B. (1982). *Miró in America*. Museum of Fine Arts, Houston, TX.

Rowell, M. (1986). *Joan Miró—Selected Writings and Interviews*. G.K. Hall, Boston, MA.

Rubin, W. (1973). *Miró in the Collection of the Museum of Modern Art*, p. 32. Museum of Modern Art, New York.

Runyan, W.M. (1984). *Life Histories and Psychobiography: Explorations in Theory and Method*. Oxford University Press, New York.

Schildkraut, J.J. (1982). Miró and the mystical in modern art: problems for research in metapsychiatry. *Am. J. Soc. Psychiat*, **II**(4), 3–20.

Schildkraut, J.J. (1993). Miró offers case in point of creativity's link to depression. Letter to the Editor, *The New York Times*, Sunday, October 24, 'The Week in Review', p. 14.

Schildkraut, J.J. & Hirshfeld, A.J. (1995). Mind and mood in modern art I: Miró and "melancolie". *Creativity Res. J.*, **8**(2), 139–156.

Schildkraut, J.J., Hirshfeld, A.J. & Murphy, J.M. (1994). Mind and mood in modern art II: depressive disorders, spirituality and early deaths in the Abstract Expressionist artists of the New York School. *Am. J. Psychiat.*, **151**, 482–488.

Serra, P.A. (1986). *Miró and Mallorca.* Rizzoli International Publications, New York.

Stich, S. (1980). *Joan Miró: The Development of a Sign Language.* Washington University, St. Louis, MO.

Tillich, P. (1964). Address on the occasion of the opening of the new galleries and sculpture garden of The Museum of Modern Art. Reprinted in *On Art and Architecture*, Paul Tillich (1987), Eds J. Dillenberger & J. Dillenberger, pp. 246–249. Crossroad Publishing Co., New York.

Wittkower, R. & Wittkower, M. (1963). *Born under Saturn.* Norton, New York.

CHAPTER 13

THE BLACK BORDER: JOAN MIRÓ SELF-PORTRAITS, 1937–42

DAVID LOMAS

Miró had been stranded in Paris for more than a year, unable to return to Spain because of the Civil War, when he announced in a letter dated 3 November 1937 to his dealer in New York, Pierre Matisse, that he had embarked several weeks earlier on a self-portrait bust "three times larger than natural size" (Miró, 1937b, cited in Rowell 1987, p. 157). The scale of Miró's ambition was evidently to match as he confidently assures the dealer to whom the picture would later be consigned for sale that "it will be the most sensational thing I have ever done". Throughout the winter of 1937–38, as he labored at this Herculean task, a steady flow of correspondence kept Matisse abreast of each new development. By February (1938), after several false starts, Miró confides that at last he is on the right track and promises to send Matisse a photograph. The following month he is so pleased with the portrait that in order to preserve it he decides to have a tracing made, allowing him the option of continuing to work on the copy should he wish to. As it now stands, *Self-Portrait I* (Figure 12-11, p. 124) is a mainly monochrome drawing in pencil and crayon with touches of oil colour. A strictly frontal head with pursed lips and an intent, riveting stare nearly fills the large canvas. The eyes are like blazing stars and the whole face is consumed by flames. With Europe itself about to erupt in con-

flagration, it is as though Miró has condensed into this apocalyptic image the self-portrait of an entire epoch. One could scarcely dispute the assessment of James Thrall Soby, one-time owner of the picture, that "this beyond question is one of the major portraits of our time" (Soby 1959, p. 93).

Between 1937 and 1942, Miró carried out more self-portraits than at any other moment of his career. In addition to *Self-Portrait I* and its more abstract pendant, *Self-Portrait II*, in 1938 Miró created jointly with Louis Marcoussis, an erstwhile cubist painter whose printmaking studio he shared, the etched *Portrait of Miró* which intriguingly straddles the genres of portrait and self-portrait (discussed by Schildkraut & Hirshfeld, Chapter 12, this volume). There are a further dozen or more self-portrait drawings from these years. Executed in some instances on mere scraps of paper and never exhibited during the years of Franco's rule because of the political sympathies Miró expresses, they are nonetheless complex and marvellously inventive images that repay our careful attention. My aim in this chapter will be to examine some of the cultural and political factors that impinge on how Miró portrays himself and which might contribute to an explanation of why it was that he turned so assiduously to self-portraiture at this moment. The dramatic, cataclysmic upheavals on the world stage had repercussions in the narrower arena of cultural politics that were of no lesser consequence for artists and which compelled even well-established painters to take stock of where they stood, to examine closely and redefine themselves. For Miró, I want to argue, the act of self-portrayal was imbued with such urgency because his identity as an artist could no longer be taken for granted. Between 1937 and 1942, Miró not only reinvents the nearly moribund genre of self-portraiture, he also reinvents himself.

Out of a desire to inspect and record his features with the utmost precision, Miró reports that as he worked on *Self-Portrait I* he used a concave shaving mirror (Miró, 1961, cited in Rowell 1987, p. 257). This is an unusual recourse for a portrait painter, since the reflected image is not only magnified but also quite grotesquely distorted and, as Soby has noted, could account for some of the oddities of the resulting self-portrait. Miró's head looms before us so abruptly foreshortened that hairs on the tip of his nose are hugely enlarged, the one comical note in an otherwise gravely serious image. He has also incorporated aberrations round the periphery of the reflection to convey in *Self-Portrait I* a striking effect of centrifugal rupture of the facial contour. I suspect that Miró would not have been aware of an essay by Goethe on Leonardo's *Last Supper* in which he alerts us to the highly disconcerting aspect of a face viewed in this manner. Asserting that the human countenance only appears beautiful when contained within strict parameters of size, Goethe instructs the reader:

"Make the experiment, and look at yourself in a concave mirror, and you will be terrified at the inanimate, unmeaning monstrosity, which, like a Medusa, meets your eye . . . Something

similar is experienced by the artist, by whose hands a colossal face is to be formed" (Goethe 1980, p. 185).

Something similar, we may imagine, was experienced by Miró at whose hands a self-portrait three times natural size was to be formed. If it were a desire to apprehend (in the etymologic sense of "to lay hold of") himself, warts and all, that drove Miró to use a concave mirror in the first place, the effect of doing so was quite the reverse of what had been intended: it was to place him, momentarily, beyond the grasp of recognition. For an uncanny instant it was as though he were someone (or something) other, an exorbitant movement in which he was propelled outside of himself. *Self-Portrait I* stands as a record of that putative moment of rupture and self-estrangement. A self-portrait, it is a portrait of the self as other.

Quite a different mode of address was recorded in Miró's youthful *Self-Portrait* of 1919 (Figure 13-1). At the time Miró was jockeying for position at the forefront of the avant-garde in Barcelona and the disjunctive styles which he combines in the picture were dictated by fashions current in those circles. The Cubist faceting of his shirt, left conspicuously unfinished, advertises his modernity and international outlook, whereas the stylized head, treated in a manner indebted to newly rediscovered Catalan Romanesque murals, aligns him with a resurgent tide of Catalan nationalism. Painted on the eve of Miró's departure for Paris, it is an image that speaks, on every level, of artistic ambition. Accordingly, in the exaggerated curves of the small globular face and open neckline are reiterated heart shapes that betray a narcissistic investment in an idealized image of what Miró himself would like to be. As the

13-1
JOAN MIRÓ
SELF-PORTRAIT, 1919
Oil on canvas, 28¾ × 23⅝ in
(73 × 60 cm)
Musée Picasso, Paris.
Photograph © R.M.N.,
Paris. © 1996 Artists
Rights Society (ARS),
NY/ADAGP, Paris

common expression has it, the like-ness seems to capture the subject. In *Self-Portrait I*, on the other hand, that intimacy with oneself which the term identity presupposes has irretrievably broken down, and along with it the cohesiveness of the self-image. Also gone is the earthy solidity and pres-ence of the earlier self-portrait, an effect of the large furrowed expanse of shirt in a fiery terracotta colour which half recalls the Catalan landscape.

Freud, in the essay on "The 'Uncanny'", recounts an incident which happened on a train journey when he caught sight of his face reflected in a swinging glass door and momentarily failed to recognize it as his own. Indeed, he recalls having felt a hearty distaste for the bearded stranger lurching towards him and wonders now if his reaction was not "a vestigial trace of the archaic reaction which feels the 'double' to be something uncanny (*unheimlich*)" (Freud, 1955a, p. 248). An initial clue to the similarly uncanny character of *Self-Portrait I* comes from a note jotted down by Miró in 1942 or thereabouts as he contemplated resuming work on the picture (in all likelihood, he is referring to the traced copy which by that stage we can assume had been made). "Think about William Blake when doing the self-portrait" he writes (Miró, 1942 in Rowell 1987, p. 190). André Masson, a long-standing artistic acquaintance of Miró's, had by that date already embarked on a series of imaginary portraits which took their cue from the work of William Blake who, at the behest of his patron John Varley, had transcribed visions of various assorted historical, or in some cases completely imaginary, personages. One of Masson's images, a 1939 ink drawing of the pre-Socratic

philosopher Heraclitus with hair in flames (Figure 13-2), is very close in conception to Miró's self-portrait. In this case, the flames apparently allude to the crucial role of fire as an agent of flux and transmutation in Heraclitus's cosmology—"Fire lives in the death of earth, air in the death of fire, water in the death of air, and earth in the death of water" is one of the adages attributed to Heraclitus. (Another source to be considered for the motif of flaming hair is alchemical illustrations with which Miró and Masson were both familiar. See, for the purposes of comparison, Klossowski de Rola, 1988, Figures 30 and 498.) It is obvious that Masson may have seen *Self-Portrait I* in Miró's studio, however the family resemblance between the images could also derive from a common ancestor, a drawing of great renown by Blake himself. *The Man Who Taught Blake Painting in His Dreams* of 1819 is one of the best known Blake–Varley

13-2
ANDRÉ MASSON
VISIONARY PORTRAIT OF HERACLITUS, 1938
India ink on paper,
19⅝ × 25⅝ in (50 × 65 cm)
Private collection.
Courtesy of Comité Andre Masson. © 1996 Artists Rights Society (ARS), NY/ADAGP, Paris

sketchbook drawings and, as Blake was a self-taught artist, it is commonly thought to be in some respect a self-portrait, the orientalized features notwithstanding (Figure 13-3, the Tate Gallery version, is a replica attributed to John Linnell). Blake, using a wiry, incisive line, represents his head in full-face in order to heighten the impact of his visionary stare. Flames of inspiration arise from the forehead and merge with contiguous locks of hair. Miró had an opportunity to see this drawing at first-hand in 1937 at an exhibition of Blake and Turner at the Bibliothèque Nationale in Paris and the visual evidence alone suggests that, independently of Masson and well before him, Miró struck upon the idea of portraying himself in the guise of Blake, a much venerated surrealist precursor. It could have been just after a visit to the exhibition that Miró wrote to Matisse setting out in unmistakably Blakean terms his aims in a picture, the *Still-life with Old Shoe* (Figure 13-4), which he was then working on: "To look nature in the face and *dominate it* ... It's as though by the strength of your eyes you bring down a panther at your feet in the middle of the jungle" (Miró, 1937a, cited in Rowell 1987, p. 147). And his comment soon afterwards in an interview with Georges Duthuit that "Each grain of dust contains the soul of something marvellous" (Miró, 1936, cited in Rowell, 1987, p. 153) is again highly redolent of Blake, whose name was often invoked by the surrealists in the wake of the International Exhibition of Surrealism in London in 1936.

Consider for a moment the mental note: "Think about William Blake when doing the self-portrait". Such a mask doubtless struck Miró as the most economical way of signalling his identity as a visionary artist. As a painter-poet, Blake would have had a special

13-3
After WILLIAM BLAKE
*THE MAN WHO TAUGHT BLAKE
PAINTING IN HIS DREAMS
(Replica), c. 1819*
*Pencil on paper, 10¼ × 8⅛ in
(26 × 20.6 cm)*
*Tate Gallery, London.
Reproduced by permission
of Sotheby's*

appeal for Miró, who in his own work sought to achieve a synthesis of painting and poetry (in fact, he would later make use of a technique of relief-etching pioneered by Blake in the illustrated books which enabled him to combine images and hand-written text on the same plate). The remark, however, is more than a little perplexing because it poses a question of whose self it is that is represented. What does it mean to paint a self-portrait with another artist *in mind*? It is as though, in the words of the poet Arthur Rimbaud, "I is an other"

13-4
JOAN MIRÓ
STILL LIFE WITH OLD SHOE,
1937
Oil on canvas, 32 × 46 in
(81.3 × 116.8 cm)
The Museum of Modern Art, New York. Gift of James Thrall Soby. Photograph © 1996 The Museum of Modern Art, New York. © 1996 Artists Rights Society (ARS), NY/ADAGP, Paris

(Rimbaud 1871/1988, p. 100).

It transpires that yet another ghost haunts the space of *Self-Portrait I*. Van Gogh, an ego ideal dating from Miró's earliest days as a painter, is paid a reverent homage in the *Still Life with Old Shoe* which was painted in Paris between January and May of 1937. Strident expressionist colours and a discarded boot alongside the rudiments of a peasant repast clearly allude to the Dutch painter, as Miró confirmed in an interview years later (Miró, 1978, cited in Rowell, 1987, p. 293). In *Self-Portrait I*, which followed close on the heels of the still-life, Miró (figuratively speaking now) steps into the boots of Van Gogh: the sunflower on his lapel is a token of this identification. Held within the precincts of the 1937 Paris World's Fair was a blockbuster exhibition of Van Gogh which opened in June and ran until October. The catalogue for this event was published as a special issue of *L'Amour de l'Art*, a popular art magazine, and contained an essay by René Huyghe,

curator of paintings at the Louvre, which predictably dwelt at length on Van Gogh's tragic persona. A caption to one of the numerous self-portraits (Figure 13-5) remarks on a background of flame-shaped arabesques that can be imagined as embroiling the artist's head, and in his catalogue essay Huyghe powerfully evokes "torches of fire, into which trees, houses, rocks, metamorphose and ascend to the sky, rejoining fires of neighbouring worlds" (p. 27). As *Self-Portrait I* was commenced in the month of October, it seems reasonable to infer that the Van Gogh exhibition gave Miró the initial spark.

Matters prove to be more complicated, however, Miró writing in a letter to his dealer on 5 February 1938 that, having *destroyed* the portrait several times, "I now feel that I am on the right track. It will be drawn in a few days, and then I will have it photographed and send you a print" (Miró, 1938a, cited in Rowell, 1987, p. 158). Thus it would appear that *Self-Portrait I* underwent substantial changes with its definitive form only being arrived at by Miró some time in the new year. Adding weight to this hypothesis is a caricatural drawing dated September 21 1937, which Miró has inscribed on the reverse side "Étude pour un portrait–autoportrait" (Study for a portrait–self-portrait) (Figure 13-6). If, as seems probable, this is an early study for the self-portrait, then as it evolved Miró has clearly jettisoned its comical spirit in favour of a far more serious, exalted conception. A factor responsible for this drastic "about face" was, indubitably, the publication of a short text by the writer Georges Bataille entitled "Van Gogh Prometheus" in the first issue of *Verve*, a new avant-garde magazine, in December 1937. That several lithographs by Miró were illustrated in the same issue of *Verve* adds to the likelihood that he knew the text in question, which takes the form of an avowedly idiosyncratic review of the recently closed Van Gogh exhibition. In the catalog, Van Gogh was cited as having said that "There are circumstances where it is better to be the vanquished than the victor, better Prometheus than Jupiter". Bataille takes this as a cue to return to the topic of sacrifice, which he had first broached in connection with Van Gogh in an essay of 1930 that bore the somewhat lugubrious title of "Sacrificial Mutilation and the Severed Ear of Vincent Van Gogh". This article had been published in *Documents*, a journal edited by Bataille, the unique character of which resulted from the involvement not only of artists and writers but also of ethnologists. This orientation is reflected in Bataille's essay, which marshalls evidence from a wide range of ethnographic as well as psychiatric sources in order to demonstrate that Van Gogh's self-mutilation, in spite of its ostensible basis in

13-5
VINCENT VAN GOGH
Self-portrait, 1889
Oil on canvas,
25⅝ × 21¼ in (65 × 54 cm)
Museé d'Orsay, Paris.
Photograph © R.M.N.

13-6
JOAN MIRÓ
Study for a Self-portrait,
1937
Ink on paper, 25¼ × 19⅛ in
(64 × 48.5 cm)
© 1996 Artists Rights
Society (ARS), NY/ADAGP,
Paris

mental illness, was no less an "expression of a veritable social function, of an institution as clearly defined, as generally human as sacrifice". The act of slicing off an ear Bataille regards as analogous to the mutilations inflicted on the body in initiatory and other rites. Both spring from a desire to rupture the limits of the self, from "the necessity of throwing oneself or part of oneself *out of oneself*" which "in certain instances can have no other end than death" (Bataille 1930/1986b, p. 67).

An important theme running through Bataille's writings in the 1930s is his attempt to valorize a principle of loss over and against the norms of utility and conservation. He contends that our existence is impoverished by instincts of self-preservation, which shore up the defensive ramparts of the ego only to confine and imprison us. With the bourgeois individual in his sights, he refers contemptuously to "all that confers on (many) faces the repugnant aspect of defensive closure". In order to achieve the brilliant radiance of light, Being in Bataille's estimation must continually risk itself, burn and consume itself. The sun—wastefully expending its energy—is a potent symbol for the unconditional, sovereign loss of self which alone can redeem the habitual emptiness of human existence. Bataille offers this as an explanation for the central role played by the sun in numerous sacrificial myths and rituals, as well as Van Gogh's obsession with it. Taking up once more the themes of rupture and ecstatic loss of oneself, in "Van Gogh Prometheus" Bataille asserts that Van Gogh went so far as to identity himself with the sun:

"Van Gogh, who decided by 1882 that it was better to be Prometheus than Jupiter, tore from within himself

rather than an ear, nothing less than a SUN . . . Van Gogh began to give to the sun a meaning which it had not yet had. He did not introduce it into his canvases as part of a decor, but rather like the sorcerer whose dance slowly rouses the crowd, transporting it in its movement. At that moment all of his painting finally became radiation, explosion, flame, and himself, lost in ecstasy before a source of radiant life, exploding, inflamed" (Bataille 1937/ 1986a, p. 59).

Self-Portrait I renders this sovereign moment as the artist "lost in ecstasy before a source of *radiant* life" becomes himself explosive, inflamed. Miró translates into visual form Bataille's recasting of a Promethean myth of the artist in terms of self-sacrifice. The flames kindled on the forehead of Blake, the Romantic poet, have grown into a self-immolating fire.

Presumed differences of temperament, as well as unwarranted preconceptions about the nature and worth of their respective enterprises, have made historians reluctant to admit of any link between Bataille and Miró until very recently. And yet we have only to look at *Music, Michel, Bataille and Myself* of 1927 (Winterthur, Kunstmuseum), a painting by Miró which takes as its anecdotal starting-point a stroll along the Seine in the company of Bataille and Michel Leiris, to remind ourselves that in truth they were part of a close-knit circle of friends; commenting on this work, Miró insisted that he had been well acquainted with Bataille in the period after his departure in 1927 from the rue Blomet (Miró, 1977, cited in Rowell, 1987, p. 101). Michel Leiris, who was a close confidant of both men, can be regarded as a sort of intermediary. His long-running autobiography, of which the first installment, *L'Age* d'Homme, was published in 1939 (see Leiris, 1968), was based on a principle of uncensored reportage akin to the psychoanalytical imperative to "tell all"—or, for that matter, the Catholic confessional—and was not unlike a sacrifice in its self-lacerating exposure. An aficionado of the bullfight, Leiris actually brought the idea of sacrifice to bear on painting in an article about André Masson, in which he envisages the canvas as an arena and the artist with palette and brushes in hand as a matador. Of course, Miró's friendship with André Masson from the moment of his arrival in Paris, when they occupied adjacent studios at 45 rue Blomet, is almost legendary. Throughout the 1930s Masson was closely involved with Bataille, and a brief consideration of his work during this period reveals a number of parallels with *Self-Portrait I* that serve to elucidate its pictorial meanings.

Sacrifices, an album of five etchings by Masson, was published in 1936 together with a prefatory text by Bataille. Masson's etchings are loosely based on Part III of Sir James Frazer's *The Golden Bough* dealing with myths of the death of God, a choice of theme that reflects his passion, shared also with Bataille, for the philosophy and aesthetics of Nietzsche. One of the plates depicts the Egyptian corn deity Osiris suspended in mid-air, his head fused with the sun, offering a visual parallel to the central image in Bataille's writings about Van Gogh. This same motif resurfaces as the frontispiece to Masson's *Mythologies* in 1946; another illustration in that volume shows a man holding open a gaping wound in his chest to reveal inside of him a sort of starry firmament *à la* Van Gogh. "Living by light / The light lives by him / A thousand fulgurating suns / Inhabit his breast", reads the caption, echoing a line from William Blake's poem *The Four Zoas* cited by Bataille in one of his essays from this period: "Son sein s'ouvre comme un ciel étoilé". In the pages of *Acéphale*, a journal they produced in 1936 and 1937, Bataille and Masson announced plans for a monograph on Blake, which never came to fruition but which indicates nonetheless the depth of their interest in the English author whose work, like Van Gogh's, they subsumed within an interpretive framework of sacrifice. Apart from the orgasmic eroticism, a virtual trademark of Masson's work at this point, his *Portrait of Blake* of 1939 in a crucifixion pose can be likened to Miró's self-portrait in a number of respects: flaming hair, explosive rupture of boundaries, and metaphoric rapports of eyes and stars convey in both an impression of a figure imprinted on cosmic space.

An event that gave a vital impetus to the theme of ecstatic fusion with the cosmos—one which, incidentally, can be located within an aesthetic discourse of the sublime—was the epiphany Masson underwent during a night in January 1935 when he was lost on the mountains of Montserrat near to Barcelona. His saga that night revived in him the traumatic memory of having been left for dead under a night sky on the battlefield of the Somme, thereby explaining his visceral sense of dread mingled with awe at the sublimity of the vista. As the artist later recalled of his experience, "it was doubly vertiginous, the cliff and the sky with spinning stars, the sky itself appeared to me like an abyss, something I had never felt before, a vertigo of height at the same time as the vertigo of depth. And I felt myself amidst a sort of maelstrom, a tempest, and quite hysterical. I believed I was going mad" (Clébert, 1971, pp. 49–51). Two paintings by Masson and a poem inspired by the event were carried by the surrealist journal *Minotaure* in June 1936, together with a commentary by Bataille who declares: "No limit, no measure can be given to the violence of those in whom a vertigo is liberated by the vault of the sky". The dizzying centrifugal expansion in *Self-Portrait I* certainly brings to mind this account, though an antecedent for the idea of projection of a figure onto cosmic space can be found within Miró's own *oeuvre* in the four variants of the *Head of a Catalan Peasant* of 1925.

Bataille further elaborates upon this distinctive spatial metaphor in the late 1930s in two essays, "Heavenly Bodies" and "Star Eaters" (Bataille, 1970, pp. 514–20, 564–68). The first of these tracts was illustrated by Masson with a great spiralling vortex, whilst in the second Bataille lavishes praise on Masson's recent figure drawings, such as his *Portrait of Heraclitus*, which appears at the head of the article—figures that, he remarks, "are not enclosed upon themselves, but explore and lose themselves in space". The static fixity of objects depicted from a stable view-point gives way in Masson's work, we are told, to a Heraclitean world of flux and interpenetration: "the visages drawn by André Masson have . . . invaded the clouds or sky. In a sort of ecstasy, which is none other than their precipitate exaltation, they annihilate themselves". A more evocative description than this of Miró's anguished self-portrait could hardly be imagined and yet, unfortunately, Bataille does not seem to have known about it, since he makes just a single, dismissive reference to Miró in the article (there is no firm evidence that *Self-Portrait I* was ever exhibited publicly in Paris before being dispatched to New York).

All the salient features of *Self-Portrait I* outlined thus far—rupture of ego boundaries, sacrifice of the self, becoming "other"—are consistent with the nature of visionary experience as it was bequeathed to surrealism. M.H. Abrams, in his classic study, *Natural Supernaturalism*, has shown brilliantly how Christian theology progressively internalizes the biblical Apocalyse, "transferring the theatre of events from the outer earth and heaven to the spirit of the single believer" (Abrams, 1971, p. 47). Typically, in religious conversion experiences, the moment of spiritual revelation comes to be portrayed as a death and rebirth of the person, for which the conversion of Paul on the road to Damascus stands as a paradigmatic instance. Rimbaud's famous declaration in the "Letter of a Seer" that "I is an other" is, hence, merely an extension into the secular domain of poetry of an age-old religious belief. Miró, as was noted, in his rebirth as a visionary, becomes literally "other" by virtue of identifying with Blake and Van Gogh, both of whom embody in different ways the visionary ideal.

Themes of the Apocalypse and Last Judgement were closely allied in Blake's work to his conception of the artist as a man of vision, a revealer of eternal truths as opposed to the contingent truths peddled by science. Blake combines in his view of the Last Judgement the biblical version of a universal, eschatological event with a notion of an equivalent event occurring in the mind of an individual person: "Whenever any Individual Rejects Error & Embraces Truth a Last Judgement passes upon that Individual" (Blake, cited in Bindman, 1977, p. 166). Blake made this remark in the context of a letter explaining one of several painted versions of the Last Judgement, all of which were studies for a much larger composition intended, David Bindman states, "as a summation of all Blake's visionary ideas" (Bindman, 1977, p. 169). Amongst the works listed in the catalog as being on display at the Bibliothèque Nationale in 1937 was the first of the watercolour versions (Pollock House, Glasgow) of the Last Judgement painted by Blake. Comparison with *Self-Portrait I* yields, in addition to the obvious thematic link, parallels of a formal and compositional nature which makes it intriguing to speculate whether Blake may have provided Miró with yet another of his visual models.

The visionary epiphanies which are described in the lives of Christian mystics routinely take the form of an apocalyptic loss of self. When Miró was asked in an interview in 1951 to name his favourite poets he replied tellingly: "The Spanish mystics. St John of the Cross and St Theresa" (Miró, 1951, cited in Rowell 1987, p. 227). His often repeated claim to have painted under the effects of hallucinations induced by hunger during his first years in Paris makes him their worthy successor. In 1948, for instance, Miró recalls that "In 1925 (the year he began painting the "dream paintings", so-called, in conformity with André Breton's doctrine of automatism) I was drawing almost entirely from hallucinations. At the time I was living on a few dried figs a day. I was too proud to ask my colleagues for help. Hunger was a great source of these hallucinations. I would sit for long periods looking at the bare walls of my studio trying to capture these shapes on paper or burlap" (Miró, 1948, cited in Rowell, 1987, p. 208). Breton, too, knowingly draws upon a discursive tradition linking fasting to spiritual revelation when he confides in the *Manifesto of Surrealism* that, at the time he and Philippe Soupault wrote their first revelatory automatic texts, "the fact is that I was not eating every day" (Breton, 1924/1972a, p. 22).

The highly dramatized accent on the loss of self in *Self-Portrait I* may bear some relation to the predicament in which Miró found himself, as an artist, in 1937. Once accused by Breton of cherishing the sole desire ". . . to give himself up utterly to painting and painting alone" (Breton, 1928/1972b, p. 36), Miró now begins echoing the rhetoric of the Left which was vocal in denouncing such an artistic stance. He speaks piously of wanting ". . . to go beyond easel painting . . . and to bring myself closer . . . to the human masses I have never stopped thinking about" (Miró, 1938b, cited in Rowell, 1987, p. 162) and in recorded interviews is at pains to make known his wish to ". . . plunge into the reality of things", the motive for which is obscure, unless it be as a concession to a social realist agenda which demanded not just a politically engaged art, but one that was accessible and in touch with reality. For the first time in 1937, Miró turned his hand to overtly propagandistic art by carrying out a mural commission (*The Reaper*, now destroyed) for the Spanish Republican Pavilion at the Paris World's Fair, further evidence that he had been forced to shift his ground radically in response to the new political exigencies.

Portrait painting had itself become a controversial issue as a result of the Left-sponsored realism debates in Paris in the mid-1930s, with the alleged neglect of this traditional, humanist genre by modern artists now being wielded as a stick to beat them with. Louis Aragon, formerly one of the surrealists but now a staunch advocate of socialist realism, gave voice to the new orthodoxy:

"The portrait is an essentially realist genre, and can scarcely be accommodated by modern theories which condemn realism. I would simply say of these theories that it suffices to condemn them to note that they are incapable of doing justice to a human phenomenon like the existence of the portrait" (Aragon, 1981, p. 57).

That Aragon's address, entitled "Socialist Realism and French Realism", was made in October 1937 could indicate that Miró's turn to self-portraiture at this moment was not unconnected with this sea-change. The most spectacular case of an avant-garde artist reviving portraiture as part of a return to realism was that of another former surrealist, Alberto Giacometti, who did so in a Cézannist portrait of his mother dated 1937. It is, moreover, fascinating to consider that as work proceeded on *Self-Portrait I* through the winter of 1937–38, all the while Miró posed with his daughter Dolorès for a portrait by the artist Balthus (Figure 13-7). Wearing the same suit and tie as in his self-portrait, Miró is seated nearly square on, one arm extended rigidly to his knee while the other supports the waist of his daughter who leans nonchalantly against his thigh, her right hand resting on top of his. Their intimacy seems as unaffected as the stylistic idiom they are depicted in, a sober naturalism of which Aragon would doubtless have approved. Balthus captures a sense of the disquiet of the epoque—a trait for which the new figuration was much praised—by isolating the wistful father and daughter in a setting that is unrelieved in its drabness. Sitting for this portrait would have given Miró ample time to reflect upon his own artistic stance which his portrayal as a visionary in *Self-Portrait I* marks out in utter contrast to the tawdry realism of Balthus.

(It is notable that in the Balthus portrait there is no indication of Miró's special status as an artist, something that his own self-portrait seems determined to preserve.) While it is plainly obvious that Miró does not meekly submit to the dictates of the prevailing realist style, neither could he blithely switch off from the political demands now being made on artists. He was not alone in being under great strain at this moment: similar pressures had surely contributed to Picasso's much publicized cessation of painting during 1935. World events aside, for artists of a modernist persuasion this really was the apocalyptic end of an era. *Self-Portrait I* vividly records the dissoluton of Miró's (artistic) identity. Uniquely possibly in the history of portraiture, it captures a moment when identity fades, evaporates and becomes, thereby, unrepresentable.

In February 1938, before he had finished work on the self-portrait, Miró painted a watercolour, *Woman in Revolt* (Figure 13-8), possibly the most rebarbative little image in his entire *oeuvre*. The subject, a peasant woman defiantly brandishing a sickle as she flees a burning village, was a stock one in realist painting of the time, but the disturbing incongruity of a phallus stretched across the picture plane in effect shifts the register of Miró's image away from external reality to the plane of psychical reality. The meaning of this grotesque intrusion into the pictorial field is evident as one's eye oscillates between it and the diminutive sickle above, between the alternatives of castration and disavowal. A quota of castration anxiety no doubt also lurks in *Self-Portrait I*, in as far as the distorted mirror reflection employed by Miró has, as Goethe reminds us, a terrifying Medusan aspect. For Freud the terror caused by the Medusa is none other than fear of castration, and such a fear is liable to be provoked in any circumstance which threatens the subject with loss of its illusory wholeness and integrity (Freud, 1955b, pp. 273–74).

Miró wrote to his dealer early in March 1938 saying, "My portrait is already drawn . . . I have now turned the canvas against the wall and will leave it there for several days so that I can begin painting with fresh eyes. I think this will be the most important work of my life. I might do a tracing to preserve the drawing, which in itself is something of considerable breadth" (Miró, 1938a cited in Rowell 1987, p. 158). When Miró did finally return to the traced copy of *Self-Portrait I* in 1960 (Figure 12-13, p. 126) he literally defaced it with daubed graffiti. His comical over-painting not only mocks the grandiose pretensions of the earlier self-portrait, seen peering out from underneath, it also defuses and recuperates an alien image of himself which was, in more than one respect, out of character. *Self-Portrait I* marks a moment of rapprochement with Bataille during a phase of the latter's work that culminated with his book *Inner Experience*, where the poetic would be equated with the uncanny; it is "the familiar dissolving into the strange, and ourselves with it" (Bataille, 1943/1988, p. 5).

Though it was not until much later that the term was coined, it seems appropriate to speak of a "politics of identity" in relation to the self-portraits Miró produced in the years 1937–1942. By internalizing the apocalypse in *Self-Portrait I* Miró effectively proclaimed his own personal fate to be inseparable from the tragedy then unfolding in Spain. The flames that engulf him would surely have been linked by contemporary viewers with graphic news footage of ransacked and burning villages relayed daily to Paris.

That such an association was fully intended is borne out by the notes Miró wrote in 1942, when he thought to undertake further work on the picture: "See to it that . . . the whole thing resembles a landscape", he remarks (Miró, 1942, cited in Rowell, 1987, p. 189). The implicit message of resistance carried by Miró's symbolic alliance with the peoples' suffering is further strengthened by clear-cut references in *Self-Portrait I* to Catalan Romanesque art. William Rubin was

13-7
BALTHUS (BALTUSZ KLOSSOWSKI DE ROLA)
JOAN MIRÓ AND HIS DAUGHTER DOLORES,
1937–38
Oil on canvas, 51¼ × 35 in (130.2 × 88.9 cm)
The Museum of Modern Art, New York. Abby Aldrich Rockefeller Fund. Photograph © 1996 The Museum of Modern Art, New York. © 1996 Artists Rights Society (ARS), NY/SPADEM, Paris

13-8
JOAN MIRÓ
WOMAN IN REVOLT, 1938
*Watercolor, pencil and
charcoal on paper,
22⅝ × 29¼ in (57.4 × 74.3 cm)
Museé National d'Art
Moderne, France. © 1996
Artists Rights Society
(ARS), NY/ADAGP, Paris*

the first to observe that the stylization of the face derives from such a source, and he notes furthermore that the Apocalypse was a common theme in early Medieval art (Rubin, 1973, p. 76). Catalonia, Miró's birthplace, fiercely maintained its separation from Castilian Spain and became a natural stronghold of opposition to the nationalist Franco. Included in the programme of cultural events sponsored by the Republican government aimed at promoting international awareness of their cause was an exhibition of "Catalan Art From the Tenth to the Fifteenth Centuries" held at the Jeu de Paume and the Chateau de Maisons-Laffitte in Paris from March to April of 1937. Picasso was on the steering committee for that event and in *Guernica*, subsequently shown in the Republican Pavilion at the Paris World's Fair, he makes conspicuous iconographic allu-

sions to the beasts of the Apocalypse. Christian Zervos, in a book published on the occasion of the Catalan art exhibition, rehearses the myth of an organic tie uniting the Catalan people with their soil, the basis of their proud independence:

"In the face of all the monuments of this art, we know that its substance is peculiar to itself, that the very temperament of the Catalans and the earth which bears them are its source and that man and earth are all of one piece. This communion of earth, man and work which it conveys is imprinted strongly in the Catalan style and explains the spiritual autonomy of the people of this part of the Iberian peninsula (Zervos, 1937).

This myth of attachment to the landscape is deployed in a highly strategic fashion by Miró in a sequence of drawings based on the terrain of Montserrat, a place of utmost spiritual and symbolic importance for Catalonia, which he made toward the end of 1938 as nationalist forces were poised to overrun Barcelona (they entered the city on January 26 1939). The Benedictine monastery at Montserrat houses an ancient wooden statue of the Virgin Mary, whose body seems to have permeated the landscape of Miró's drawings: the rocky outcrops which are a striking feature of the mountains have become her nurturing breasts, and a sign for the female genitals occupies the space between them. In the penultimate drawing (Figure 13-9), dated December 31 1938, the female sex has been replaced by a cyclopic eye, that of the artist; a written inscription on this astonishing drawing informs the viewer that it is a "self-portrait" metamorphosed into the rocks of Montserrat! Unlike the works produced by Masson several years earlier in response to the same location, here

the quasi-mystical fusion with landscape carries an unmistakable message of political solidarity.

Political considerations were also paramount in the cluster of self-portrait drawings which Miró made after the capitulation of France forced his return to Spain. In concluding, I wish to consider one such image (Figure 13-10) which was pencilled onto a rather shabby envelope addressed to Miró at 4 Pasage del Credito in Barcelona—his birthplace and where, in a sort of return to origins in 1942, he had again taken up a studio. A far cry from a conventional portrait likeness, Miró uses a vocabulary of signs which are explained in notes appended to both sides of the sheet. The motifs hark back repeatedly to the 1920s, a mood of retrospection that lends to the image an autobiographical character: a dog barks at the moon, while an inscription informs us that the grooves of the postal mark symbolize the tilled field—a reference back to his

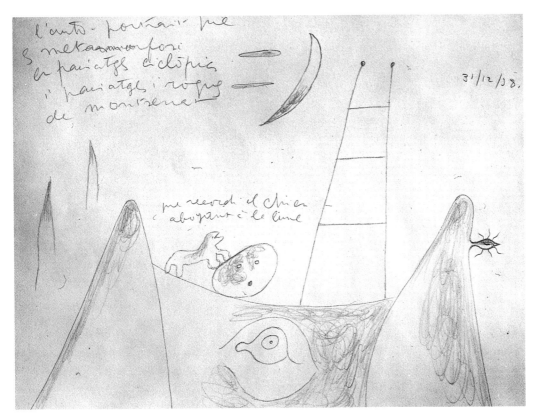

13-9
JOAN MIRÓ
Self-portrait, 1938
Graphite pencil on paper,
6¾ × 8⅝ in (17 × 22 cm)
Fundació Joan Miró,
Barcelona. © 1996 Artists
Rights Society (ARS),
NY/ADAGP, Paris

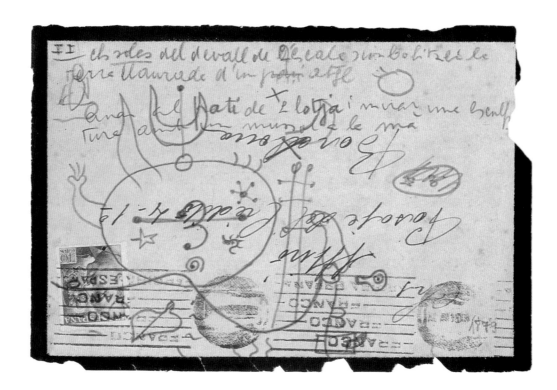

13-10
JOAN MIRÓ
SELF-PORTRAIT, 1942
*Graphite pencil on
envelope paper, 4⅞ × 6⅞ in
(12.4 × 17.5 cm)
Fundació Joan Miró,
Barcelona. © 1996 Artists
Rights Society (ARS),
NY/ADAGP, Paris*

landmark picture of 1923. Super-imposed upon this Catalan soil is the undulating contour of the artist's shoulders, a fusion of body and land-scape that was implicit way back in the 1919 *Self-Portrait* but which by 1942 had taken on greater poignancy since, in the wake of Franco's victory, all public expressions of Catalan-ness were brutally suppressed and even to speak in Catalan was a punishable offence. (For an informative account of the reign of terror after the Civil War, when it is estimated that upwards of 4000 people were summarily executed in Catalonia, and of the "culture of resistance" that arose at this time, see Kaplan, 1992.) It was perhaps only in these very private drawings which remained for years in his possession that Miró could have voiced his opposition, which he does overtly in a self-portrait drawn onto a newspaper cutout from 1938, reporting on the last ditch stand of Republican forces in the Aragon region. A political message can also be read into the *Self-Portrait on an Envelope* which actually contains

not one portrait but two: in addition to Miró's self-portrait, there is a portrait of the dictator Franco in the form of a stamp. Miró signals his hostility to the regime by tipping the envelope upside down in a deliberate gesture that sets his own features against those of the dictator.

The ladder is a motif which recurs in every one of the 1942 self-portrait drawings, where it connotes transcendence, a consistent driving impulse in Miró's work of the war years from the *Flight of a Bird Over the Plain* to the *Constellation* series. At root, his yearning for transcendence is nothing more than a heartfelt protest against conditions he found intolerable: the *Constellations*, Breton wrote memorably, are like ". . . the note of wild defiance of the hunter expressed by the grouse's love-song" (Breton, 1972b, p. 263). In reply to a *Cahiers d'Art* questionnaire in 1939, Miró restated his belief that the forms chosen by the artist ". . . must reveal the movement of a soul trying to escape the reality of the present, which is particularly ignoble

. . . in order to approach new realities, to offer other men the possibility of rising above the present" (Miró, 1939, cited in Rowell, 1987, p. 166). The task confronting a painter, as Miró saw it, was not to portray an "ignoble" reality—as life under Franco must have been for an ardent Catalan like Miró—but to negate it by trying to envision a new and better reality.

That a Catalan identity was, publicly, dead and buried may have some bearing on a marginal detail of the *Self-Portrait on an Envelope* that we have yet to address: the black border of the envelope, to which my title refers. This was traditionally used to send a death notice (though there is no indication in the present case as to the source of the letter). With a deft economy of means, Miró takes advantage of this border which he uses as a makeshift frame. But it also means that his own self-portrait is addressed to him, bizarrely, in the form of a death notice. Miró mourns for an identity lost, a concern at the heart of this tiny image just as it was seen to be in the majestic *Self-Portrait I*.

CHRONOLOGY

1936

July 17–18 Outbreak of Civil War in Spain.

1937

January 15–February 15 "Aquarelles de Turner. Oeuvres de Blake", exhibition at the Bibliothèque Nationale which includes *The Man Who Taught Blake Painting In His Dreams*, c. 1819, and a watercolour of the *Last Judgment*, 1806.

January 24–May 29 Paints *Still-life with Old Shoe*.

March–April "L'Art Catalan du Xe au XVe Siècle", exhibition at the Jeu de Paume connected with the Paris World's Fair.

June Work on *The Reaper* mural for Spanish Republican Pavilion of Paris World's Fair which opened July 12. Received the commission in April.

June–October Van Gogh exhibition at the Palais de Tokyo (226 items).

October Work on *Self-Portrait I* commences. At the same time sits for a portrait in a realist style of himself and daughter Dolorès by the painter Balthus, which is completed the following January.

December "Van Gogh Prometheus", by Georges Bataille, appears in first issue of *Verve*.

1938

February 5 "The work moves ahead. I have destroyed my portrait several times; I now feel that I am on the right track. It will be drawn in a few days . . ."

February Paints *Woman in Revolt*.

March 3 Engraves *Portrait of Miró* with Louis Marcoussis. Second phase of work on the plate in November.

March Ceases work on *Self-Portrait I*. "I might do a tracing to preserve the drawing, which in itself is something of considerable breadth".

Paints *Self-Portrait II*.

December Sequence of self-portrait drawings metamorphosed into rocks of Montserrat.

1939

January 26 Franco troops occupy Barcelona.

1942

Having returned to Spain in 1940, executes a cluster of symbolic self-portraits in Barcelona, including the *Self-Portrait on an Envelope*. Notebook entries indicate that he contemplates resuming work on *Self-Portrait I* probably at this time.

1960

Reworks traced copy of *Self-Portrait I*.

REFERENCES

Abrams, M.H. (1971). *Natural Supernaturalism*. Norton, New York.

Aragon, L. (1981). *Écrits sur l'Art Moderne*. Flammarion, Paris.

Bataille, G. (1970). *Oeuvres Complètes*, Vol. 1, Gallimard, Paris.

Bataille, G. (1986a). Van Gogh Prometheus [1937], *October* 36, **Spring 1986**, pp. 58–60.

Bataille, G. (1930/1986b). *Visions of Excess. Selected Writings, 1927–1939* (Trans. A. Stoekl, 1930). University of Minnesota Press, Minneapolis.

Bataille, G. (1943/1988). *Inner Experience* (Trans. L. Boldt).

Bindman, D. (1977). *Blake as an Artist*. Oxford University Press, Oxford.

Breton, A. (1924/1972a). *Manifestoes of Surrealism* (Trans. R. Seaver & H. Lane). University of Michigan Press, Ann Arbor.

Breton, A. (1928/1972b). *Surrealism and Painting* (Trans. S. Taylor). Macdonald, London.

Clébert, J.-P. (1971). *Mythologie d'André Masson*. Pierre Cailler, Geneva.

Freud, S. (1955a). The Uncanny [1919]. *The Standard Edition of the Complete Psychological Works of Sigmund Freud*, Vol. XVII. Hogarth Press and the Institute of Psycho-Analysis, London.

Freud, S. (1955b). Medusa's Head [1940/1922]. *The Standard Edition of the Complete Psychological Works of Sigmund Freud*, Vol. XVIII. Hogarth Press and the Institute of Psycho-Analysis, London.

Goethe, J. (1980). *Goethe on Art* (Trans. J. Gage). Scolar Press, London.

Kaplan, T. (1992). *Red City, Blue Period: Social Movements in Picasso's Barcelona*. University of California Press, Berkeley, Los Angeles, Oxford.

Klossowski de Rola, S. (1988). *The Golden Game. Alchemical Engravings of the Seventeenth Century*.

Leiris, M. (1968). *Manhood. Preceded by the Autobiographer as Torero* (Trans. R. Howard). Jonathan Cape, London.

Miró J. (1936). Interview with Georges Duthuit in *Cahiers d'Art*, **XI** (8–10). Cited in Rowell, M. (1987: see below), pp. 150–55.

Miró J. (1937a). Letter to Pierre Matisse, February 12 1937. Cited in Rowell, M. (1987: see below), pp. 146–47.

Miró J. (1937b). Letter to Pierre Matisse, November 3 1937. Cited in Rowell, M. (1987: see below), p. 157.

Miró J. (1938a). Letter to Pierre Matisse, February 5 1938. Cited in Rowell, M. (1987: see below), p. 158.

Miró J. (1938b). I Dream of a Large Studio. *XXe siècle*, **May 1938**. Cited in Rowell, M. (1987: see below), pp. 161-2.

Miró J. (1939). Statement in *Cahiers d'Art*, **April–May**. Cited in Rowell, M. (1987: see below), p. 166.

Miró J. (1942). Working notes, 1941–42. Cited in Rowell, M. (1987: see below), pp. 175–95.

Miró J. (1948). Interview with James Johnson Sweeney. Cited in Rowell, M. (1987: see below), pp. 207–11.

Miró J. (1951). Interview with Raphael Santos Torroella, cited in Rowell, M. (1987: see below), pp. 226–27.

Miró J. (1961). Comments by Joan Miró. Rosamond Bernier, cited in Rowell, M. (1987: see below), pp. 257–60.

Miró J. (1977). Memories of the rue Blomet. Cited in Rowell, M. (1987: see below), pp. 100–104.

Miró J. (1978). Interview with Lluis Permanyer. Cited in Rowell, M. (1987: see below), pp. 290–95.

Rimbaud, A. (1871/1988). Letter to Georges Izambard ("Letter of a Seer") May 13 1871. Cited in Rimbaud, A. (1988). *Complete Works* (Trans. P. Schmidt), pp. 100–101.

Rowell, M. (1987). *Joan Miró. Selected Writings and Interviews*. Thames and Hudson, London.

Rubin, W. (1973). *Miró in the Collections of the Museum of Modern Art*. Museum of Modern Art, New York.

Soby, J. (1959). *Joan Miró*. Museum of Modern Art, New York.

Zervos, C (ed). (1937). *Catalan Art From the Ninth to the Fifteenth Centuries*. Heinemann, London and Toronto.

CHAPTER 14

CHAOS AS A STIMULUS

ROSA MARIA MALET

I use the term "chaos" in the title of this chapter to refer to the state of confusion and disorder which in some cases is the origin of the creative act, impelling the artist to work in his desire to control this state of confusion.

I refer to "chaos" as a contrast to those well-balanced and organized contexts in which, as is the case in certain countries dominated by order, cleanliness and civilized behavior, examples of artistic creation are few and of little or no importance.

In this chapter I relate the idea of chaos to Joan Miró because I feel that his creativity was stimulated more by difficulty and the desire to overcome it than by any alterations in his state of mind. Although I do not intend to trespass on the field of medicine, and certainly have no right to do so, I would simply like to say that I do not agree with the hypothesis that psychic alterations enhanced Miró's creativity. Certainly, the problems that either affected him personally or affected the world around him could not have left him indifferent. I believe, though, that the reaction they provoked was not one of discouragement, but of strength to confront adversity. Joan Miró's work and the development of his artistic personality can thus be seen as a parallel to the conflicts he was forced to confront throughout his lifetime.

When his father enrolled him in a commercial college, Miró reacted in a way that was to be a constant throughout his life: the greater the difficulty, the greater the stimulus. The more important the crisis, the more determined his efforts to overcome it. Joan Miró himself described his reaction by saying, "The life I led as a child made me strong, I am very happy about that. I had a very hard life and that helped me. I don't regret it. My problems have made me strong" (Raillard, 1977).

In referring to the problems that made him strong, Miró was referring to the efforts he had to make to reconcile the long hours of classes dedicated to learning the secrets of business with his art classes at the Llotja. His father continued imposing his will when the time came to find a job for young Joan, who went to work at the Droguería Dalmau Oliveres, a large shop that sold hardware and chemical products.

At the beginning of this century adolescent rebellion must have involved tremendous conflict, but nevertheless Miró soon informed his father in no uncertain terms that he planned to dedicate himself entirely to painting. Although one cannot say that Miró's father was understanding, he at least accepted his son's position. For Joan this was a challenge rather than a victory. The obstacle race was just beginning, and from then on it became increasingly clear that Miró was motivated much more by problems than by success. This brings us to 1911.

He encountered his first difficulties as a full-time painter when he exhibited his work at the Galeries Dalmau in Barcelona between February 16 and March 3 1918. The critics were divided:

some supported him, chiefly Josep Maria Junoy, who wrote the introduction to the exhibition catalogue; others, like Josep Llorens i Artigas and Pere Oliver, were somewhat disconcerted and still others were radically opposed, particularly Joan Sacs, one of the pseudonyms of the painter Feliu Elies, who signed his caricatures in *La Publicidad* as Apa.

Joan Sacs' widely circulated articles, which appeared not only in *La Publicidad* but also in *Revista Nova*, *Vell i Nou* and *Mirador*, and the labels he attached to Miró on the occasion of his first exhibition, among them "nervy egoist" and "detestable colorist", would have caused a weaker spirit to crumble. Miró's reaction was just the opposite.

His wounds were still open that summer when he retreated to Montroig to continue working, determined not to veer from his path. He wrote to his friend E.C. Ricart, "No simplifications or abstractions, my friend. Right now what interests me most is the calligraphy of a tree or a rooftop, leaf by leaf, twig by twig, blade of grass by blade of grass, tile by tile. This does not mean that these landscapes will not finally end up being cubist or wildly synthetic. But we shall see. What I do plan to do is work a long time on the canvases until they are as finished as possible so that at the end of the season and after having worked hard, if I only appear with a few canvases, it won't matter. Next winter the gentlemen critics will continue to say that I persist in my disorientation" (Miró, 1918). During 1918 he painted just four landscapes— *Vegetable Garden with Donkey* (Figure 14-1), *The Tile Works, House with Palm Tree* (Figure 14-2), and *The Trail*—all of which are radically different from his previous works. In these new canvases his work was very painstaking and his use of color subordinate to the composition.

14-1
JOAN MIRÓ
VEGETABLE GARDEN WITH DONKEY, 1918
Oil on canvas, 25¼ × 27½ in (64 × 70 cm)
Moderna Museet, Stockholm. Photograph courtesy of Fundació Joan Miró, Barcelona. © 1996 Artists Rights Society (ARS), NY/ADAGP, Paris

Uncomfortable in the artistic climate of Barcelona, which he found utterly suffocating, Miró continued working patiently, producing what he called "calligraphy" and thinking about a desire that was fast becoming a need: to go to Paris.

Miró went to Paris for the first time in March 1920. He had never been in a city larger than Barcelona nor, it goes without saying, in a place that offered such a wide range of opportunities. He went to museums, galleries, and attended the Dada Festival in the Salle Gaveau in the spring of 1920. He reported almost everything he had done to J.F. Ràfols in a letter written in March 1920. Referring to his contemporaries, he wrote: "I have seen exhibitions of the moderns. The French are asleep—Rosenberg Exhibition. Works by Picasso and Charlot—Picasso very fine, very sensitive, a great painter" (Miró, 1920a). From his comments it is

14-2
JOAN MIRÓ
HOUSE WITH PALM TREE,
1918
*Oil on canvas, 25⅝ × 28¾ in
(65 × 73 cm)*
*Private collection.
Photograph courtesy of
Fundació Joan Miró,
Barcelona. © 1996 Artists
Rights Society (ARS),
NY/ADAGP, Paris*

not hard to deduce that he found Paris more interesting for its museums than for its contemporary French painters. Only Picasso impressed him. This posed a new problem. Picasso who was already well known and comfortably well-off, was surrounded by a circle of artists, some of his own generation, others slightly younger, who were aligned with Cubism.

Although he recognized Picasso's worth and his contribution to art, Miró clearly realized that if he joined the cubist movement he would be doomed to be a second-rate artist. As he wrote in another letter to Ràfols, "I only admire those who are ready to lay down their lives in the struggle. I am not interested in the ones who reap glory from something for which others before them risked everything" (Miró, 1920b).

He knew that he had to struggle; he wasn't sure if he was on the right track, but he was always absolutely certain

that he wanted to explore his own paths. Miró made a great leap forward in the summer of 1923 when, after having painted *The Farm* (1921–22) (Figure 12-5, p. 119), he painted *The Tilled Field* (Figure 14-4) and *Catalan Landscape (The Hunter)* (Figure 16-6, p. 182), works which marked his break with figurative art and his move towards symbols, a moment so aptly described by Sebastià Gasch:

"Miró has discovered spiritual splendour in real objects. He then appropriates this object, installs it in his mind, works with it, polishes it, deforms it, transfigures it, in order to fix it in his work, the whole thing resplendent with that spirit that hides behind material appearances and which the artist has perceived or, rather, intuited in the actual object before starting his painting. Joan Miró could be said to be the only artist of our time who brings objectivism and subjectivism together in a full, pure and intense merger" (Gasch, 1929).

Miró was fascinated by surrealist poetry and through his friendship with André Masson, who also had a studio in rue Blomet, he soon met André Breton and the circle of writers and poets who brought the surrealist movement to life.

Breton said about Miró:

"For every thousand problems that don't concern him in the least, even though they might be the ones that fill the human spirit, there may be only a single desire in Joan Miró, that of abandoning himself to painting, and only to paint (which for him means clinging to the only terrain in which we are certain there are means available to him) that pure automatism which I, for my part, have never stopped referring to, but whose value

and profound reasons I fear Miró has only verified for himself in a very superficial fashion. It is perhaps, in truth, for that very reason that he can pass as the most 'surrealist' of us all" (Breton, 1929/1965).

Possibly somewhat disconcerted by Miró's paintings and his way of working, Breton labeled him the most surrealist of the entire group without being fully aware at the time that what Miró was essentially doing was working with the greatest possible freedom, in which there was obviously no room for formulas and precepts. It is no wonder then that when the group was affected by a serious crisis in 1929, Miró reacted by saying that "painting had to be assassinated".

The crisis erupted after some members of the surrealist group had joined the Communist Party. Breton called a meeting at the Bar du Château, at 53 rue du Château, ostensibly to discuss the fate of Lev Trotsky, whom Stalin had ousted from power. The real reason for the meeting was that Breton wanted to propose that various groups and individuals overlook the possible ideological distances that separated them and engage in a joint action that would be based on a previously accepted program to which they would all be committed.

The initial subject was definitely shelved and the meeting served to clarify positions. George Bataille was among the most radically opposed to Breton. Among those who also spoke out against him were Miró and his friends Michel Leiris and André Masson.

Under no circumstances would Miró commit himself to anything that might constrain his work; it was through his work that he maintained a permanent commitment with day-to-day reality throughout his entire life and in the

different political circumstances in which it fell to him to live, always managing to do this without ever producing pamphleteering art.

Although Miró did not take the pressures of the radical surrealists as a frontal attack, he was nevertheless not totally indifferent to them. A man of few words, he could only participate in the struggle by using his own weapon: painting. This is how he explained his reaction to the journalist Francisco Melgar in 1931:

"I personally don't know where we are heading. The only thing that's clear to me is that I intend to destroy, destroy everything that exists in painting. I have an utter contempt for painting.

14-3
JOAN MIRÓ
VILLAGE AND CHURCH OF MONT-ROIG, 1919
Oil on canvas, 28¾ × 24 in (73 × 61 cm)
Collection of Maria Dolors Miró. Photograph courtesy of Fundació Joan Miró, Barcelona.
© 1996 Artists Rights Society (ARS), NY/ADAGP, Paris

The only thing that interests me is the spirit itself and I only use the customary artist's tools—brushes, canvas, paints—in order to get the best effects. The only reason I abide by the rules of pictorial art is because they're essential for expressing what I feel, just as grammar is essential for expressing yourself" (Melgar, 1931).

For a time, Miró seemed to have completely abandoned brushes and paint in favor of the drawing pencil and the collage. His efforts were not in vain. His research was not useless: the path along which he was moving gradually led to new alternatives, as described by Georges Hugnet:

"It was then he made his 1929 collages, collage-symbols, a challenge to art, whose techniques and stripped-down qualities presaged, on the one hand, the sculptures and objects of 1930 and, on the other, his drawings, which were pure plasticity" (Hugnet 1931).

Miró's reaction to painting is openly and obviously expressed in the *Constructions*, produced during the summer of 1930. These were a logical outgrowth of the previous year's collages, in which he went beyond the two dimensions of painting.

As was to occur so many times in his life, chance provided Miró with a new, enriching and exceptional experience:

the opportunity to design the sets and costumes for the production of *Jeux d'Enfants*, that Léonide de Massine was preparing for the Ballets Russes de Montecarlo.

Miró experienced both the Spanish Civil War and World War II at close quarters and reacted to the two conflicts very differently, although in both cases his reactions led to new milestones in his career.

Miró was with his family in Montroig when the Spanish Civil War broke out in 1936. During that entire summer he worked on the 27 *Paintings on Masonite* that Jacques Dupin has described as violent exorcisms of war. (See Figures 14-5 and 14-6) The fact is that Miró expressed himself violently in this series, not through the use of aggressive colors or abrupt forms, but because the materials themselves and the way he used them are violent. Instead of canvas he used a hard support—masonite, a wood conglomerate that he boldly left uncovered and used as the background. It was the masonite itself that demanded materials that were more consistent than just pure paint. That is why he used tar, sand, casein and shoepolish on top of the masonite.

At the end of the year he went to Paris for an exhibition at the Galerie Pierre and decided to remain there with his family. Nevertheless, he followed the war in Spain as closely as possible. The distance, his straitened circumstances, and his limited space caused him to react differently now. To use his own expression, he felt the need to control reality. And he managed to do this through the still-life he painted at that time, *Still Life with Old Shoe* (1937) (Figure 13-4, p. 136). Atop a table, a bottle, an apple pierced by a fork, a crust of bread and an old shoe that Miró painted from life. What was he trying to convey by using

such a traditional form of painting as the still-life and treating it in such an iconoclastic way? He explained his intentions to Pierre Matisse, his New York dealer:

"I am going to push this painting to the limit, for I want it to hold up against a good still-life by Velázquez.

It is somewhat reminiscent of The Farm *and* Table with Glove—*less*

14-6
JOAN MIRÓ
*PAINTING ON "MASONITE",
1936*

*Oil, tar, casein and sand on wood conglomerate,
30⅞ × 42⅜ in
(78.3 × 107.7 cm)*

Photograph courtesy of Fundació Joan Miró, Barcelona. © 1996 Artists Rights Society (ARS), NY/ADAGP, Paris anecdotal than the first and more powerful than the second. No sentimentalism. Realism that is far from being photographic and also far from the realism exploited by some of the Surrealists. Profound and fascinating reality.

To look nature in the face and dominate it is enormously attractive and exciting.

. . . Human events have precipitated this need in my mind. An inner necessity, not at all to show off and prove that I can paint, which would be a pretentious and tendentious parlour game" (Miró, 1937).

Unlike what he had done when the Spanish Civil War was imminent, Miró did not express his repulsion for World War II in painting. Instead he used purely pictorial resources to exteriorize his process of introspection, his virtual reclusion when painting the Constellations in 1940–41. This is how he described his state of mind that time:

"I felt a deep desire to escape. I closed myself within myself purposely. The night, music, and the stars began to play a major role in my paintings. Music had always appealed to me, and now music in this period began to take on the role poetry had played in the early twenties" (Sweeney, 1948).

The Constellations, born of a conflict Miró was forced to confront, marked the start of a new period. Their iconography, which recurs in all Miró's subsequent work, is an apparent attempt to represent the entire cosmic order. The figures symbolize the earth. The stars refer to the unreachable world of the heavens, of which our experience can only be visual. The birds and the ladder of escape serve as a link between the earthly world and the celestial world that is the fruit of the imagination.

If we understand poetry as the form of expression best able to move the imagination and evoke feelings, Miró unquestionably reached the peak of

14-7
JOAN MIRÓ
WOMAN WITH THREE HAIRS, BIRDS AND CONSTELLATIONS, 1973
Acrylic on canvas, 76⅜ × 146⅝ in (194 × 372.5 cm)
Fundació Joan Miró, Barcelona. © 1996 Artists Rights Society (ARS), NY/ADAGP, Paris

his artistic career with the *Constellations*, whose poetic tone stems from the symbolic nature of the images he borrowed from reality.

While the wartime crisis led Miró to express his state of mind in visual form, the post-war crisis caused him to reflect on the meaning of art and its validity. Faced with the growing commercialization of art, he turned to a more primitive form—ceramics—as a more valid and honest alternative. Miró was unable to find a justification for art as pure aesthetics, as no more than a mere medium of exchange, at a time when human beings had just proven that they were capable of "scientifically" killing one another. That was why he decided to flee from the references that were closest to him, but linked to a contradictory culture, and explore others that were equally close to him, but linked to tradition rather than culture. Ceramics gave Miró back the authenticity he feared he had lost. It was also ceramics that enabled him to go beyond easel painting, as he had professed his desire to do in a text that dated from 1938 (Miró, 1938), and reach the largest possible number of people, which he did with his ceramic murals. It was also ceramics that led him a few years later to begin sculpting in bronze.

The long years of the Franco regime more or less coincided with the first international recognition of Joan Miró at the beginning of the 1940s. Far from leading him into easy, pleasant formulas, these years distanced him from the iconographic path that would have assured his success. Miró always distrusted success because of its inherent danger of stagnation. Instead, his work became increasingly concentrated, more essential and frequently even more violent.

Miró said, "My desire is to attain a maximum intensity with a minimum of means. That is why my painting has gradually become more spare" (Miró, 1959). Indeed, his work is immediately identified by his palette, which he limited to primary colors used as a counterpoint to the black that served him as a writing tool. His efforts to concentrate on the essentials also led him to use a limited code of symbols that allude to an extremely concrete and meaningful iconography. (Figure 14-7)

The keenness and even the aggressiveness we find in Miró's last works are like a materialization of what he meant when he said that he wanted to die, saying "*merdre!*", just like that, with an *r* between the *d* and the *e*, just as a way to express rebellion on wishing good luck for the performance that starts when life finishes.

REFERENCES

Breton, A. (1929/1965). *Le Surrealisme et la Peinture*, pp. 36–37. Ed. Gallimard, Paris.

Gasch, S. (1929). Joan Miró. *Gaseta de les Arts* (Barcelona), **7**, (March).

Hugnet, G. (1931). Joan Miró ou l'enfance de l'art, *Cahiers d'Art* (Paris), **7–8**, 335–340.

Melgar, F. (1931). Interview with Joan Miró. *Ahora* (Madrid), January 24.

Miró, J. (1918). Letter to E.C. Ricart, July 16 1918. Fundació Joan Miró, Barcelona.

Miró, J. (1920a). Letter to J.F. Ràfols, March 1920. Fundació Joan Miró, Barcelona.

Miró, J. (1920b). Letter to J.F. Ràfols.

Miró, J. (1937). Letter to Pierre Matisse, Paris, February 12 1937 (English trans. Paul Auster). In *Joan Miró, Selected Writings and Interviews*, Ed. M. Rowell, p. 147. G.K. Hall, Boston.

Miró, J. (1938). Je rêve d'un grand atelier. *XXème Siècle* (Paris), **2**, May–June 1938 (English trans. Paul Auster). In *Joan Miró, Selected Writings and Interviews*, Ed. M. Rowell, p. 162. G.K. Hall, Boston.

Miró, J. (1959). Je travaille comme un jardinier, propos recueillis par Yvon Taillandier *XXème Siècle* (Paris), mensual, **1**(1), February 15, 1959. (English trans. Paul Auster). In *Joan Miró, Selected Writings and Interviews*, Ed. M. Rowell, p. 251. G.K. Hall, Boston.

Raillard, G. (1977). *Ceci est la Coleur des mes Rêves*. Éditions du Seuil, Paris, p. 18.

Sweeney, J.J. (1948). Joan Miró: comment and interview. *Partisan Review* (New York), **15**(2), **February**, 209.

CHAPTER 15

ASSASSINATING PAINTING: COLLAGE AND SCULPTURE AS A CRISIS OF IDENTITY?

WILLIAM JEFFETT

Miró arrived in Paris for the first time in the spring of 1920 at the height of the Dadaists' rejection of established artistic and cultural values. Cubism had thrown academic and realistic forms of representation into question through the invention of collage in the years prior to the onset of World War I. Before coming to Paris, Miró had explored a visual language rooted in the depiction of the rural landscape of his native Catalonia; it was one in part resulting from his awareness of the French and Italian avant-garde movements Fauvism, Cubism and Futurism. Following the upheaval of the war, an entire generation of artists questioned not only the legitimacy of the culture which had produced the war, but challenged both the means of art and the very identity of the artist. This perceived crisis, bolstered by the growing interest in Freud's revolutionary model of the unconscious mind, reverberated through the vanguard movements of the 1920s, especially the surrealist movement which was founded by André Breton in 1924. Miró's participation in Surrealism paradoxically brought him success and notoriety as a painter operating within a post-cubist language informed by a flagrantly literary poetics. Suspicious of such success within the Parisian art market—and responding to the exigencies of Breton's position—Miró aggressively proclaimed the destruction of painting. By the last years of the decade he produced a number of collages striking for their inclusion of non-artistic materials and their overtly crude construction. This anti-art strategy echoed the widespread sense of social, economic and cultural crisis, and at the same time it sought to provoke a new model of artistic identity.

Miró's often-quoted dictum calling for the "assassination of painting" has most typically been associated with his work just before and after 1930. Indeed, this was a time when he explored unorthodox approaches involving collage, construction and assemblage-objects, and repeatedly called for "the assassination of painting", claiming that his work was "más allá de la pintura" (beyond painting), as he told Francesco Melgar in 1931 (Melgar, 1931). Likewise, his work was understood in these terms by critics, poets and other like-minded artists in Paris, Barcelona, New York and Brussels. Louis Aragon included him in the surrealist exhibition of collages "La Peinture au Défi" (Challenge to Painting) at the Galerie Goemans in March 1930, and Tériade quoted the phrase as emblematic of the surrealist position in the newspaper *L'Intransigeant* the following month (Tériade, 1930). More recently, it has become clear that this rhetorical stance predated Miró's crisis of actual artistic strategy in the years 1928–1932. Even in 1925 Miró was situated within the avant-garde discourse of anti-art by critics like Sebastià Gasch (Gasch, 1925), and by 1927 Raynal could confidently attribute to Miró the authorship of the slogan "Je veux assassiner la peinture" ("I want to assassinate painting") (Raynal, 1927).

What then might this slogan mean and how might its meaning change between 1927 and 1930? Between 1925 and 1928 Miró went through a prolific period of painting, and he produced increasingly reductive and schematic figurations in his painting. Thus it would seem rather paradoxical that he made this statement at the very moment that he was so prolific and perceived, rightly or wrongly, as the "leader of the surrealist school" as Raynal claimed in the very same breath that he pointed to Miró's murderous intentions (Raynal, 1927). Could it then be that Miró initially directed his plot not at his own painting in the years 1925–1927, but at a certain idea of painting? It is evident that by this time all avant-garde strategies stood in opposition to the "*cuisine*" of painting which was academic painting. What is less clear, but equally important, as Christopher Green has pointed out, was that Surrealism stood in opposition to cubist painting; and although that very painting had opened the way forward for the surrealist artists, especially in the introduction of collage into painting, it had by the 1920s become established and, therefore, the object of derision by the younger surrealist generation, including Miró and Masson (Green, 1987).

How can Miró's adoption of anti-artistic strategies be understood in terms of crisis? Consider, for example, the deliberate crudeness of Miró's col-

lages of the summer of 1929, the way in which they incorporate roughly cut shapes from ordinary materials such as sandpaper, as in the *Collage* (1929) shown in Figure 15-1 and the *Head of George Auric* (1929) shown in Figure 15-2. Here the placement of the collage elements replaces the act of drawing with a pencil and the idea of poetic discovery is introduced as the locus of creativity.

15-1
JOAN MIRÓ
PAPER COLLAGE, 1929
Pencil and collage on paper, 39¾ × 26 in (101 × 66 cm)
Private collection.
Photograph courtesy of Fundació Joan Miró, Barcelona. © 1996 Artists Rights Society (ARS), NY/ADAGP, Paris

The collage entitled *The Spanish Dancer* (1928) of the previous summer similarly presents the conjunction of a hatpin and a feather as a representation of the dancer. Here Miró substitutes the objects, hatpin and feather, for the body of the dancer in order to suggest the totality of her presence; just as in bringing these two objects together, within the frame of the support, he suggests the motion and gesture of the dance. In one way, this is an extension of the schematic language which he had been evolving; in another, it was a step beyond painting: a step which moved physically into the realm of the real, which adopted the previously discredited means of poetry and literature, and necessarily involved the utilization of literary strategies.

Collage heralded the onset of this artistic crisis which only found its logical fulfilment in the three-dimensional works. Miró's constructions of the summer of 1930 extended the idea that the locus of creation lay beyond the artist, somewhere in the world itself, and as if to prove this point, Miró had the wooden components for these works fabricated by a carpenter to his specifications, as in the example of the *Construction* (1930) in the Museum of Modern Art (Figure 15-3). We know this because the art critic Sebastià Gasch reported in the October 15 1930 edition of the newspaper, *La Publicitat*, that Miró "has limited himself to trace only the plan of the discovered construction, to designate its measurement and deliver it to a common carpenter for fabrication" (Gasch, 1930). Furthermore, Miró's plans and notations regarding these sculptures, housed in the archives of the Fundació Joan Miró, bear this out.

Removing himself, and any trace of the presence or touch of the artist, from the artistic object is itself suggestive of crisis, but a crisis in many ways more directed at the public persona of the artistic subject: "the artist Joan Miró". Here we are in the presence of the second moment of artistic crisis; the assassination of painting is turned not against painting or the institution of art, but against the previous painterly output produced by Miró. How could this happen? How could an artist repudiate, in a manner of speaking, his own work, and what is the significance of this repudiation?

It might be read as a challenge to the established notion of the artistic

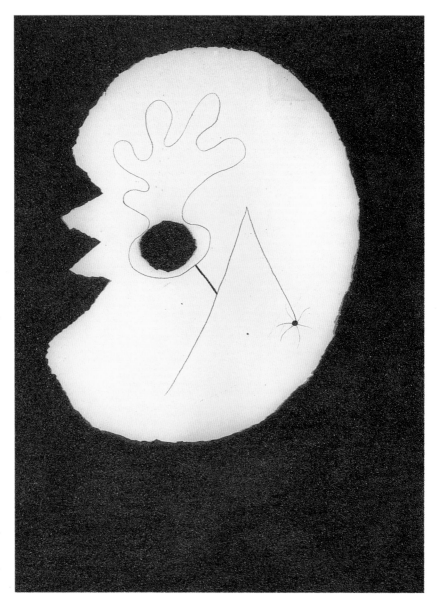

15-2
JOAN MIRÓ
HEAD OF GEORGES AURIC,
1929
Tarboard, chalk, India ink
and pencil on card,
43¼ × 29½ in (110 × 75 cm)
Kunsthaus Zürich. © 1996
Artists Rights Society
(ARS), NY/ADAGP, Paris

personality. Just as collage itself had offered the possibility of a challenge to painting, so Miró's assassination attempt could be read as offering a challenge to the artistic construction of the artist's personality as ego. This would seem to be the case with the earlier surrealist strategy of "automatic writing", although such a precedent must be qualified in Miró's instance in so far as his work of the early 1920s was related to surrealist artistic processes at the same time that it was carefully reasoned. This calculated procedure is also a feature of

15-3
JOAN MIRÓ
RELIEF CONSTRUCTION, 1930
Wood and metal,
35⅞ × 27⅝ × 6⅜ in
(91.1 × 70.2 × 16.2 cm)
The Museum of Modern
Art, New York. Purchase.
Photograph © 1996 The
Museum of Modern Art,
New York. © 1996 Artists
Rights Society (ARS),
NY/ADAGP, Paris

Miró's increasingly anti-art works of the early 1930s, and would suggest a denial, or at least a removal, of the persona of the artist as the central determining force in the act of making the artwork. Rather, the notion of the artist as creating something from nothing is replaced by the idea of the spark or shock of poetic "discovery" of something disturbing or unusual embedded in the world, or perhaps buried in the unconscious mind of the artist. This act of discovery would then entail the annulment of the artist and his personality, which would in turn be replaced by the spontaneous spark originating in the world of things and provoking inspiration in the magnetic field of the artist's now receptive mind.

The other distinguishing feature of these constructions is the explicitly violent relationship that they establish with the viewer, especially as regards the use of staples and nails; the former attack the figures represented in the construction, the latter assault the viewer, returning his/her gaze in a threatening gesture. The crisis represented in these works may be understood as a crisis turned not only inward at the artist Miró, but aggressively outward at the viewer. This is all the more clear in Miró's defiant and provocative *Personnage* (1930 or 1931), which flaunts all established pictorial and sculptural conventions (Figure 15-4). It was ironically classified in 1931 as "sculpture" by the editors of the surrealist review *Surréalisme au Service de la Révolution*, a designation which separated it from the "symbolic object". Indeed, Miró can here be seen to be using the means of sculpture to dismantle the idea of sculpture, just as at the same time the brazenly phallic imagery seems to subvert conventional social propriety and morality in the presentation of a bourgeois gentleman.

The paintings Miró executed at the same time as these constructions similarly reveal a deliberate strategy, even as they feign the look of spontaneity, immediacy and chaotic organization. As with the constructions, they were the product of a reasoned process intended to disrupt the normal modes of thinking and painting (Figure 15-5). Here there are drawings for the paintings which carefully transfer the result of the drawing process into the final, meticulously realized painting. Yet, on the level of the drawing, Miró has proceeded from an initial image, which was relatively conventional and legible,

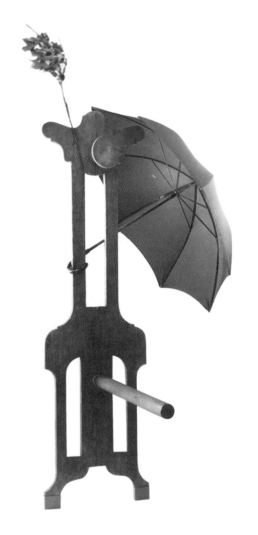

15-4
JOAN MIRÓ
PERSONAGE WITH UMBRELLA
(Replica of lost original of 1930)
Assemblage, 78 in high (198 cm high)
Fundació Joan Miró, Barcelona. © F. Catala-Roca, Barcelona. © 1996 Artists Rights Society (ARS), NY/ADAGP, Paris

to an effacement and eradication of these initial images (Figure 15-6). The result is a crossed-out or cancelled image presented as painting.

Miró's "assassination of painting" functions as a provocation within the social construction of the idea of art. The poets Tristan Tzara and Georges Hugnet had both pointed out this singular feature of Miró's strategy, and noted that if Miró sought to destroy painting, he did so with the means proper to the medium (Tzara, 1931; Hugnet, 1931). What then was the nature of this crisis within art itself, of which Miró's paintings and sculptures are an instance? As noted, Miró's collages were featured as part of the surrealist exhibition of collages, conceived by Louis Aragon and organized

15-5
JOAN MIRÓ
COMPOSITION, 1930
Oil on canvas,
90½ × 65 in (230 × 165 cm)
Photograph courtesy
Museé de Grenoble.
© 1996 Artists Rights
Society (ARS), NY/ADAGP,
Paris

scandalous and unsaleable, and it was left for Pierre Loeb to exhibit them privately at his own home (Anon., 1931). This was in part the result of the conservative artistic climate born of the neo-classical revivals typical of the decade, just as it was symptomatic of the shock to the Parisian art market resulting from the world-wide economic collapse. Can Miró's "assassination of painting" be understood as a crisis in the confidence of the monetary and cultural value of painting, and if so at what point does this sociological crisis parallel a more subjective crisis? Miró's strategy, it seems to me, forms part of a larger surrealist project to undermine the financial value of works of art in order to affirm that it was only in terms of the mind and its processes that a work of art could be valued. Accordingly, the value of a work of art derived specifically from its appeal to the workings of the mind. Miró's artistic crisis might then be understood as being mediated through the context of Surrealism, in which he played a central role.

Would it then be possible to conceive of Miró's artistic crisis in terms of a crisis in Surrealism? At the end of the 1920s Surrealism was indeed embroiled in a crisis of identity, in which the aims of the movement and the means to action were questioned, a crisis, indeed, which led many artists to part company with André Breton (Figure 15-7). Miró, somewhat curiously, never broke with Breton through these difficult years which saw the expulsion of many of Miró's friends from the ranks of the movement, and the very real tensions and conflicts which emerged between the publication of Breton's two all-important tracts: *Le Surréalisme et la Peinture* (1928) and the *Second Manifeste du Surréalisme* (1930).

Miró's own position within Sur-

at the Galerie Goemans in March 1930. There Aragon likened art to a jewel, and noted that it was domesticated by money. Collage, on the other hand, was "poor" and reflected the "refusal of a certain reality" (Aragon, 1930/1965). Miró's own development as an artist mirrored this observation. Though his work was enigmatic, there was certainly a market for his paintings in the late 1920s, and his show at the right bank Galerie Georges Bernheim in May 1928 was a particularly notable success. By the summer of 1930 Bernheim refused to exhibit Miró's constructions, which he considered realism may be understood as being inscribed between these two documents, the one aesthetic, the other essentially political, that is as occurring at the same time that he moved, by way of collage, into three dimensions. Breton had not publicly committed himself to any particular position with regard to Miró's painting until the appearance in 1928 of the expanded version of *Le Surréalisme et la Peinture*, where his newly formulated remarks regarding Miró are paradoxical and equivocal. On the one hand, Breton called Miró "the most surrealist of us all", praised him for most closely embodying a "pure automatism", noting that "on his own ground Miró is invincible" and that "no-one else has the same ability to bring together the incompatible, and to disrupt calmly what we do not dare, even hope, to see disrupted"; but, on the other hand, he was critical of Miró for a kind of mindlessness removed from a "chemistry of the intellect" and a simple symbolism expressive "in its most child-like sense" (Breton, 1928/1965; pp. 37, 40).

Breton's judgments have double meanings: just as Miró is the most spontaneous of the surrealists, so he is painterly in a superficial sense; just as he can make the most startling juxtapositions, so they are the least sophisticated of substitutions. Breton goes on to caution Miró that the artist is only an instrument of pure imagination, and he states ". . . I take this opportunity of affirming the indefensibility of certain rights other than that of painting . . ." (Breton, 1928/1965, p. 41), which amounts to both a denial of painting as mere retinal sensation and an affirmation of painting as a vehicle for thought, as a poetic locus for mental activity. Breton's reservations express the concern that Miró simply likes paint-

ing too much, that Miró's paintings are often lacking in intellectual substance. Miró's response, as has often been noted, was almost as ambiguous; while he never broke openly with Breton, his allegiance remained tenuous and distant at best, and his affirmation of Breton's political program equivocal. While the names of his close friends Aragon, Dalí, Ernst, Goemans and Tzara are among the signatories of the manifesto, Miró's name is absent. The source of Miró's "assassination of painting" lay in the Dada roots of Surrealism, and it was to this root that Miró's surrealist friends returned in

15-6
JOAN MIRÓ
PRELIMINARY SKETCH FOR PAINTING, 1930
Graphite pencil on paper, 8½ × 6⅝ in (21.7 × 16.7 cm)
Fundació Joan Miró, Barcelona. © F. Catala-Roca, Barcelona. © 1996 Artists Rights Society (ARS), NY/ADAGP, Paris

1930. What is less frequently said, although Anne Umland also has recently taken this position, is that while Miró's "assassination of painting" was in part a return to a Dada strategy, its application to his own works, may also be a positive response to Breton's criticism (Umland, 1992, p. 53).

How then did Miró turn this crisis in Surrealism inward? His approach to this crisis was indeed a response to the crisis of art within the terms of painting, as we have seen Hugnet (1931) and Tzara (1931) had argued; so perhaps it is in artistic strategies that we must look to answer the question, where does the artistic event interface with the subject of the artist? While Miró had evolved a highly productive

working method through the course of the 1920s, there was the danger that the very facility he had achieved with his medium was the principal impediment to authentic inspiration, that the process of painting itself threatened to degenerate into facile repetition and the production of a signature style. Carl Einstein pointed out this danger in the pages of Georges Bataille's *Documents*, where, in a review of the Goemans' show of collages, he wrote that collage was a weapon by which one "combats precious and individual writing", by which he meant collage was an aid in subverting style. Likewise, collage was of assistance in combating a decrepit conception of individuality, which he called "this old SELF . . .", and he went on to describe the latter as the psychic equivalent to petty bourgeois financial security, "The SELF is psychic interest: the little, unearned income" (Einstein, 1930). For Miró the "assassination of painting" entailed the destruction of a particular attitude to painting within his own approach to art, but at the same time it offered a means whereby he generated new and provocative images. The destruction of this old attitude to painting entailed a disruption of all traits and habits which might be identified with the personality of Miró, the artist.

In what sense might it be appropriate to speak of a crisis in Miró's art as an identity crisis? In the very act of finding and assembling what would otherwise appear as merely random and arbitrary objects, Miró found a means of realizing a visual form of poetry, and he did this as a deliberate way of avoiding the serial form of repetition which had come to characterize much of early modern painting and, indeed, his own painting. What are the implications of this strategy, and in what way are they a form of

15-7
MAN RAY
ANDRÉ BRETON, 1935
*ADAGP/Man Ray Trust,
Paris, 1995. © 1996
Artists Rights Society
(ARS), NY/ADAGP, Paris*

murder? The psychoanalyst Jacques Lacan has noted, within the context of a discussion of the surrealist approach to metaphor, "So, it is between the signifier in the form of the proper name of a man and the signifier that metaphorically abolishes him that the poetic spark is produced" (Lacan, 1966/1977, p. 158). Lacan's remarks echo those of the philosopher Alexandre Kojève, for whom, "the *conceptual* understanding of empirical reality is equivalent to a *murder*" (Kojève, 1947/1969/1980, p. 140), by which he meant that any living thing dies as it passes into language and is understood as abstract concept. Surely it is not without significance that Bataille, Breton, Lacan and many of the surrealists attended Kojève's lectures at the Sorbonne in the 1930s. As for Miró's artistic strategy, there is no meaning signified in any single component in the collages, for they take on meaning only as signifiers in the context of the collage. Likewise, the presence of the artist in the work is only achieved in his absence, in the measure of the difference separating one work from another and each work from the artist.

This situation becomes more acute if we examine an instance of self-portraiture. Sometime about 1930, Man Ray made a photographic portrait of Miró in which he placed the artist before a black backdrop on which he provocatively and tantalizingly placed a rope; here an instance, I would argue, of metaphoric juxtaposition, and pictorial collage worked out in photography with Miró and a piece of rope as somewhat enigmatic signifiers (Figure 15-8). Man Ray has recalled in his autobiography, entitled *Self-Portrait*, the context of this portrait:

"Joan Miró brought his first stylized, bucolic scenes from Spain, but very

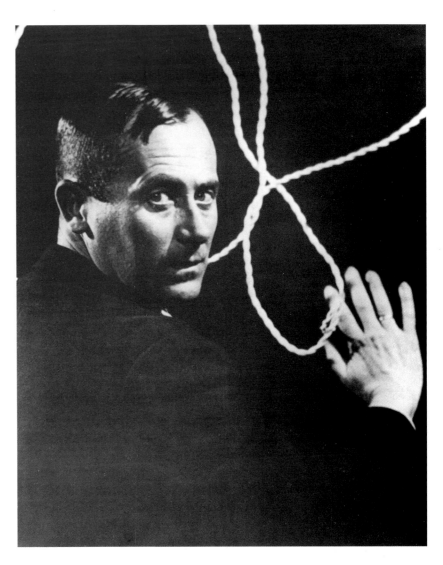

15-8
MAN RAY
JOAN MIRÓ, c. 1930
ADAGP/Man Ray Trust, Paris, 1995. © 1996 Artists Rights Society (ARS), NY/ADAGP, Paris

soon entered completely into the Dada and Surrealist spirit . . . He assembled heterogeneous objects, combining them with his painting. Sometimes a large coil of rope was attached to the composition. It reminded me of an episode where several of us were visiting Ernst's studio. Miró was very taciturn; it was difficult to get him to talk. A violent discussion was going on; he was pressed to give his opinion but remained obstinately mute. Max seized a coil of rope, threw it over a beam, tied a slip knot at the end, and, while the others pinioned his arms, put it around his neck and threatened to hang him if he did not speak. Miró did not struggle but remained silent;

he was ravished with being the center of so much attention. When he came to pose for me, I perfidiously hung a rope in back of him as an accessory. He did not comment on this, but the rope then figured in his later works" (Ray, 1963, pp. 251–252).

This incident is interesting in a number of different ways and offers access to the idea of crisis and assassination in terms of art, Surrealism and the artistic subject: Miró. Interestingly, it is not because of what he says, but because of what he does *not* say that Miró's surrealist friends sought to murder him. In other words Miró's role in Surrealism was one in which he removed himself from the center of intellectual discourse by *not* speaking, just as he increasingly removed any evidence of his own presence from his work by incorporating seemingly arbitrary things in his collages, constructions and assemblages. That the surrealists sought *actually* to murder Miró for this non-act of silence is interesting. In doing so they adopted the artist's own artistic strategy to make their point, even if they did not really mean it, since, if they meant it, they would have actually executed Miró on the spot. Who would have been the wiser? Miró's own acquiescence and delight at being the center of attention in this event raises yet further the question of the degree to which he sought to undermine painting by plastic means, since this entailed some equivalent procedure which would also dispense with the artist? Without art there is no further need for the artist!

Also at the beginning of the 1930s, the photographer Rogi André depicted Miró in two photographs singular for their seeming banality (Figures 15-9 and 15-10). In the full-length version we see the diminutive Miró standing with his hands in his pockets, carefully attired and distractedly staring away from the camera lens into space. Miró's careful attention to dress, especially his somewhat dandyish tie and neatly cut hair are worth noting, as is the nondescript room and the stark side lighting towards which he is looking. The shoulder-length version is even more striking and partakes of greater artifice. Here we find Miró again before a black backdrop, not at all dissimilar to the one to be found in Man Ray's portrait. The lighting is even more dramatic and from the side so that one side of Miró's face is bathed in light and the other engulfed in shadow, as if to emphasize the presence of the artist as something ghost-like, or spectral.

15-9
ROGI ANDRÉ
JOAN MIRÓ, c. 1930
Photograph courtesy of Bibliothèque Nationale de France. © Cliché Bibliothèque Nationale de France, Paris

15-10
ROGI ANDRÉ
JOAN MIRÓ, c. 1930
Photograph courtesy of
Bibliothèque Nationale de
France. © Cliché
Bibliothèque Nationale de
France, Paris

While seemingly uncomplicated, this portrait, like the one by Man Ray, must be read in a larger context, especially when we consider Miró's own exploration of self-portraiture. Here Miró ceases to be the artist-subject exploring the mysterious world of nature and becomes the object of an *other*'s work. Miró himself may well have been deeply fascinated with André's portrait and apparently considered making a collage based on the portrait. Whether such a collage was executed, or whether it still exists, is not clear, but

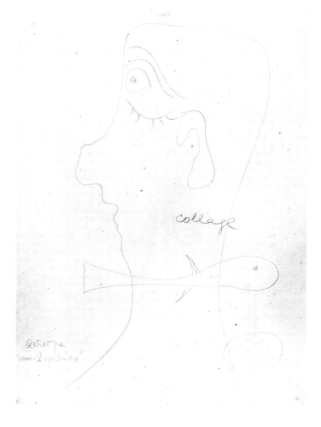

15-11
JOAN MIRÓ
SELF-PORTRAIT, 1936
Graphite pencil on
paper, 15½ × 12⅜ in
(39.5 × 31.5 cm)
Fundació Joan Miró,
Barcelona. © 1996 Artists
Rights Society (ARS),
NY/ADAGP, Paris

jectivity and artistic identity. Indeed, if his use of collage was understood as an assault on reality, as perceived through the mirror of art, then we might understand this murder plot as a call for the abolition of the distinction between art and life, and one not without dangers for the artist himself. For Miró, such a process would not only entail the destruction of the persona of the artist as socially constructed, but it would likewise require a cutting up and rearrangement of his own subjectivity.

DEDICATION

This chapter is dedicated to Pilar Baos.

REFERENCES

Anon. (1931). Joan Miró a Barcelona. *L'Opinió* (Barcelona), 3 July.

Aragon, L. (1930/1965). La peinture au défi. In *Les Collages*, Ed. Louis Aragon, pp. 36–37. Hermann, Paris.

Breton, A. (1928/1965). *Surrealism and Painting.* Harper & Row, New York.

Breton, A. (1930). *Second manifeste du Surréalisme.* Simon Kra. Paris.

Einstein, C. (1930). Exposition des collages (Galerie Goemans). *Documents* (Paris), **II**(4), 244.

Gasch, S. (1925). Els pintors d'avant-guardia: Joan Miró. *Gaceta de les Arts* (Barcelona), **II**(39), 15 December, 3–5.

Gasch, S. (1930). Escultures de Joan Miró. *La Publicitat* (Barcelona), 15 October, 5.

Green, C. (1987). *Cubism and Its Enemies.* Yale University Press, London.

a drawing after the André portrait remains which is labeled "collage" and dedicated "retrat par Mme Rogi André", as if Miró is adopting André's perspective with regard to himself (Figure 15-11). Careful attention is given to his eyes, ears and even to the tie, which is represented as a fish from which a sphere hangs by a thread. Miró positions himself with regard to the viewer in profile, thereby treating his own facial features as something schematic and transparent. The designation "collage" would seem to liken the attributes of the artist to found objects, and suggest that the structure of the artistic subject is as arbitrary as the arrangement of the components in a collage.

As we have seen, Miró's call for the murder of painting was a strategy with ramifications which reached far beyond the limited confines of art, but it was one which called for a radical re-thinking of our understanding of sub-

Hugnet, G. (1931). Joan Miró ou l'enfance de l'art. *Cahiers d'Art* (Paris), **VI**(7–8), 335–340.

Kojève, A. (1947/1969/1980). *Introduction to the Reading of Hegel: Lectures on the Phenomenology of Spirit.* Cornell University Press, Ithaca.

Lacan, J. (1966/1977). Agency of the letter in the unconscious. *Ecrits: A Selection.* Routledge, London.

Melgar, F. (1931). Los artistas españoles en Paris: Juan [sic] Miró. *Ahora* (Madrid), 24 January, 18.

Ray, M. (1963). *Self-Portrait.* Little, Brown, Boston.

Raynal, M. (1927). *Anthologie de la Peinture en France de 1905 à nos Jours,* p. 37. Editions Montaigne. Paris.

Tériade, E. (1930). La peinture, le surréalisme et la pêche à l'instinct. *L'Intransigeant* (Paris), 7 April, 5.

Tzara, T. (1931). Le papier collé ou le proverbe en peinture. *Cahiers d'Art* (Paris), **VI**(2), 61–64.

Umland, A. (1992). Joan Miró's *Collage* of Summer 1929: La peinture au défi?. In *Essays on Assemblage,* Ed. John Elderfield, Studies in Modern Art No. 2, Museum of Modern Art, New York.

CHAPTER 16

MIRÓ FINDS HIS VOCATION
AS AN ARTIST

BARBARA ROSE

Three years after Joan Miró was born, the American philosopher and psychologist William James delivered the Lowell Lectures on exceptional mental states at Harvard (James, 1896, cited in Taylor, 1984). James' interests in extending the new discipline of psychology to the study of psychic phenomena, including religious consciousness, made him a unique thinker who bridged the gap between science, art and religion. In the Lowell lectures, James examined the relationship between artists and "lunatics", criminals and visionaries. He also considered altered states of consciousness and paranormal phenomena. These extraordinary lectures covered topics only now beginning to be thought about in a thorough scientific manner. The first was on dreams, the second on automatism, the third on hysteria, the fourth on multiple personality, the fifth on diabolic possession and the sixth on witchcraft.

In the literature of the late nineteenth century, genius was equated with insanity (Nordau, 1968, p. 155). The idea that genius was a morbid and pathological expression of a degenerate insanity was the prevailing view of continental researchers such as Jacques Moreau and Cesare Lombroso, but James did not agree with this definition of creativity. He had other explanations for visionary phenomena and ecstatic states—including mystical hallucinations—than psycho-

pathic tendencies. The oldest son of the Swedenborgian religious philosopher Henry James, William James was determined to prove that genius was healthy rather than morbid, despite the life-long mental illness of his father and his siblings, including Alice, the female dysfunctional member of a family of melancholic male geniuses (Jamison, 1993, pp. 207–216). "The prevailing opinion of our time supposes that a psychotic condition is the foundation for genius", James observed. He noted further that:

"We make a common distinction between healthy and morbid, but the true fact is that we can not make it sharp. No one symptom by itself is a morbid one—it depends rather on the part that it plays. We speak of melancholy and moral tendencies, but he would be a bold man who should say that the melancholy was not an essential part of every character . . . A life healthy on the whole must have some morbid elements" (James, 1896, cited in Taylor, 1984, p. 15).

Other writers who have studied the relationship between genius and mental disorders include Otto Rank, whose book *The Psychology of the Artist* is among the most provocative analyses of the relationship between creativity and neurosis (Rank, 1984, pp. 25–26). Rank saw in both the neurotic and the artist a similar drive toward totality. He identified the bifurcation between art and neurosis as the capacity to act. In his view, the neurotic may have the same fantasies, dreams, etc. as the artist, but the neurotic, unlike the artist, cannot act. Like neurotics, artists may have breakdowns or crises. The artist, however, gets out of bed. The neurotic remains incapacitated. Both the artist and the neurotic may at times be bedridden, but the neurotic is paralyzed by unresolved conflict, whereas the artist transforms psychic material into aesthetic experience.

In *Born under Saturn*, Rudolph and Margot Wittkower collected anecdotes and material that related genius to insanity (Wittkower & Wittkower, 1963). It was the first time a leading art historian trod into this territory of psychological malfunction among artists throughout history. Most of the material was assembled from existing texts, printed without interpretation. Interestingly, there are no Spanish artists in this collection of various types of perverse, antisocial, disintegrated and pathological behavior. The reason, I believe, is that Spanish culture traditionally has considered paranormal experiences—visions, ecstasies, hallucinations et al—a normal part of daily life (Gallego, 1968).

In Spain, the vividness and also the frequency of hallucinations and visions were greater than in any other part of Europe. Identifying literally and physically with the passion of Christ is a major theme in Spanish religious thought. This identification inspires the writings of St Ignatius Loyola and St Francis Xavier, as well as the poems of San Juan de la Cruz. There is a vast literature of the visions, ecstasies and epiphanies of the various saints. In other words, "seeing things" was a normal part of the Spanish mental life.

Miró's obsession with numbers reflects a long tradition of folk superstition dating back to the Middle Ages that continued well into the twentieth century, as did the visions and hallucinations. When I asked Miró why he did not become a surrealist he said, "A Spaniard does not need to become a Surrealist: he is already irrational" (Rose, 1982, p. 11). We may conjecture that the acceptance of the irrational as rational and of the paranormal as normal was far easier for a man like Miró than it would have been, for example, for a Cartesian rationalist like Matisse.

As we know, Joan Miró was profoundly influenced by medieval Catalan art. To understand the relationship between Miró's adolescent illness and the resolution of his adolescent crisis of identity through art, we need to see his artistic choices in relation to Spanish and Catalan culture to appreciate the basis of the integration of the personality of a genius. As a youth, Miró visited not only the local churches and cathedrals, but also the Museo de Catalunya, where the monumental Catalan Romanesque frescoes were installed. The powerful fresco paintings of *Christ Pantocrater* (Figure 16-1) and of the *Virgin in Majesty*, which Miró first saw as a child, communicate a sense of awe and immanence that no modern work of art can deliver. "Before I was even ten years old I was going by myself on Sunday mornings to the Museum of Romanesque Art" (Miró, 1978, cited in Rowell, 1992, p. 297).

Disembodied eyes are one of the characteristic images in Catalan Romanesque frescoes. There are animals covered by staring eyes. "They come from a Romanesque chapel where there is an angel whose wings have been replaced by eyes. Another

16-1
CHRIST PANTOCRATOR
from Sant Climent de
Taüll
© *Museu Nacional D'Art*
de Catalunya, Barcelona.
MNAC Photographic
Service
(Calveras/Sagristà)

and wonder he felt in the presence of these frescoes in his paintings, especially in the later large-scale works in which the viewer feels lost in the field of luminous color. In Miró's work, there is no shadow (Figure 16-3). All is light. Even when the canvas is occupied by a large black figure, as in the later works, the surroundings are a startling blaze of light. The viewer is immersed, surrounded by color as light. The result is an eclipse of distance between subject and object, i.e. spectator and artwork, that gives the spectator the illusion of merging with the work, as in a mystical experience (Rose, 1982, pp. 18–19).

Sensitivity to light varies from individual to individual. There is no proof of physiognomic or genetic predisposition to certain kinds of mystical experience that exposure to intense light creates, but it is an interesting hypothesis. In his famous *Self-Portrait I* of 1937–38 (Figure 12-11, p. 124), Miró painted his eyes as suns with large staring pupils. At midday, the light on the coast of Catalunya is so intense that there is a blinding brilliance that one sees in Miró's late paintings, in which the sun becomes a kind of blazing eyeball. That blinding light is different qualitatively, but in terms of intensity it is similar to the merciless bright light of Jerusalem, where so many mystical epiphanies took place. It appears that relentless burning light may induce a kind of trance state. Both Miró and his admirer, Jackson Pollock, alluded to working like shamans in an unconscious trance state. "When I am *in* my painting, I'm not aware of what I'm doing. It is only after a sort of "get acquainted" period that I see what I have been about. I have no fears about making changes, destroying the image, etc., because the painting has a life of its own" (O'Connor & Thaw, 1978, p. 241). Indeed, there is evidence that

Romanesque angel has eyes in its hand, right in the palm" (Miró, 1974, cited in Rowell, 1992, p. 282) (Figure 16-2).

The great Pantocraters and robed Virgins in Catalan apses loom like awesome *personnages*. To a child they must have seemed terrifying indeed. When recollected by the adult Miró, the looming *personnages*, surrounded by signs representing stars or angels with eyes on their wings, became powerful signs imbued with their original majesty and distant might. Miró wished to communicate and was successful in communicating the awe

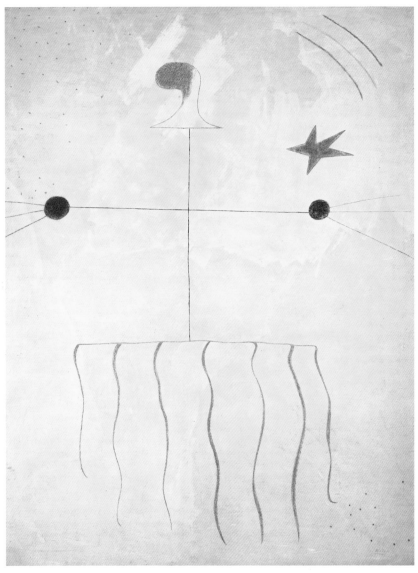

creative associations and connections take place in such a state of withdrawal from the world.

Creative play involves the ability to regress to the early days of childhood when creation was a free-flowing activity, an uninterrupted stream of freely associated material not held back by the inhibition of criticism. If the artist who strives for perfection has his semiformed ideas criticized, the result may be an inability to free-associate for fear of critical rejection. As Nancy Andreasen has observed, (Chapter One, this volume) the primary act of creation occurs in the security of that other "place" where creation flows without judgment. In that mental state of otherness, the artist is entirely alone. We may define the capacity to endure such loneliness, and to tolerate the emotional chaos that unformed or partially formed concepts stir up, as the mark of the successful creative personality. New concepts are born in this privileged zone from which the artist cannot be sure how to exit. In weaker people, fear inhibits or stops

the creative urge from continuing to express itself.

There is understandable fear of entering this "place" or mental state where creativity is fluid, which is characterized by regression and the disorder of chaotic and unformed feeling and thought. The difference between the artist and the neurotic is that the artist or the genuinely creative individual has the ego strength to risk failing, and to go on experimenting in a zone of uncertainty without knowing whether these experiments are valid or substantive. Indeed, the consistent and relentless pursuit of experimenta-

16-2 *(above left)*
Santa Maria d'Aneu
(detail of cherubim)
© *Museu National D'Art de Catalunya, Barcelona. MNAC Photographic Service (Calveras/Sagrista)*

16-3 *(above)*
Joan Miró
Head of Catalan Peasant, 1924. Oil on canvas, 57½ × 45 in (146 × 114.2 cm). National Gallery of Art, Washington. Gift of the Collector's Committee. © *1995 Board of Trustees, National Gallery of Art, Washington.* © *1996 Artists Rights Society (ARS), NY/ADAGP, Paris*

tion *without the security of validation* appears to characterize high levels of risk-taking creativity in general, whether in art or in science.

Miró, for example, worked for years without material or critical success. Yet he persevered in expressing his vision. When Miró sold his first painting *The Farm* to Ernest Hemingway in 1923, he was already in his 30s. We know from his own words that when he showed *The Farm* (Figure 12-5, p. 119) to Eluard and Breton, they stared at it and had no reaction whatsoever. He felt rejected by Paris—but he did not care, because he had something within himself that was far stronger than the ordinary artist's drive to be famous, rich or immortal. Although the period between the two World Wars was essentially conservative, Miró was able to continue creating new forms. In the 1930s, he began to fill up his canvas again with the *personnages* of his parallel universe, which we may enter as Alice entered Wonderland or crossed over to the other side of the Looking Glass. Like Alice, Miró was able to enter and to leave the Wonderland fantasy and to step back and forth through the mirror of reality.

In 1987 I participated in the seminar "Success and Failure" held at the 37th International Design Conference in Aspen, Colorado, organized by novelist Michael Crichton. Participants included architect Frank Gehry and artist Milton Glaser. We found that transcending the fear of failure was the *sine qua non* for success and that those unable to transcend the fear of failure could not take the great risks that innovation requires. In other words, the willingness to fail repeatedly characterizes the highest creative achievement. Clearly Miró did not fear either failure or rejection. The question is, why? We must return to specific biographical data in Miró's life to

understand why he could risk failure and experiment constantly without knowing what the results might lead to in advance.

During the years of painting and drawing in isolation at his family's farm in Montroig, Miró solved his initial crisis of identity by identifying his work as a project greater than himself—driven or inspired by forces beyond his individual ego. This sense of fulfilling destiny permitted Miró to rid himself of the responsibility or the guilt feelings that might accompany taking up as a life's work the vocation of an artist.

The stylistic breaks in Miró's work permit us to reconstitute the development of his ability to transcend the fear of failure and rejection. The first important break occurs in 1917–18 when he begins to use the farm at Montroig, in the vicinity of Tarragona, to create agricultural and folkloric symbols opposed to the industrialism and commercialism of modern life. Rejecting the urban metropolis of Barcelona, Miró finds refuge in an agricultural tradition still alive in Tarragona where his paternal grandparents lived only a short way from the farm of Montroig. At this point, ancient agricultural traditions become more real and more valid to him than the industrial machine forms of modern life that alienate man from nature, work from craft, art from life. The connection to this tradition through his peasant grandparents was vital to the integration of his personality as an artist.

In the case of every successful creator, one finds a validating experience, a relationship with a close relative, a teacher, or someone the artist respects who validates the creative enterprise or gives permission to transgress the bourgeois conventions. In Miró's case, that validating figure was his maternal grandfather. Miró writes about his relationship to his family in a letter to Jacques Dupin, written in 1957. In this letter, Miró speaks affectionately about his grandparents as well as about his own father's rejection of his ambition to become an artist.

"I know that my maternal grandfather was very fond of me. Starting as a simple cabinet maker's assistant, he finally had his own business. He did not know how to read or write and he only spoke the Majorquin dialect . . . My maternal grandmother was very intelligent and romantic . . . My paternal grandparents had no personality; they were blacksmiths and peasants, and just good people" (Miró, 1957, cited in Rowell, 1992, p. 45).

In developmental terms, resolution of the problem of personal identity signals the end of adolescence and the beginning of maturity. Not resolved, this problem continues to haunt the artist, impeding development, and re-emerging over and over again in a series of ever more insistent and debilitating crises. When we speak of the formation of personal identity, we refer to a specific moment in the evolution of that personality. Adolescence coincides with a crisis of identity and is resolved only through the resolution of the identity crisis. In Chapter Twelve, Schildkraut and Hirshfeld note the period in Miró's life between the ages of 17 and 26, during which the sickly Miró found health in his vocation as an artist. Miró's illness served a specific purpose: illness permitted him to persuade his father reluctantly to accept that his son was too sick to work. Picasso had a similar adolescent crisis expressed in illness (Richardson, 1991, p. 97). The identity crisis of an artist begins with the first rejection of the artist's vocation because the bour-geois family realistically suspects that the life of an artist is insecure: it is a path that will produce no material good, but will in fact permit the off-spring to lead a life of leisure, like an aristocrat or a loafer, as opposed to working regularly like the good bour-geois (Figure 13-1, p. 133).

There is a collective sense that crea-tion is a playful activity, so privileged that a price must be paid for this more and more expensive freedom to be impractical and non-materialistic. Thus, leisure required to dream must be paid for dearly, often in economic misery and emotional suffering. In this context of bourgeois culture, the artist must suffer. Traditionally, the artist must suffer for other reasons as well. In creating, the artist challenges and competes with the gods. Such hubris is punishable by torment, possibly even death, or according to traditional myths by being maimed or transformed into an animal, plant or a lower form of life. The relationship between the artist and suffering is perhaps best expressed by Edmund Wilson (1965) in his study of creativity, *The Wound and the Bow*. Wilson focuses on the story of Philoctetes, the warrior who carried the bow of Heracles abandoned by the Greeks when he was wounded by Apollo. It is Wilson's thesis that every artist has a deep wound. Wilson does not specify whether it is psychic or physical, but theorizes that to com-pensate for this wound, the artist becomes devoted to fabricating a weapon to fight back against those who have rejected or wounded him or her.

Applying Wilson's concept of the wound and the bow, we may ask what could be the critical "wound" in Miró's case? Was there a physical trait in Miró remarkable enough to create psycho-logical problems, including problems of rejection in school, and of difficulty in totally accepting himself? We may observe that Miró was very diminutive in stature. In a culture in which height is equated with masculinity, this can be painful. The capacity to transcend a physical circumstance—to push beyond the limit—is something that great artists appear to have in common. Given his smallness, it is noteworthy, indeed superhuman, that well into his 80s, Miró was painting works twice as big as himself (Figure 16-4).

I was fortunate enough to spend a few days with Joan Miró in Barcelona and to observe him working. Miró did not confuse art with life. In a sense, he was two people: the man of the world, wearing a dark conservative business suit, white shirt and close-cropped hair, who changed into the completely self-absorbed artist once inside the studio. In the *taller* (studio), Miró donned a worker's costume. He exchanged his bourgeois business attire for a white jumpsuit, the way a surgeon scrubs up and puts on a sterile uniform before operating. Once transformed, Miró became completely lost in his work in a trance-like state of total concentration. This state of withdrawal was described by Nancy Andreasen (Chapter 1, this volume) as a "place" or space into which the artist

16-4
JOAN MIRÓ
WOMAN IN FRONT OF A SHOOTING STAR III, 1974
Acrylic on canvas, 80½ × 76⅝ in (204.5 × 194.5 cm)
Fundació Joan Miró, Barcelona. © 1996 Artists Rights Society (ARS), NY/ADAGP, Paris

retreats when he or she begins to create. Entering the "space" of creation entails a temporary rejection of the external world.

When withdrawal from the world into an interior space is manifested by non-creative people, we interpret shutting out the world as pathological. During this period of intense concentration and lack of interest in the outside world, the artist, on the other hand, seems driven by forces external to the self that move him or her to break through conventions and received ideas to conceive genuinely original projects. Indifference to physical discomfort, including indifference to hunger, is characteristic of this "trance" state. Normal instincts are suppressed when the formless takes form. To take an example of such indifference to physical suffering in Miró's life, we may recall that he fainted from hunger and hallucinated when he first came to Paris in 1921.

It has been suggested that the artist is motivated by desire for fame, money and the beautiful lovers they buy. This may be true, in many cases, for Renaissance and post-Renaissance artists, who were indeed driven by the desire for immortality, economic security and sexual fulfillment. There are cases, however, in which the motivation is not material, but spiritual fulfillment, and the goal is not immortality but salvation. This is true of artistic motivation from the fall of the Roman empire until the Renaissance. During the height of the Renaissance, spirituality sometimes was less important than worldliness, nevertheless, geniuses continued to be perturbed by intense mood swings. The "terribilità" of Michelangelo may be the earliest recorded manifestation of the mood swings and melancholia that appear to be the price of artistic glory (Wittkower & Wittkower, 1963, p. 73).

However, the desire for fame, money and the beautiful lovers they buy does not explain Miró's drives or ambitions. Miró wrote off success as cheap, and the pursuit of it even cheaper. He criticized Picasso's drive to succeed and to make money as typically French (Miró, 1928, cited in Rowell, 1992, pp. 97–98). The only pursuit of the artist, according to Miró, should be the perfection of his craft (Rowell, 1992, pp. 97–98). Miró's identification of his work with the anonymity of the medieval artisan was, in a sense, another shield against rejection. This drive to annihilate the ego, to efface the self, is characteristic of mystics. Self-effacement, leading to the ritualization of the act of painting and its understanding as a devotional activity, as opposed to the romantic or sentimental concept of self-expression, was the focus of Miró's quest for spiritual transcendence.

Miró identified with the anonymity of the pious artisan. There are many citations in Miró's letters of his sense of painting, not as a paying job, but as a mystical vocation or calling that parallels a priest, martyr or saint assuming his vocation. Miró's concept of art as a devotional activity was in decided contrast with the self-important posturing of the romantic genius, the dominant model of creativity at the time Miró became an artist.

The identification of genius with depression and suffering which we have noted is not necessarily pejorative, however; the romantic genius is destined to play out the drama of life in public. The public at large wants to believe that the artist is "other", and that the artist is capable of expressing the anti-social and uninhibited actions forbidden to the god-fearing and law-abiding conventional man. In a famous letter that Miró wrote in 1915, he observes that mortals cannot aspire to complete happiness:

"That would be rebelling against God, who was man and suffered for us. Pain is the inseparable brother of pleasure. The one cannot exist without the other. La souffrance, c'est le sacrement de la vie" (Miró, 1915, cited in Rowell, 1992, p. 49).

Suffering in this context becomes a very important part of the artistic process. In Edmund Wilson's (1965) hypothesis regarding creativity, every wound serves as a reminder that we are mortal beings doomed never to know complete happiness. Joseph Schildkraut has spoken about this fatalistic aspect of Miró's temperament. It is a constant thread in his work. In his studio in the Rue Blomet in Paris, the young Catalan artist had a sign which said in French, *"Train passant sans arrêt"* (Train passing through without stopping). This is how Miró the mystic conceived of the *fugaz de la vida* (transitoriness of life) that is one of the great themes of Spanish literature and art.

Towards the end of his life, Miró made a series of imaginary portraits titled *The Hope of Man Condemned to Death* (Figure 16-5). That hope could only be of an afterlife in the mystical sense.

In this context, we may understand the resolution of Miró's adolescent identity crisis as the acceptance of his mission or his vocation as an artist–shaman–priest. He is "called" to serve divine purposes in the sense that the saint is "called". In his writings, Miró refers many times to living like a monk. He describes the drawing classes that he took in Barcelona as a young man:

"That class was like a religious ceremony for me; I washed my hands carefully before touching the paper and pencils. The implements were like

sacred objects, and I worked as though I were performing a religious rite" (Miró, 1957, cited in Rowell, 1992, p. 44).

We have seen that Miró identified himself with the agricultural work of the peasant rather than with the commercial trading of the businessman and the capitalist. In this identification, as well as his later activities, it appears that Miró had a highly evolved sense of class consciousness. Miró's revolutionary fervor expressed itself not in specific political actions, but in making a radical kind of art which broke conventions, transgressed boundaries and challenged taboos. The formation by Miró in the early 1920s of a specific personal vocabulary of signs and symbols—a private secret language—was a personal parallel to the transmission of the taboo Catalan language and culture. Miró's identification of his art with Catalan culture and history gives his work wholeness and integrity.

For Miró, art was a type of labor identified with farming and with anonymous medieval artisanship. His view of Catalan nationalism as a personal crusade reconciled the conflicts of a revolutionary personality who was not violent with his historical moment. This is not a coincidence. To go on creating his art without external approbation, Miró had to have the conviction of faith. By identifying himself with the revolutionary project of Catalan nationalism, Miró was able to escape the inner critic. He was able to silence the inhibition that rejection by others would normally have created.

It was during the winter of 1923–24 that Miró made the decisive leap from Cubist-Realism to a new style of signs and symbols, a picture-writing that was a secret code, like the Catalan language or the crypto-Judaism practised

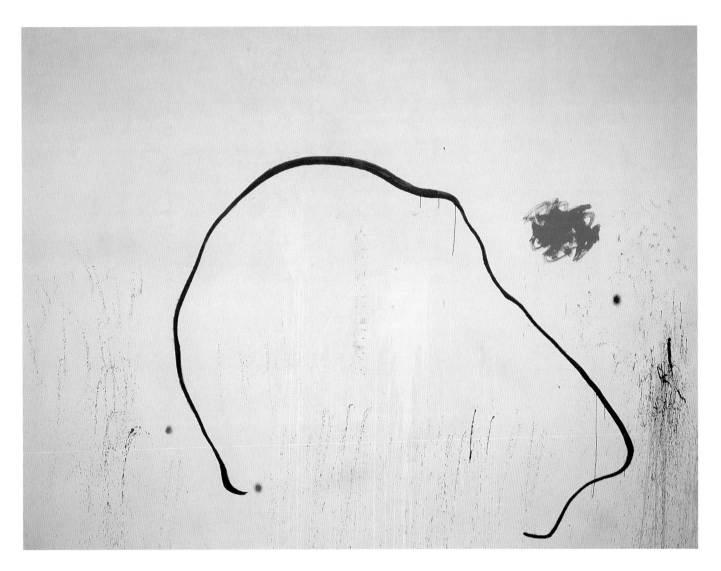

by the *Marranos* in Mallorca. We know how totally Miró identified his symbolic language with the suppressed Catalan language and culture. Indeed, William Rubin persuaded Miró to decode his pictographic symbols, so specifically we see that he was literally creating a private sign-language form of picture-writing, which referred both to paleontology and ancient ideogramatic languages as well as the forbidden Catalan language. We may interpret Miró's formation of a new vocabulary of signs and symbols as a shamanistic invocation, a vision of the reconstitution of the Catalan language and culture (Rubin, 1973) (Figures 16-6a, 16-6b).

Miró's voice found an echo in America as it could nowhere else in the world. His basic concerns coincided, for cultural and historical reasons, with those of the American avantgarde, who were as romantic and radical as he himself. The lack of a continuous artistic tradition, and in particular absence of classical roots, gave rise to the idea that American artists had to reach far back behind antiquity to the prehistoric past to find its antecedents. For what America did possess was remnants of a Paleolithic culture, and a landscape as dramatic and awesome as the great looming peaks of the Pyrenees.

Miró's tradition was deeper and more

16-5
JOAN MIRÓ
HOPE OF THE MAN CONDEMNED TO DEATH I,
1974
Acrylic on canvas, 105¼ × 138⅜ in (267.5 × 351.5 cm)
Fundació Joan Miró, Barcelona. © 1996 Artists Rights Society (ARS), NY/ADAGP, Paris

16-6a
JOAN MIRÓ
*CATALAN LANDSCAPE [THE
HUNTER], 1923–24*
*Oil on canvas, 25½ × 39½ in
(64.8 × 100.3 cm)*
*The Museum of Modern
Art, New York. Purchase.
Photograph © 1996 The
Museum of Modern Art,
New York. © 1996 Artists
Rights Society (ARS),
NY/ADAGP, Paris*

16-6b
*Chart identifying
iconographical elements
in the painting,* CATALAN
LANDSCAPE (THE HUNTER)
*(1923–24) by Joan Miró.
9 × 8 in (22.9 × 20.3 cm)*
*From William S. Rubin
(1973),* MIRÓ IN THE
COLLECTION OF THE MUSEUM
OF MODERN ART, *p. 22. The
Museum of Modern Art,
New York. © 1973 The
Museum of Modern Art,
New York*

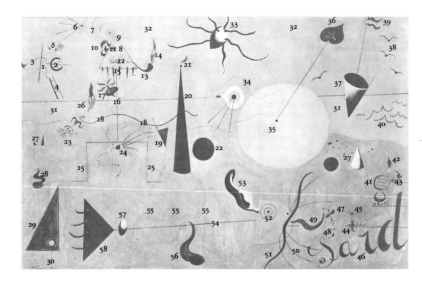

THE HUNTER

1. Bird-airplane
2. Propeller
3. Fuselage
4. Rope ladder
5. French and Catalan flags
6. Star
7. Rainbow
8. Hunter's head
9. Hunter's Catalan cap
10. Hunter's ear
11. Hunter's eye
12. Hunter's moustache
13. Hunter's pipe
14. Smoke
15. Hunter's beard
16. Hunter's body
17. Hunter's heart
18. Hunter's arm
19. Knife
20. Gun
21. Smoke from gun
22. Bullet (shot)
23. Rabbit
24. Hunter's sex organ
25. Hunter's leg
26. Flame
27. Landscape elements
28. Turd
29. Vine
30. Stem
31. Mediterranean Sea
32. Sky
33. Sun-egg
34. Eye
35. Carob tree
36. Carob leaf
37. Small boat
38. Seagulls
39. Spanish flag
40. Waves
41. Grill
42. Hunter's campfire to cook lunch
43. Pepper
44. Potato
45. Potato flower
46. First four letters of word "Sardine"
47. Fly
48. Defecation of fly
49. Sardine's tongue
50. Sardine's whiskers
51. Surface of water
52. Sardine's eye
53. Sardine's ear
54. Sardine's spine
55. Sardine's bones
56. Sardine's bowel
57. Sardine's eggs (reproductive organ)
58. Sardine's tail

complex than that of his Parisian contemporaries because it embraced the Mozarabic roots of Catalan culture and the medieval tradition that was still alive in folklore and art as a living reality in the present. The only important American artist to be inspired by similar childhood memories was Arshile Gorky, whose style came so close to Miró's that on at least one occasion, Miró himself became confused. Like Miró, Gorky, who was born Vosdanig Adaoian in the province of Van in Armenia, had roots in an intensely pious medieval culture far from the European mainstream. Gorky did not proclaim his Armenian roots publicly, as Miró constantly propagandized for Catalan culture; however, in emotional letters to his family written in Armenian, Gorky spoke of the profound influence on his art of the medieval illustrated manuscripts and wall paintings of his native province of Van, and certainly there is some coincidence between ornate orientalism of filigree and finial and the hypnotic Mozarabic element that remains in Catalonian *art nouveau* (Auping, 1995, p. 173).

One may perhaps attribute Miró's literalism to the concreteness of Spanish mysticism, in which he was steeped. Like Spaniards, Americans frequently manifest a taste for an extremely literal realism. The popularity in America of *trompe l'oeil* painting around the turn of the century, and of Magic Realism in the 1930s and Photo-Realism in the 1970s are expressions of this taste. Miró's hyper-realism of the *detailist* period (Figure 16-7), however, is based neither on photography, like American *trompe l'oeil* styles, nor involved with bizarre juxtapositions. With the exception of his Dada constructions and collages of the 1930s, Miró does not create strangeness by juxtaposing unlikely images.

Instead of collaging fragments in imitation of cinematic montage, Miró creates an entire "other" world, which is unreal, but within its own context, entirely consistent.

The two other artists one thinks of who have fashioned similar parallel universes are Dubuffet and Oldenburg, who were both influenced by Miró's capacity to homogenize landscape, figure, still-life and architecture into a single physical consistency. In all these artists, there is a certain element of caricature, but it is caricature in the grand manner—a kind of medieval carnival of masked and costumed actors. Coincidentally, Miró, Dubuffet and Oldenburg realized themselves as public artists, and all three were involved with the popular spectacle of theater.

America's unique and intense appreciation of Miró before 1960 depended on a perception of his art as youthful, fresh, experimental and innovative. It was all of these things. But it was also rooted in a culture absolutely unknown and unknowable to the fans in New York and California, that of Catalan nationalism and medieval Catalan art. For, paradoxically, the extreme radicality and revolutionary daring of Miró's art were rooted in ancient traditions and a culture and language that had been officially declared dead.

The admiration of Americans for the Catalan resistance to Franco notwithstanding, there was no way his American public could understand how closely Miró identified his art with the project of the restitution of the Catalan language and nation, nor how he resolved his crises of identity by looking not forward but backward, to the Paleolithic origins of work in hunting and gathering and in farming, the life-affirming activity of his beloved grandfather who validated his own

16-7
JOAN MIRÓ
HORSE, PIPE AND RED
FLOWER, 1920
*Oil on canvas, 32½ × 29½ in
(82.6 × 74.9 cm)*
*Philadelphia Museum of
Art. Gift of Mr and Mrs
Earle Miller. © 1996
Artists Rights Society
(ARS), NY/ADAGP, Paris*

anti-bourgeois choice. A society whose central myth was frontier would find it difficult to comprehend the morality of looking backward toward medieval piety, and the anti-industrial (and therefore anti-progressive) identification of art not with alienation, but with the humble life of the heroic Catalan peasant.

REFERENCES

Auping, M. (1995). *Arshile Gorky: The Breakthrough Years*. National Gallery of Art, Washington, D.C.

Gallego, J. (1968). *Vision et Symboles dans la Peinture Espangnole du Siecle d'Or*. Editions Klinckseck, Paris.

Jamison, K.R. (1993). *Touched with Fire: Manic-depressive Illness and the Artistic Temperament*, pp. 207–216. Free Press Macmillan, New York.

Miró, J. (1915). Letter to E.C. Ricart. Cited in Rowell (1992: see below), pp. 48, 49.

Miró, J. (1928). A Conversation with Joan Miró, by Frances C Trabal. Cited in Rowell (1992: see below), pp. 92–97.

Miró, J. (1957). To Jacques Dupin. Cited in Rowell (1992: see below), pp. 44, 45.

Miró, J. (1974). Miró: Now I Work on the Floor, by Yvon Taillandier. Cited in Rowell (1992: see below), p. 282.

Miró, J. (1978). Three Hours with Joan Miró, by Santiago Amón. Cited in Rowell (1992: see below), p. 297.

Nordau, M. (1968). *Degeneration*. H. Fertig, New York.

O'Connor, F.V. & Thaw, E.V. (1978). *Jackson Pollock: A Catalogue Raisonné of Paintings, Drawings, and Other Works*, Vol. 4. Yale University Press, New Haven.

Rank, O. (1984). *The Psychology of the Artist*.

Rank, O. (1989). *Art and Artists: Creative Urge and Personality Development*. W.W. Norton, New York.

Richardson, J. (1991). *A Life of Picasso*, Vol. I. Random House, New York.

Rose, B. (1982) *Miró in America*. The Museum of Fine Arts, Houston.

Rowell, M. (Ed.) (1992). *Joan Miró: Selected Writings and Interviews*. DeCapo Press, New York.

Rubin, W. (1973). *Miró in the Collection of The Museum of Modern Art*. The Museum of Modern Art, New York.

Taylor, E. (1984). *William James on Exceptional Mental States: the 1896 Lowell Lectures*. University of Massachusetts Press, Amherst, MA.

Wilson, E. (1965). *The Wound and the Bow*. Oxford University Press, London.

Wittkower, R. & Wittkower, M. (1963). *Born under Saturn*. W.W. Norton, New York.

PART IV
ABSTRACT EXPRESSIONISTS OF THE NEW YORK SCHOOL

INTRODUCTION

JOSEPH J. SCHILDKRAUT

In the first chapter of Part IV we have reprinted (with slight modifications) Robert Rosenblum's classic paper of 1961, "The Abstract Sublime", a harbinger of his highly acclaimed book, *Modern Painting and the Northern Romantic Tradition: Friedrich to Rothko* (Rosenblum, 1975). In this paper, Rosenblum demonstrated the relationship of Abstract Expressionist painting to "the visionary nature-painting of a century ago". Comparing the Abstract Expressionists to the great nineteenth century romantic painters, Caspar David Friedrich and J.M.W. Turner, Rosenblum writes of their "heroic search for a private myth to embody the sublime power of the supernatural . . ."

The following chapter by Joseph J. Schildkraut, Alissa J. Hirshfeld & Jane M. Murphy, "Depressive Disorders, Spirituality and Early Deaths in the Abstract Expressionists of the New York School", presents a "case study" of the high prevalence of depression and depression-related disorders in a group of 15 of these artists. Using the technique of psychic automatism (based on free association) in order to reveal unconscious material, the Abstract Expressionists aspired to produce an art that addressed the mythic themes of creation, birth, life and death, an art that was "tragic and timeless".

The last chapter is "Abstract Expressionism as Psychobiography: The Life and Suicide of Arshile Gorky" by Kareen K. Akiskal and Hagop S. Akiskal. A pioneer in the development of the new abstract art in America, Gorky provided a "vital link between European modern art and American Abstract Expressionism". In this chapter, the Akiskals examine "the life history and circumstances of the suicide of Arshile Gorky, from a psychological perspective", with the aim of documenting "his cyclical melancholy which contributed to his becoming one of America's greatest painters". They conclude, "In the end he lost everything—his life included—to give birth to . . . Abstract Expressionism."

REFERENCE

Rosenblum, R. (1975). *Modern Painting and the Northern Romantic Tradition: Friedrich to Rothko.* Harper & Row, New York.

CHAPTER 17

THE ABSTRACT SUBLIME

ROBERT ROSENBLUM

"It's like a religious experience!" With such words, a pilgrim I met in Buffalo last winter attempted to describe his unfamiliar sensations before the awesome phenomenon created by 72 Clyfford Stills at the Albright Art Gallery. A century and a half ago, the Irish romantic poet, Thomas Moore, also made a pilgrimage to the Buffalo area, except that his goal was Niagara Falls. His experience, as recorded in a letter to his mother of July 24 1804, similarly beggared prosaic response:

"I felt as if approaching the very residence of the Deity; the tears started into my eyes; and I remained, for moments after we had lost sight of the scene, in that delicious absorption which pious enthusiasm alone can produce. We arrived at the New Ladder and descended to the bottom. Here all its awful sublimities rushed full upon me ... My whole heart and soul ascended towards the Divinity in a swell of devout admiration, which I never before experienced. Oh! Bring the atheist here, and he cannot return an atheist! I pity the man who can coldly sit down to write a description of these ineffable wonders: much more do I pity him who can submit them to the admeasurement of gallons and yards ... We must have new combinations of language to describe the Fall of Niagara."

Moore's bafflement before a unique spectacle, his need to abandon measurable reason for mystical empathy, are the very ingredients of the mid-twentieth-century spectator's "religious experience" before the work of Still. During the romantic movement, Moore's response to Niagara would have been called an experience of the "Sublime", an aesthetic category that suddenly acquires fresh relevance in the face of the most astonishing summits of pictorial heresy attained in America in the last 15 years.

Originating with Longinus, the Sublime was fervently explored in the later eighteenth and early nineteenth centuries and recurs constantly in the aesthetics of such writers as Burke, Reynolds, Kant, Diderot and Delacroix. For them and for their contemporaries, the Sublime provided a flexible semantic container for the murky new romantic experiences of awe, terror, boundlessness and divinity that began to rupture the decorous confines of earlier aesthetic systems. As imprecise and irrational as the feelings it tried to name, the Sublime could be extended to art as well as to nature. One of its major expressions, in fact, was the painting of sublime landscapes.

A case in point is the dwarfing immensity of Gordale Scar, a natural wonder of Yorkshire and a goal of many Romantic tourists. Re-created on canvas between 1811 and 1815 by the British painter James Ward (1769–1855), *Gordale Scar* (Figure 17-1) is meant to stun the spectator into an experience of the Sublime that may well be unparalleled in painting until

17-1
JAMES WARD
A VIEW OF GORDALE, IN THE
MANOR OF EAST MALHAM IN
CRAVEN, YORKSHIRE, THE
PROPERTY OF LORD
RIBBLESDALE (GORDALE
SCAR), (c. 1812–14)
Oil on canvas, 10 ft 11 in
× 13 ft 10 in (332.7 ×
421.6 cm)
Tate Gallery, London/Art
Resource, New York

a work like Clyfford Still's *Untitled, 1957* (Figure 17-2). In the words of Edmund Burke, whose *Philosophical Enquiry into the Origin of Our Ideas of the Sublime and the Beautiful* (1757) was the most influential analysis of such feelings: "Greatness of dimension is a powerful cause of the sublime". Indeed, in both the Ward and the Still, the spectator is first awed by the sheer magnitude of the sight before him (Ward's canvas is 131 × 166 inches; Still's, 112 × 154 inches). At the same time, his breath is held by the dizzy drop to the pit of an abyss; and then, shuddering like Moore at the

bottom of Niagara, he can only look up with what senses are left him and gasp before something akin to divinity.

Lest the dumbfounding size of these paintings prove insufficient to paralyze the spectator's traditional habits of seeing and thinking, both Ward and Still insist on a comparably bewildering structure. In the Ward, the chasms and cascades, whose vertiginous heights transform the ox, deer and cattle into Lilliputian toys, are spread out into unpredictable patterns of jagged silhouettes. No laws of man or man-made beauty can account for these God-made shapes; their mysterious, dark

188

formations (echoing Burke's belief that obscurity is another cause of the Sublime) lie outside the intelligible boundaries of aesthetic law. In the Still, Ward's limestone cliffs have been translated into an abstract geology, but the effects are substantially the same. We move physically across such a picture like a visitor touring the Grand Canyon or journeying to the center of the earth. Suddenly, a wall of black rock is split by a searing crevice of light, or a stalactite threatens the approach to a precipice. No less than caverns and waterfalls, Still's paintings seem the product of eons of change; and their flaking surfaces, parched like bark or slate, almost promise that this natural process will continue, as unsusceptible to human order as the immeasurable patterns of ocean, sky, earth or water. And not the least awesome thing about Still's work is the paradox that the more elemental and monolithic its vocabulary becomes, the more complex and mysterious are

its effects. As the romantics discovered, all the sublimity of God can be found in the simplest natural phenomena, whether a blade of grass or an expanse of sky.

In his *Critique of Judgment* (1790), Kant tells us that whereas "the Beautiful in nature is connected with the form of the object, which consists in having boundaries, the Sublime is to be found in a formless object, so far as in it, or by occasion of it, *boundlessness* is represented". Indeed, such a breathtaking confrontation with a boundlessness in which we also experience an equally powerful totality is a motif that continually links the painters of the Romantic Sublime with a group of recent American painters who seek out what might be called the "Abstract Sublime". In the context of two sea meditations by two great romantic painters, Caspar David Friedrich's *Monk by the Sea* of about 1809 (Figure 17-3), and Joseph Mallord William Turner's *Evening Star*

17-3
CASPAR DAVID FRIEDRICH
THE MONK BY THE SEA,
1808–10
43¼ × 67½ in
(110 × 171.5 cm)
Nationalgalerie,
Staatliche Museen, Berlin.
Photograph by Jörg P.
Anders. Foto Marburg/Art
Resource, New York

(Figure 17-4), Mark Rothko's *Green on Blue* of 1954 (Figure 17-5) reveals affinities of vision and feeling. Replacing the abrasive, ragged fissures of Ward's and Still's real and abstract gorges with a no less numbing phenomenon of light and void, Rothko, like Friedrich and Turner, places us on the threshold of those shapeless infinities discussed by the aestheticians of the Sublime. The tiny monk in the Friedrich and the fisher in the Turner establish, like the cattle in *Gordale Scar,* a poignant contrast between the infinite vastness of a pantheistic God and the infinite smallness of His creatures. In the abstract language of Rothko, such literal detail—a bridge of empathy between the real spectator and the presentation of a transcendental landscape—is no

longer necessary; we ourselves are the monk before the sea, standing silently and contemplatively before these huge and soundless pictures as if we were looking at a sunset or a moonlit night. Like the mystic trinity of sky, water and earth that, in the Friedrich and Turner, appears to emanate from one unseen source, the floating, horizontal tiers of veiled light in the Rothko seem to conceal a total, remote presence that we can only intuit and never fully grasp. These infinite, glowing voids carry us beyond reason to the Sublime; we can only submit to them in an act of faith and let ourselves be absorbed into their radiant depths.

If the Sublime can be attained by saturating such limitless expanses with a luminous, hushed stillness, it can also be reached inversely by filling this void

with a teeming, unleashed power. Turner's art, for one, presents both of these sublime extremes. In his *Snowstorm* of 1842 (Figure 17-6), the infinities are dynamic rather than static, and the most extravagant of nature's phenomena are sought out as metaphors for this experience of cosmic energy. Steam, wind, water, snow and fire spin wildly around the pitiful work of man—the ghost of a boat—in vortical rhythms that suck one into a sublime whirlpool before reason can intervene. And if the immeasurable spaces and incalculable energies of such a Turner evoke the elemental power of creation, other work of the period grapples even more literally with these primordial forces. Turner's contemporary, John Martin (1779–1854), dedicated his erratic life to the pursuit of an art which, in the words of the *Edinburgh Review* (1829), ". . . awakes a sense of awe and sublimity, beneath which the mind seems overpowered". Of the cataclysmic themes that alone satisfied him, *The Creation*, an engraving of 1831 (Figure 17-7), is characteristically sublime. With Turner, it aims at nothing short of God's full power, upheaving rock, sky, cloud, sun, moon, stars and sea in the primal act. With its torrential description of molten paths of energy, it locates us once more on a near-hysterical brink of sublime chaos.

That brink is again reached when we stand before a *perpetuum mobile* of Jackson Pollock, whose gyrating labyrinths recreate in the metaphorical language of abstraction the super-human turbulence depicted more literally in Turner and Martin. In *Number 1, 1948* (Figure 17-8), we are as immediately plunged into divine fury as we are drenched in Turner's sea; in neither case can our minds provide systems of navigation. Again, sheer magnitude can help produce the Sublime. Here, the very size of the Pollock—68 × 104 inches—permits no pause before the engulfing; we are almost physically

17-5
MARK ROTHKO
GREEN ON BLUE, 1956
*Oil on canvas, 89¾ ×
63½ in (228 × 161 cm)
Collection of the
University of Arizona
Museum of Art, Tucson.
Gift of Edward J.
Gallagher, Jr. © 1996 Kate
Rothko–Prizel &
Christopher
Rothko/Artists Rights
Society (ARS), NY*

the awesome vistas of telescope and microscope, his pictures leave us dazzled before the imponderables of galaxy and atom.

The fourth master of the Abstract Sublime, Barnett Newman, explores a realm of sublimity so perilous that it defies comparison with even the most adventurous romantic explorations into sublime nature. Yet it is worth noting that in the 1940s Newman, like Still, Rothko and Pollock, painted pictures with more literal references to an elemental nature; and that subsequently he spoke of a strong desire to visit the tundra, so that he might have the sensation of being surrounded by four horizons in a total surrender to spatial infinity. In abstract terms, at least, some of his paintings of the 1950s already approach this sublime goal. In its all-embracing width, Newman's *Vir Heroicus Sublimis* (Figure 17-9) puts us before a void as terrifying, if exhilarating, as the arctic emptiness of the tundra; and in its passionate reduction of pictorial means to a single hue (warm red) and a single kind of structural division (vertical) for some one hundred and forty-four square feet, it likewise achieves a simplicity as heroic and sublime as the protagonist of its title. Yet again, as with Still, Rothko and Pollock, such a rudimentary vocabulary creates bafflingly complex results. Thus the single hue is varied by an extremely wide range of light values; and these unexpected mutations occur at intervals that thoroughly elude any rational system. Like the other three masters of the Abstract Sublime, Newman bravely abandons the securities of familiar pictorial geometries in favor of the risks of untested pictorial intuitions; and like them, he produces awesomely simple mysteries that evoke the primeval moment of creation. His very titles (*Onement, The Beginning, Pagan*

lost in this boundless web of inexhaustible energy. To be sure, Pollock's generally abstract vocabulary allows multiple readings of its mood and imagery, although occasional titles (*Full Fathom Five, Ocean Greyness, The Deep, Greyed Rainbow*) may indicate a more explicit region of nature. But whether achieved by the most blinding of blizzards or the most gentle of winds and rains, Pollock invariably evokes the sublime mysteries of nature's untamable forces. Like

Void, Death of Euclid, Adam, Day One) attest to this sublime intention. Indeed, a quartet of the largest canvases by Newman, Still, Rothko and Pollock might well be interpreted as a post-World-War-II myth of Genesis. During the romantic era, the sublimities of nature gave proof of the divine; today, such supernatural experiences are conveyed through the abstract medium of paint alone. What used to be pantheism has now become a kind of "paint-theism".

Much has been written about how these four masters of the Abstract Sublime rejected the cubist tradition and replaced its geometric vocabulary and intellectual structure with a new kind of space created by flattened, spreading expanses of light, color and plane. Yet it should not be overlooked that this denial of the cubist tradition was not only determined by formal needs, but also by emotional ones that, in the anxieties of the atomic age, suddenly seemed to correspond with a romantic tradition of the irrational and the awesome as well as with a romantic vocabulary of boundless energies and limitless spaces. The line from the Romantic Sublime to the Abstract Sublime is broken and devious, for its tradition is more one of erratic, private feeling than submis-

17-6
JOSEPH MALLORD WILLIAM
TURNER
STEAMBOAT (SNOWSTORM),
1842
Oil on canvas, 36 × 48 in
(91.4 × 121.9 cm)
Tate Gallery, London/Art
Resource, New York

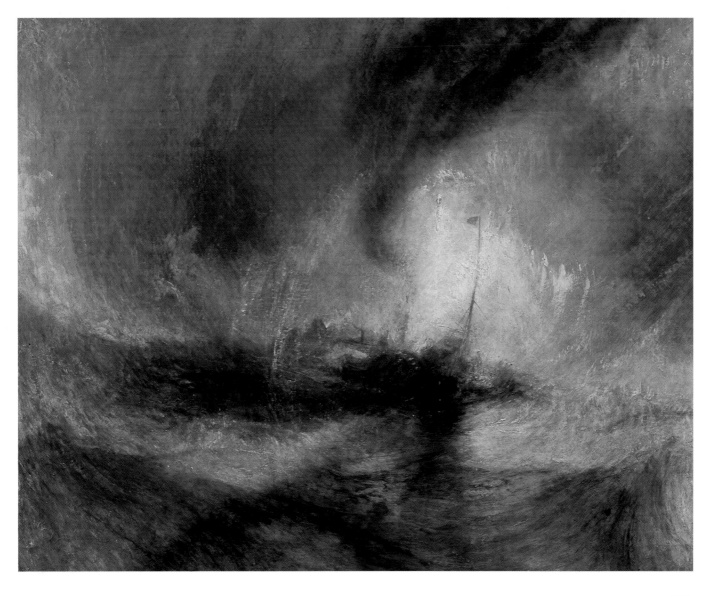

17-7
JOHN MARTIN
THE CREATION, FROM
ILLUSTRATIONS OF THE BIBLE,
1831
Mezzotint, 10½ × 14⅛ in
(26.7 × 35.9 cm)
Print collection, Miriam
and Ira D. Wallach
Division of Art, Prints and
Photographs. The New
York Public Library. Astor,
Lenox and Tilden
Foundations

sion to objective disciplines. If certain vestiges of sublime landscape painting linger into the later nineteenth century in the popularized panoramic travelogues of Americans like Bierstadt and Church (with whom Dore Ashton has compared Still), the tradition was generally suppressed by the international domination of the French tradition, with its familiar values of reason, intellect and objectivity. At times, the counter-values of the northern romantic tradition have been partially reasserted (with a strong admixture of French pictorial discipline) by such masters as van Gogh, Ryder, Marc, Klee, Feininger and Mondrian; but its most spectacular manifestations—the sublimities of British and German romantic landscape—have only been resurrected after 1945 in America, where the authority of Parisian painting has been challenged to an unprecedented degree. In its heroic search for a private myth to embody the sublime power of the supernatural, the art of Still, Rothko, Pollock and Newman should remind us once more that the disturbing heritage of the romantics has not yet been exhausted.

ACKNOWLEDGEMENT

This essay originally appeared in Art News, **59** (10) (February, 1961), pp. 38–41 and 56–57. Copyright © 1961 ART NEWS, February, reprinted by courtesy of the publisher.

17-8
JACKSON POLLOCK
NUMBER 1, 1948, 1948
Oil and enamel on unprimed canvas, 68 × 104 in (172.7 × 264.2 cm)
The Museum of Modern Art, New York. Purchase. Photograph © 1995 The Museum of
Modern Art, New York. © 1996 The Pollock–Krasner Foundation/Artists Rights Society (ARS), NY

17-9
BARNETT NEWMAN
VIR HEROICUS SUBLIMIS, 1950–51
Oil on canvas, 7 ft 11⅜ in × 17 ft 9¼ in (242.2 × 541.7 cm). The Museum of Modern Art,
New York. Gift of Mr and Mrs Ben Heller. Photograph © 1996 The Museum of Modern Art, New York

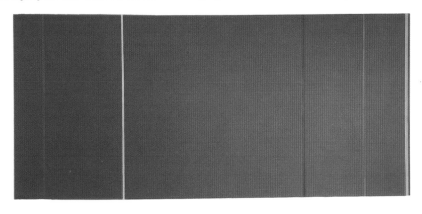

CHAPTER 18

DEPRESSIVE DISORDERS, SPIRITUALITY AND EARLY DEATHS IN THE ABSTRACT EXPRESSIONIST ARTISTS OF THE NEW YORK SCHOOL

Joseph J. Schildkraut, Alissa J. Hirshfeld and Jane M. Murphy

In a previous study (Schildkraut & Hirshfeld, 1995, see also Chapter 12, this volume), we showed how depression played a crucial role in the artistic development of the twentieth-century Spanish artist Joan Miró; and we discussed the relationship of Miró's spiritual beliefs and yearnings for transcendence both to his depression and to his art-making. Following up on this line of inquiry, we have gone on to explore similar issues in the lives and works of the mid-twentieth-century abstract expressionist artists of the New York School (many of whom were strongly influenced by Miró).

This chapter will present a case study of the prevalence of psychopathology, particularly mood disorders, in 15 of the abstract expressionist artists who, after the end of World War II, effectively shifted the center of gravity of modern Western art from Paris to New York, while establishing themselves among the masters of twentieth-century art. As well as documenting the prevalence of psychopathology found in a group of these artists, we shall consider how their psychopathology may have been related to, or even have contributed to, the pathfinding art that they produced.

The 15 artists in this group include: Jackson Pollock, Mark Rothko, Robert Motherwell, Barnett Newman, Arshile Gorky, Franz Kline, Willem de Kooning, Philip Guston, William Baziotes, Adolph Gottlieb, Clyfford Still, Ad Reinhardt, James Brooks, Bradley Walker Tomlin and David Smith (see Note, p. 209).

"WHERE DO WE COME FROM? WHAT ARE WE? WHERE ARE WE GOING?"

Although they have been classified as a school, the abstract expressionist artists came from a variety of cultural backgrounds and emerged with divergent styles. However, all were intent on creating an art with psychological and spiritual significance addressing mythical themes and confronting the elemental issues of creation, birth, life and death.

From the surrealists they borrowed the techniques of psychic automatism, based on free association, which involved painting without preplanning in order to reveal unconscious material. In both form and content these artists were strongly influenced by Miró, whose 1925 painting, *Birth of the World* (Figure 12-4, p. 117), may be seen as a precursor of Abstract Expressionism (Schildkraut, 1982). Looking back to the end of the previous century, in Paul Gauguin's masterpiece of 1897 (Figure 18-1), some 50 years before the abstract expressionists, we find an explicit statement of what would become the subject of their art: "Where do we come from? What are we? Where are we going?" A few examples may be illustrative here.

Where do we come from? Mark Rothko gives us a glimpse of the magic and mystery of our origins in his 1944 painting, *Slow Swirl by the Edge of the Sea* (Figure 18-2). *What are we?* Tragic and inseparable, intimations of human grandeur and human frailty may be revealed in Rothko's painting, *Green and Tangerine on Red* of 1956 (Figure 18-3). *Where are we going?* The inevitability of death confronts the viewer of the black and gray works (Figure 18-4) Rothko painted during a period of depression in 1969 and 1970, shortly before he killed himself.

Turning to the work of Barnett Newman, we are again brought back to our origins in his painting *Pagan Void* of 1946 (Figure 18-5). Moving ahead to his work of 1950–51, Figure 17-9, p. 195 shows Newman's extraordinary large-scale celebration of humanity,

Vir Heroicus Sublimis (Man Heroic Sublime); while in *Stations of the Cross, Number 1* of 1958 (Figure 18-6), the first in his series of meditations on Christ's Passion, on man's suffering and death, Newman begins to ask the age-old question, "Lema Sabachthani?" (Why have you forsaken me?) (Newman, 1966).

Jackson Pollock, too, explores our mythic origins in his mysterious and compelling painting, *Guardians of the Secret* of 1943 (Figure 18-7); and in *Autumn Rhythm* (Figure 18-8), one of three large-scale abstract poured paintings created in 1950 during an extended period of relative sobriety (see below), we see one of Pollock's rarely revealed visions of expansive natural grandeur and human vitality. But it is in *Number 32* (Figure 18-9), with his palette restricted to black, that Pollock achieved the most open and graceful yet hauntingly mysterious of his 1950 abstract masterpieces. After resuming his drinking in 1951 and 1952, Pollock produced a series of black poured paintings in which figures re-emerged, illustrated by *Echo, Number 25* of 1951 (Figure 18-10). Overtones of death and mourning are conveyed in these enigmatic black paintings.

18-1
PAUL GAUGUIN
WHERE DO WE COME FROM? WHAT ARE WE? WHERE ARE WE GOING?, 1897
Oil on canvas, 54¾ × 147½ in (139.1 × 374.6 cm)
Tompkins Collection. Courtesy, Museum of Fine Arts, Boston

18-2
MARK ROTHKO
SLOW SWIRL BY THE EDGE OF THE SEA, 1944
Oil on canvas, 6 ft 3⅜ in × 7 ft ¾ in (191.4 × 215.2 cm)
The Museum of Modern Art, New York. Bequest of Mrs Mark Rothko through the Mark Rothko Foundation, Inc. Photograph © 1996 The Museum of Modern Art, New York. © 1996 Kate Rothko–Prizel and Christopher Rothko/Artists Rights Society (ARS), NY

18.3
MARK ROTHKO
GREEN AND TANGERINE ON RED, 1956
Oil on canvas, 93½ × 69⅛ in (237.4 × 175.5 cm)
The Phillips Collection, Washington D.C. © 1996 Kate Rothko–Prizel and Christopher Rothko/Artists Rights Society (ARS), NY

18-4
MARK ROTHKO
UNTITLED, 1970
Acrylic on canvas,
80¼ × 69⅛ in
(203.7 × 175.6 cm)
Photograph courtesy of
PaceWildenstein. © 1996
Kate Rothko–Prizel and
Christopher
Rothko/Artists Rights
Society (ARS), NY

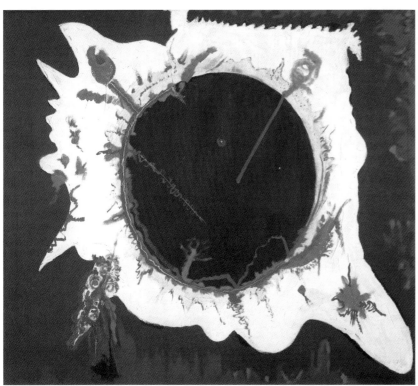

18-5
BARNETT NEWMAN
PAGAN VOID, 1946
Oil on canvas,
33 × 38 in (83.8 × 96.5 cm)
Gift of Annalee Newman
in honor of the 50th
anniversary of the
National Gallery of Art.
© 1995 Board of Trustees,
National Gallery of Art,
Washington

18-6 *(Overleaf)*
BARNETT NEWMAN
STATIONS OF THE CROSS, FIRST
STATION, 1958
Magna on canvas,
77⅞ × 60½ in
(197.8 × 153.7 cm)
National Gallery of Art,
Washington. Robert and
Jane Meyerhoff
Collection. © 1995 Board
of Trustees, National
Gallery of Art, Washington

18-7 (above)
JACKSON POLLOCK
The Guardians of the Secret, 1943
Oil on canvas,
40⅜ × 75⅜ in
(122.6 × 191.5 cm)
San Francisco Museum of Modern Art, Albert M. Bender Collection. Albert M. Bender Bequest Fund Purchase. © 1996 The Pollock–Krasner Foundation/Artists Rights Society (ARS), NY

18-8 (left)
JACKSON POLLOCK
Autumn Rhythm, 1950
Oil on canvas, 105 × 207 in
(266.7 × 525.8 cm)
The Metropolitan Museum of Art. George A. Hearn Fund, 1957. © 1996 The Pollock–Krasner Foundation/Artists Rights Society (ARS), NY

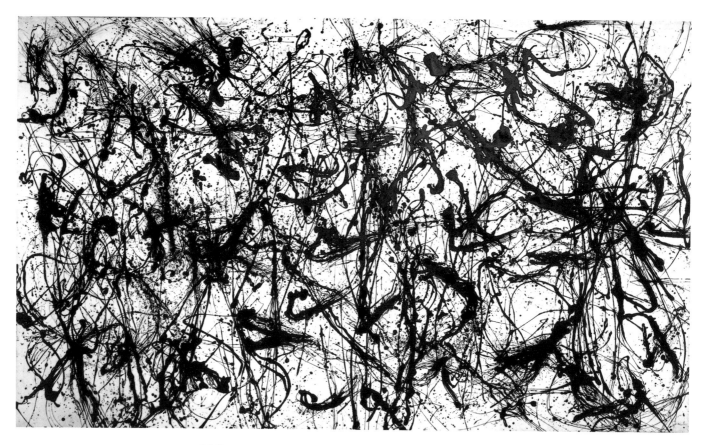

18-9
JACKSON POLLOCK
NUMBER 32, 1950, 1950
*Enamel on canvas,
8 ft 10 in × 15 ft
(269 × 457.5 cm)*
*Kunstsammlung
Nordrhein–Westfalen,
Düsseldorf. Photograph
© VG Bild-Kunst, Bonn.
© 1996 The
Pollock–Krasner
Foundation/Artists Rights
Society (ARS), NY*

18-10
JACKSON POLLOCK
*ECHO (NUMBER 25, 1951),
1951*
*Enamel on unprimed
canvas, 7 ft 7⅞ in × 7ft 2 in
(233.4 × 218.4 cm)*
*The Museum of Modern
Art, New York. Acquired
through the Lillie P. Bliss
Bequest and the Mr and
Mrs David Rockefeller
Fund. Photograph © 1995
The Museum of Modern
Art, New York. © 1996 The
Pollock–Krasner
Foundation/Artists Rights
Society (ARS), NY*

PSYCHOPATHOLOGY AND EARLY DEATHS

As shown in Table 18-1, a strikingly high prevalence of psychopathology, predominantly depressions and depressive spectrum disorders, i.e. depressive or cyclothymic personalities or temperaments, was found in this group. These findings are documented in a series of brief biographical summaries that are included as an Appendix to this chapter. Confirmatory data may also be found in Kingsley (1992).

Wysuph, 1970), Rothko (Ashton, 1983; Seldes, 1974), Guston (Mayer, 1988; Storr, 1986; Ashton, 1976, pp. 76–84), and Baziotes (Paneth, 1951–62)—suffered from recurrent episodes of depressions, in several cases compounded by alcohol abuse. Gorky, one of the two artists in this sample who ended his life by suicide, appears to have had what the Akiskals have called a "depressive temperament", with cyclothymic features (Akiskal & Akiskal, personal communication and

TABLE 18-1
PSYCHOPATHOLOGY IN ABSTRACT EXPRESSIONIST ARTISTS

Artist	Depression or depressive spectrum disorder[a]	Alcoholism or alcohol abuse	Psychiatric treatment[b]	Suicide or single-vehicle accident	Father committed suicide
WILLIAM BAZIOTES	Yes				
JAMES BROOKS					
ARSHILE GORKY	Yes			Yes[c]	
ADOLPH GOTTLIEB					
PHILIP GUSTON	Yes	Yes	Yes		Yes
FRANZ KLINE	Yes(?)	Yes			Yes
WILLEM DE KOONING		Yes	Yes		
ROBERT MOTHERWELL	Yes	Yes(?)	Yes		
BARNETT NEWMAN					
JACKSON POLLOCK	Yes	Yes	Yes	Yes[d]	
AD REINHARDT		Yes			
MARK ROTHKO	Yes	Yes	Yes	Yes[c]	
DAVID SMITH	Yes(?)	Yes(?)		Yes[d]	
CLYFFORD STILL					
BRADLEY WALKER TOMLIN					

[a] Depressive spectrum disorder includes depressive, hyperthymic, and cyclothymic personalities or temperaments (Akiskal & Akiskal, 1992).
[b] Includes psychotherapy, psychoactive drug treatment, and hospitalization.
[c] Suicide.
[d] Single-vehicle accident while driving.

Four of these artists—Pollock (Naifeh & Smith, 1989; Landau, 1989; Solomon, 1987; Potter, 1985; O'Connor, 1980; O'Connor & Thaw, 1978; Kligman, 1974; Friedman, 1972; Chapter 19, this volume). In his book on Robert Motherwell's formative years as an artist, Mattison (1987, p. 96) writes of Motherwell's "introspective, often depressed personality" and his well documented, life-long obsession with death. Two other artists in our sample, Franz Kline and David Smith, also may have had depressive or cyclothymic temperaments, although in these instances documentation is less certain.

In addition, Pollock (Wysuph, 1970, pp. 9–10, 14) and Guston (Mayer, 1988, pp. 172, 173, 179) are described by relatives as having experienced swings of depression and elation (often accompanied by heightened productivity). And Baziotes (Paneth, 1951–62, pp. 27, 30) and Smith (Wilkin, 1984, p. 78) themselves described periods of markedly heightened productivity. While such periods of heightened productivity would be compatible with a hypomanic state, it should be recognized that the productivity of creative furor may not be identical with hypomanic excitement.

At least five of these 15 artists abused alcohol: they include Pollock (Naifeh & Smith, 1989; Landau, 1989; Solomon, 1987; Potter, 1985; Kligman, 1974), Rothko (Seldes, 1974), Kline (Gruen, 1989, pp. 212, 219, 240), Guston (Mayer, 1988), and de Kooning (Gruen, 1989, pp. 213, 221). And most likely others did as well (Schildkraut et al, 1994).

Six of the 15 artists in our sample are known to have had psychiatric treatment. Three were hospitalized for psychiatric problems: Pollock for alcoholism at least twice, once accompanied by depression (Potter, 1985, pp. 57, 67); Guston once for alcoholism and once for depression (Mayer, 1988, pp. 136, 172); and Reinhardt for what was termed "anxiety" (the nature of the underlying problem is not clear), which led to his discharge from the U.S. Navy during World War II (Lippard, 1981, p. 42). Two, Pollock (O'Connor, 1980, p. 3) and Rothko (Seldes, 1974, pp. 72, 92, 99), were treated with "psychoactive" drugs, while at least three, Pollock (Potter, 1985, pp. 58, 63, 221–222), Motherwell (Mattison, 1987, p. 178; Motherwell, personal communication), and de Kooning (Gruen, 1989, p. 203), were treated by psychotherapists.

Two of these artists, Gorky and Rothko, committed suicide; two, Pollock and Smith, died in single-vehicle accidents, Pollock while driving under the influence of alcohol and Smith while chasing a sports car in his truck, leading to the speculation that these accidents were suicide equivalents; and, two, Guston (Mayer, 1988, p. 12) and Kline (Gaugh, 1985, pp. 127–128), had fathers who killed themselves when their sons were young boys.

Thus, over 50% of these 15 artists had some form of documented psychopathology which included six definite and two possible depressive spectrum disorders. At least five abused alcohol. At least 40% received psychiatric treatment and 20% were hospitalized for psychiatric disorders. Two committed suicide. Two died in single-vehicle accidents while driving, and two had histories of paternal suicides (Table 18-1).

Of the 15 artists in the present study, all but Tomlin married. Ten of these 14 men—Rothko (Seldes, 1974, pp. 78–81), Pollock (Kligman, 1974), Gorky (Mooradian, 1980, p. 9; Rand, 1980, pp. 5, 8), Guston (Mayer, 1988, pp. 132–134), Motherwell (Arnason, 1977, pp. 230–237), Smith (Gray, 1968, p. 15; Marcus, 1983, pp. 24, 137), Kline (Dawson, 1967), de Kooning (Gruen, 1989, p. 208), Reinhardt (Chronology of A. Reinhardt), and Brooks (James Brooks, 1972)—had broken, tumultuous or multiple marriages. With regard to these data, it is of interest that Akiskal & Akiskal (1988) have commented on the stormy interpersonal relations, as well as the greater prevalence of artistic creativity, that they observed in the sub-group of depressive disorders that they classify as the "soft" bipolar spectrum.

Many of these artists died early deaths and close to 50% of the sample (7 of 15) were dead before the age of 60. As shown in Table 18-2, these included Gorky, Pollock, Baziotes, Kline, Reinhardt, Tomlin and Smith. Robert Motherwell, in a moving recollection of David Smith after ". . . he killed himself in his truck . . . chasing Ken Noland in his English Lotus sports car", noted (Gruen, 1989, p. 194): "And we both knew damn well the black abyss in each of us . . . the demons of guilt and depression that largely destroyed in one way or another the abstract expressionist generation".

Using procedures developed by Monson (1974), a standardized mortality ratio (SMR) was determined to compare the frequency of deaths before the age of 60 observed in this sample of abstract expressionist artists with the expected frequency based on age-, time-, sex- and race-specific mortality rates for the USA population. The year of entry selected for this analysis was 1945, the year that Ashton (1962, p. 9) cited as "the date often given for the identification of a new American painting", and the year in which World War II ended and these artists began to gain recognition in the New York art world.

The number of deaths before age 60 in this group of abstract expressionist artists was seven, whereas the expected number of deaths based on appropriately matched U.S. population data was 2.3, resulting in a standardized mortality ratio of 3.0—indicating that the rate of death by age 60 in this group was 3 times higher than expected ($\chi^2=7.42$, $P=0.006$). As shown in Table 18-2, of the seven deaths

TABLE 18-2
MORTALITY DATA ON ABSTRACT EXPRESSIONIST ARTISTS

Artist	Year of birth	Year of death	Age at death (years)	Cause of death
ARSHILE GORKY	1904	1948	44	Suicide
JACKSON POLLOCK	1912	1956	44	Single-vehicle accident
WILLIAM BAZIOTES	1912	1963	50	Lung cancer
FRANZ KLINE	1910	1962	51	Heart disease
AD REINHARDT	1913	1967	53	Heart attack
BRADLEY WALKER TOMLIN	1899	1953	53	Heart attack
DAVID SMITH	1906	1965	59	Single-vehicle accident
BARNETT NEWMAN	1905	1970	65	Heart attack
MARK ROTHKO	1903	1970	66	Suicide
PHILIP GUSTON	1913	1980	66	Heart attack
ADOLPH GOTTLIEB	1903	1974	70	Stroke
CLYFFORD STILL	1904	1980	75	Cancer
ROBERT MOTHERWELL	1915	1991	76	Heart attack or stroke
JAMES BROOKS	1906	1992	85	Alzheimer's disease
WILLEM DE KOONING	1904	Living		

before age 60, three were due to suicide or single-vehicle accidents and three due to heart disease, causes of death shown in other studies (Murphy et al, 1987, 1989) to account for the excess mortality seen in depressive disorders.

DISCUSSION

How may we relate the facts that the work of these abstract expressionist artists achieved a place of prominence in the history of modern Western art, and that so many of the artists themselves, like Miró (Schildkraut & Hirshfeld, 1995; Chapter 12, this volume), suffered from depressions or depression spectrum disorders? Before attempting to address this question, it is useful to consider some recent commentary on the role of art and the artist in society.

In her book, *What Is Art For?*, Dissanayake (1988) develops a hypothesis concerning the bioevolutionary significance of art. Based on anthropological evidence, she asserts that the function of art originally was to make communal rituals physically and emotionally gratifying, and that art thus reinforced selectively valuable behaviors that served to promote group cohesion and to reduce anxiety. Although modern Western industrial society lacks a communal belief system, and a coherent myth, as well as the shared rituals and religious symbols of significance that existed in the cultures she studied, Dissanayake (1988, p. 200) suggests that humanity may continue its biological craving for "socially shared significances", and that art can still provide a path to the sacred and spiritual even in a profane and fragmented world.

Along these lines, Gablik (1984, pp. 11–35), in her book *Has Modernism Failed?*, writes that before the rise of the independent artist during the modern era, artists were always thought to have a spiritual, "moral, and social mission". Art, like religion and ritual, "existed primarily to support the social order". The abstract expressionists, she notes, were the last generation of modern artists who challenged the secular materialism of society resulting from industrialization, and they were thus among "the last active carrier[s] of spiritual value in a materialist age".

Jung, whose ideas were well known to the abstract expressionists (Polcari, 1991), also wrote of the artist's role in putting the viewer back in touch with the spiritual forces repressed by the culture and in giving shape to the human yearning for transcendence. The artist, he asserted, "makes it possible for us to find our way back to the deepest springs of life". And he noted: "Therein lies the social significance of art: it is constantly at work educating the spirit of the age, conjuring up the forms in which the age is most lacking" (Jung, 1966a, p. 82). He continued:

"Art is a kind of innate drive that seizes a human being and makes him its instrument. The artist . . . is a 'collective man', a vehicle and moulder of the unconscious psychic life of mankind. That is his office and it is sometimes so heavy a burden that he is fated to sacrifice happiness and everything that makes life worth living for the ordinary human being" (Jung, 1966b, p. 101).

Csikszentmihalyi (1988, p. 217) similarly has stated that the absence of "transforming cultural symbols", which in earlier, more traditional societies enabled the artist both to express and to alleviate existential pain, forces the modern artist to reach into his own psyche "to deal directly with the raw suffering of human existence". And, as they explained in their own public statements, the abstract expressionists sought to transcend the pain inherent in their tragic subject matter and to create from it an art with spiritual significance.

Asserting that all art deals with "intimations of mortality" (Chave, 1989, pp. 191–192) and "the fact that man is born to die" (Ashton, 1983, p. 187)—(see Figure 18-11, Rothko, *Entombment I* of 1946), Rothko decried the demise of myth in a society in which "the urge for transcendental" experience is no longer granted "official status" (Rothko, 1947–48). And when asked about the meaning of his art on one occasion, Rothko replied (Rodman, 1957, pp. 93–94):

"I am interested only in expressing the basic human emotions—tragedy, ecstasy, doom, and so on. . . . The people who weep before my paintings are having the same religious experience I had when I painted them" (see Figure 18-12, Rothko, *Untitled* of 1967 #1261.67).

Moreover, in their famous letter of June 7, 1943, to a *New York Times* art critic, Gottlieb and Rothko (in collaboration with Newman) further proclaimed (Seldes, 1974, pp. 18–19; Ross, 1990, pp. 205–207): "We assert that the subject [of art] is crucial and only that subject is valid which is tragic and timeless" (see Figure 18-13, Gottlieb, *T* of 1950). "That", they noted, "is why we profess spiritual kinship with primitive and archaic art" (see Figure 18-14, Gottlieb, *Divisions of Darkness* of 1945).

And in his introduction to the catalog of *The Ideographic Picture* at Betty Parsons Gallery, New York, January 20–February 8 1947, Barnett Newman stated that "the basis of an

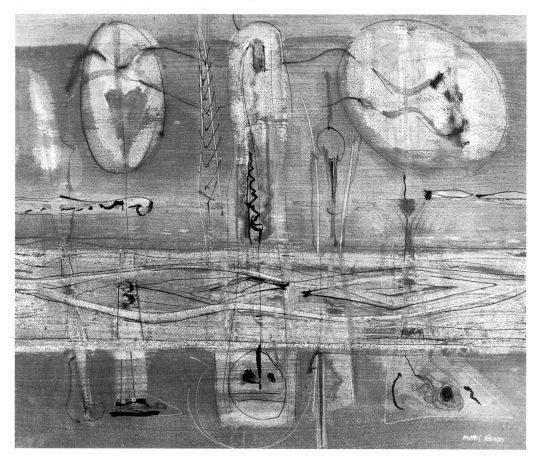

18-11
MARK ROTHKO
ENTOMBMENT I, 1946
Gouache on paper,
20⅜ × 25¾ in
(51.8 × 65.4 cm)
Purchase. Collection of Whitney Museum of American Art, New York. © 1995 Whitney Museum of American Art. © 1996 Kate Rothko–Prizel and Christopher Rothko/Artists Rights Society (ARS), NY

18-12
MARK ROTHKO
UNTITLED, 1967
Acrylic on paper, mounted on masonite, 29⅞ × 22 in (75.9 × 55.9 cm)
The Metropolitan Museum of Art, Gift of The Mark Rothko Foundation, Inc., 1985 (1985.63.1). Photograph by Lynton Gardiner. © 1996 Kate Rothko–Prizel and Christopher Rothko/Artists Rights Society (ARS), NY

18-13
ADOLPH GOTTLIEB
T, 1950
Oil on canvas, 48 × 36 in (121.9 × 91.4 cm)
The Metropolitan Museum of Art. Purchase, 1952, Mr and Mrs David M. Solinger Gift

aesthetic act is the pure idea . . . that makes contact with mystery—of life, of men, of nature, of the hard, black chaos that is death, or the grayer, softer chaos that is tragedy" (quoted by Sandler, 1970 p. 187).

The other abstract expressionists had similar concerns and voiced similar missions. Motherwell (1951, pp. 12–13) explained:

"I think that one's art is just one's effort to wed oneself to the universe, to unify oneself through union . . . . For make no mistake, abstract art is a form of mysticism. . . . that grew up in the historical circumstances that all mysticisms do, from a primary sense of gulf, an abyss, a void between one's lonely self and the world. Abstract art is an effort to close the void that modern men feel" (see Figure 18-15, Motherwell, *The Homely Protestant* of 1948).

And, speaking of his extensive series of paintings "Elegies to the Spanish Republic", his black and white meditations on the inevitability of death in life, Motherwell noted (Flam, 1983, p. 22), "Making an Elegy is like building a temple, an altar, a ritual place. . . . I seem to have hit on an archetypal image" (see Figure 18-16, Motherwell, *Elegy to the Spanish Republic No. 70* of 1961).

For some of these artists, the vision of art-making as a spiritual act grew from religious feelings stemming from childhood. Gorky, for example, influenced by his mother's pre-Christian Armenian hylozoic, pantheistic philosophy, believed that "painting is divine work" (Mooradian, 1978, p. 287) that can "harmonize sadness with beauty and thus discover life's essential reality" (Mooradian, 1978, p. 251). Newman, who was raised in a traditional Jewish household, titled his paintings with allusions to Jewish

biblical texts (Hess, 1969, p. 55) and occasionally even worked out dimensions for his canvases according to the Kabbalistic system of numerology (Hess, 1971, p. 69).

Others of these artists, not religious in a conventional sense, nevertheless created personal systems of meaning and values. Pollock, influenced by theosophical ideas, felt a mystical connection to nature (Potter, 1985, pp. 77, 115, 160) that he tried to convey in his art. Baziotes believed in the Taoist principle that the function of art is to communicate spiritual insight (Cavaliere, 1978, p. 28). And even Reinhardt, although he disapproved of organized religion, called painting a ritual process and had religious associations to his black canvases, based on his extensive reading in mystical philosophies. Quoting Meister Eckhardt, he called black "the divine dark" and, quoting Lao Tzu, "the dim and dark of Tao" (Lippard, 1981, p. 172).

Let us now reframe our earlier question and ask once again how the high prevalence of depressions or depressive spectrum disorders might have related to, and possibly even contributed to, the pathfinding art of the abstract expressionists. While there are many relevant issues which we have not considered (Schildkraut et al, 1994), based on the material presented in this chapter, we suggest what is clearly a reductionistic formulation, focusing on but one aspect of this complex relationship.

Depression inevitably leads to a turning inward and to the painful re-examination of the purpose of living and the possibility of dying. In our secular age, which lacks mediating communal belief systems and transforming cultural symbols, depression may have been particularly destructive to these artists at a personal level; yet, in instances such as those described in this chapter, depression in the artist may be of adaptive value to society at large. Thus, in bringing the abstract expressionist artists into direct and lonely confrontation with the ultimate existential question, whether to live or to die, depression may have put them in touch with the inexplicable mystery

18-14
ADOLPH GOTTLIEB
DIVISIONS OF DARKNESS, 1945
Oil on canvas, 24 × 30 in (61 × 76.2 cm)
The Everest Group Ltd, St. Paul, Minnesota, Photograph © 1990 Sotheby's Inc.

that lies at the very heart of the "tragic and timeless" art that they aspired to produce.

NOTE

The criteria for including artists in a group are always somewhat arbitrary. The specific artists we selected for our group are 14 of the 15 abstract expressionist painters defined as members of the New York School by Sandler (1970) in his seminal work, *The Triumph of American Painting: A History of Abstract Expressionism* (Sandler, 1970). They include William Baziotes, James Brooks, Arshile Gorky, Adolph Gottlieb, Philip Guston, Franz Kline, Willem de Kooning, Robert Motherwell, Barnett Newman, Jackson Pollock, Ad Reinhardt, Mark Rothko, Clyfford Still and Bradley Walker Tomlin. All of these artists were born between 1899 and 1915. (We have excluded Hans Hofmann from our group because, having been born in 1880, he was a generation older than the other artists and had matured as a painter in Europe before arriving in the

18-15
ROBERT MOTHERWELL
THE HOMELY PROTESTANT,
1948
Oil on canvas, 96 × 48¼ in
(243.8 × 121.9 cm)
The Metropolitan Museum
of Art. Gift of Robert
Motherwell, 1987. © 1996
Dedalus Foundation,
Inc./Licensed by VAGA,
New York, NY

USA. In addition, we have included David Smith (born in 1906), a sculptor closely associated with these painters (Ross, 1990), because his philosophy of art-making was similar to that of the painters in our group and, after Smith's death, Robert Motherwell identified him as a member of the first generation of abstract expressionists (Gruen, 1989, p. 194).

We have collected information on these artists from published biographies and from archival material such as letters and diary entries located at the Boston branch of the Archives of American Art, associated with the Smithsonian Institution. Diagnoses were made on the basis of this information following the principles and guidelines of DSM-III-R (American Psychiatric Association, 1987) for mood disorders and alcoholism and Akiskal & Akiskal (1992) for the affective temperaments. Since the subjects were not available for direct clinical interviews, however, we did not necessarily have access to specific details of the clinical history and documentation of specific signs and symptoms that are customarily ascertained during a clinical evaluation. In some cases, this limited our capacity to subclassify mood disorders to the extent specified by DSM-III-R. Retrospective diagnoses made on the basis of historical sources, in the absence of direct clinical examinations, are often problematic; and the problems and pitfalls of the historical approach have been discussed extensively by Runyan (1984). With the awareness that terms such as "depressed" or "melancholy" may be used metaphorically or in a romantic or nostalgic sense, we have sought to validate reports of "depression" by objective criteria such as suicide attempts, hospitalizations or other forms of treatment, loss of function (occupationally or socially) and other evidence that the person was disabled. Since we have tried to err on the conservative side, it is possible that artists whom we are reporting to have been free of significant psychopathology did, in fact, have such problems even though we have not found their illness to have been documented.

In order to compare the mortality experiences of the men in this group with an appropriate reference population, procedures developed by Monson (1974) were used. Implemented as a computer program, these procedures use cause-, age-, time-, gender- and race-specific mortality

18-16
ROBERT MOTHERWELL
ELEGY TO THE SPANISH
REPUBLIC, 70, 1961
Oil on canvas, 69 × 114 in
(175.3 × 289.6 cm)
The Metropolitan Museum
of Art. Anonymous Gift,
1965 (65.247). © 1996
Dedalus Foundation,
Inc./Licensed by VAGA,
New York, NY

rates for the USA during the period 1925–1980. The observed number of deaths among the artists is compared to the expected number of deaths based on vital statistics information for the U.S. population as a whole in order to provide a standardized mortality ratio.

APPENDIX
Biographical Summaries

Mark Rothko was born in 1903 in Vitebsk, Russia. His father, Jacob, emigrated to America in 1910, leaving his impoverished family in Russia. Three years later, Jacob died, shortly after his family was reunited in America. Attributing his melancholic disposition to his tragic childhood, Rothko experienced depressive episodes throughout his life (Ashton, 1983, p. 6). He briefly attended college at Yale, dropping out after his second year. He married for the first time at age 29.

Rothko's chronic depressions are described in detail by his biographers (Ashton, 1983; Seldes, 1974). Preoccupied with death throughout his life (Ashton, 1983, p. 43), Rothko suffered for years from insomnia and hypochondriasis. By the mid-1950s, Seldes writes, his "melancholic moods deepened into depressions", and he was addicted to alcohol and nicotine (Seldes, 1974, p. 37). After a heart attack in 1968, according to Seldes, a "pervasive melancholia" overtook him. He became obsessed with his health, believing his death to be imminent, and was plagued with self-pity, self-doubt, guilt and paranoia (Seldes, 1974, p. 71). He was treated with anti-depressant medication at that time (Seldes, 1974, pp. 72, 92, 99). One month prior to his death by suicide, Rothko reported to a doctor waking in the middle of the night, significant weight loss, inability to work and preoccupation with death (Seldes, 1974, pp. 99–100). Rothko committed suicide in 1970 at age 66.

Jackson Pollock was born in 1912 in Cody, Wyoming, to a working-class family. After high school, Pollock studied at New York's Art Students League. He married at age 33. Pollock's emotional problems have been extensively documented by many biographers (Naifeh & Smith, 1989; Landau, 1989; Solomon, 1987; Potter, 1985; O'Connor, 1980; O'Connor & Thaw, 1978; Kligman, 1974; Friedman, 1972; Wysuph, 1970). Beginning at age 25 and continuing throughout his life, Pollock saw a variety of psychotherapists—including Jungian analysts—to treat his depression and alcoholism (Naifeh & Smith, 1989; Potter, 1985). In 1938, he required hospitalization for alcoholism and depression (Potter, 1985, p. 57), and he was subsequently rehospitalized for alcoholism (Potter, 1985, p. 67).

Pollock's life-long despair can be traced to letters written during high school, a period of life Pollock described as a "damnable hell" (O'Connor & Thaw, 1978, p. 209). At 15, Pollock began drinking regularly, having been introduced to liquor by his father five years earlier. His drinking continued unabated throughout his life, except for two comparatively sober years (1948–50). While Pollock and his therapists commonly linked his problems to his overprotective yet emotionally cold mother, in fact his father, Roy, who was often on the road working, appears to have been aloof and possibly abusive. His sons remember that Roy drank heavily and that he suffered from what they called a "depressive mania" (Potter, 1985, pp. 21–23; O'Connor & Thaw, 1978, p. 226). When drunk, Jackson Pollock became destructive of people and property, and

he often required physical intervention by family, friends and even by the law (Potter, 1985, pp. 40–41, 53; Mayer, 1988, p. 65). Pollock died in a single-vehicle car crash in 1956 at age 44—driving while intoxicated, a risk he took on many occasions—leading to speculation that the accident was a suicide equivalent.

Arshile Gorky (originally named Vosdanig Adoian) was born in 1904 in Khorkom, Armenia, into a noble family (Mooradian, 1980, p. 12), which became impoverished during the Turkish siege of 1914. When Gorky was four, his father emigrated to America to avoid the draft, leaving his young son to witness the destruction of his country and the genocide of his people. Although the two were briefly reunited when Gorky came to America at age 16, they remained virtual strangers (Rand, 1980, p. 3). Fifteen-year-old Gorky's efforts to support his mother during the Turkish siege failed when she died in his arms as a result of starvation. Gorky had one year of high school education in America. He married for the first time at age 31.

In a series of letters written to his sister over the years 1937–1948, Gorky described moods of "melancholy" (Mooradian, 1978, pp. 255, 288), mental "agonies and torments" (Mooradian, 1978, p. 257), emotional struggles (Mooradian, 1978, p. 310), an inconsolable loneliness and emptiness (Mooradian, 1978, pp. 257–258), and nostalgia for his country; and he bitterly and vividly recalled the circumstances of his mother's death (Mooradian, 1978, p. 269). A series of catastrophes during the last two years of Gorky's life preceded his suicide. His studio barn burned down; he underwent a colostomy for cancer; his neck was broken and his painting arm temporarily paralyzed in a car accident; and his wife of seven years left him, taking their children with her. Gorky ended his tragic life in 1948, at age 44, when he hanged himself (see Akiskal & Akiskal, Chapter 19, this volume).

Philip Guston was born in 1913 in Montreal, Canada, to a family of poor Jewish immigrants. His father committed suicide when Philip was ten years old by hanging himself in the family shed—where Philip discovered the body (Mayer, 1988, p. 12). Guston completed two years of high school. He married at age 23.

Given to "morose introspection" (Mayer, 1988, p. 67), Guston suffered from life-long chronic depressions (Mayer, 1988; Storr, 1986; Ashton, 1976, pp. 76–84), insomnia and anxiety (Mayer, 1988, p. 191). In 1947, after receiving much public success, Guston experienced one of his periodic painting blocks, which resulted from self-doubts, and suffered deepening depression, which lasted into the mid-1950s (Guston, 1945; Mayer, 1988, pp. 37–48; Ashton, 1976, pp. 76–84). In 1961, he entered a depression which incapacitated him and kept him from painting for a year (Mayer, 1988, p. 99). In 1965, he was hospitalized to control his long-standing alcohol abuse (Mayer, 1988, p. 132). Letters Guston wrote during the early 1970s describe moving from despair to elation and back again. In 1974, he was hospitalized for "crippling depressions" and an ulcer (Mayer, 1988, pp. 172–173). Guston died following a heart attack in 1980 at age 66.

William Baziotes was born in 1912 in Pittsburgh, Pennsylvania, to an "ambitiously middle class" Greek immigrant family (Paneth, 1951–62, p. 13). Baziotes left high school in the middle of his second year, but later took art classes at the National Academy of Design in New York. He married at age 28. Baziotes described many periods of depression, interspersed with times of heightened productivity, throughout his life. At age 20, after deliberating for a year, during which he felt depressed and had trouble sleeping, Baziotes moved to New York (Paneth, 1951–62, p. 23).

Baziotes described feeling alienated from most people since his childhood, when he was teased by his classmates (Cavaliere, 1978, p. 31). The sense of alienation encountered when he first arrived in New York remained with him (Paneth, 1951–62, p. 23), and he frequently escaped to the solitude of his home town. Believing that isolation is important for the modern artist (Cavaliere, 1978, p. 49), during the 1950s he and his wife stopped socializing with other artists altogether (Hadler, 1978, p. 77). Baziotes died of lung cancer in 1963 at age 50.

Robert Motherwell was born in 1915 in Aberdeen, Washington, to upper-middle-class Protestant parents. After graduating from Stanford, he did graduate work in philosophy at Harvard and in art history at Columbia. He was married for the first time at age 26. Motherwell spoke often of his life-long "obsession with death" (Mattison, 1987, p. 42; Terenzio, 1980, p. 132). He recalled struggling to breathe as a child with asthma and attending a grand celebration on his sixteenth birthday "because nobody expected me to live [that long]" (Mattison, 1987, p. 42).

This preoccupation with death may account in part for his "introspective, often depressed personality" (Mattison, 1987, p. 96) and for his first-hand knowledge of what he called "the black abyss . . . that . . . the bounty and the drink could alleviate but not begin to fill" (Gruen, 1989, p. 194). He described himself as "filled with a self-torment and an anxiety" (Baur, 1957, p. 11), and he sought extensive psychotherapy (Mattison, 1987, p. 178). Motherwell also recounted a few specific instances of depression. The loneliness and unhappiness he felt in 1945–46 (Mattison, 1987, p. 142) was intensified by the break-up of the first of his marriages. After his first wife left him in the winter of 1948, feelings of abandonment, desperation and helplessness fueled 18-hour painting sessions, as well as contemplations of suicide (Mattison, 1987, p. 204). During the course of his life he periodically used alcohol to excess. Motherwell died of a heart attack (or stroke) in 1991 at age 76.

David Smith was born in 1906 in Decatur, Indiana, to middle-class Methodist parents. He attended college at Ohio University and Notre Dame for a brief period of time and then took classes at the Art Students League. He married for the first time at age 21.

Smith, who lived most of his adult life in the country, believed that isolation was crucial for his work, yet his loneliness often led to terrible despair (Gray, 1968, p. 16; Marcus, 1983, pp. 82, 190; Wilkin, 1984, p. 8; Merkert, 1986, pp. 44, 48). Motherwell, a close friend of Smith's during the last decade of his life, wrote that Smith (like Motherwell himself) "knew damned well the black abyss. . . . The demons of guilt and depression that largely destroyed in one way or another the abstract expressionist generation" (Gruen, 1989, p. 194). A diary from the winter of 1951–52 (written after the separation from his wife of 25 years), cited by many of his biographers (McCoy, 1973, p. 25; Wilkin, 1984, pp. 56–61; Merkert, 1986, pp. 44, 48) is worth quoting here at length:

"And so this being the happiest – is disappointing, the heights come seldom – the times of true height are so rare some seemingly high spots being suspected later as illusion – such being those contacts with people wherein elation comes related to or in dependence with others – the worth of existence is doubtful but if stuck with it – seems no other way but to proceed . . . and nothing has been as great or as wonderful as I have envisioned . . . in what do I lack balance – ability to live with another person – that ability to have acquaintances – and no friends . . . it would be nice not to be so lonesome sometimes – months pass without even the acquaintance of a mind. Acquaintances are pure waste – why do I measure my life by works – the other time seems waste – Can the life measured by work be illusion? . . . If I walk fifteen miles through mountains I'm exhausted enough to want to rest, and the mind won't . . . I hate to go to bed – to stay alive longer – I've slipped up on time – it all didn't get in – the warpage is in me."

In 1962, invited by the Italian government to create one or two sculptures for an upcoming festival, Smith created 27 sculptures, of which all but four were large-scale, in 30 days—a fact which raises the possibility of a hypomanic episode. Smith died in 1965 at age 59, when he drove his truck into a ditch while chasing artist Kenneth Noland's sports car. This ultimate act points to Smith's destructive energy, of which his biographers often speak—a violence which, according to biographers Gray (1968, p. 15) and Marcus (1983, pp. 24, 137), drove away his two wives.

Franz Kline was born in 1910 in Wilkes-Barre, Pennsylvania. When Kline was seven, his father, a saloon owner, committed suicide, at which point young Franz was sent to boarding school by his mother. Later, he would recall his unhappy childhood, exaggerating the number of years he was away from home (Gaugh, 1985, pp. 127–128). Kline interrupted his education at Boston University to study at professional art schools in Boston and London.

After his wife of 11 years, Elizabeth, was hospitalized in 1948 for a recurring psychiatric disorder, Kline began a series of affairs and years of alcohol abuse (Dawson, 1967; Gruen, 1989, pp. 212, 219, 240). Kline himself once noted, in regard to his series of sad clown portraits, "I have always felt that I'm like a clown and that my life might work out like a tragedy—a clown's tragedy" (Gaugh, 1985, p. 68). Motherwell believed that Kline was always "deeply alienated" from the world around him, his humor and affection covering "something deeper and blacker" (Gaugh, 1979, p. 43). After Kline was diagnosed with severe rheumatic heart disease in April 1961, Motherwell suggested that Kline brought about his own death by ignoring his doctor's orders to stop painting, drinking and smoking, lest he be dead within a year (Gaugh, 1979, p. 43). According to painter Elaine de Kooning, Kline "was kind of devoured" by drinking and painting too hard (Gruen, 1989, p. 212). He died in 1962 at age 51.

Barnett Newman was born in 1905 in New York City, to a well-to-do family of Russian immigrants. Newman graduated from New York's City College and took classes at the Art Students League. He married at age 31. Newman experienced a depression in February 1961, after the death of his brother, which left him unable to work for several months (Davies, 1983, pp. 13,

24). After a heart attack in 1957, which he later described as "instant psychoanalysis" (Hess, 1969, p. 58), Newman began his painting series entitled *Stations of the Cross: Lema Sabachthani* (Why have You forsaken me?), his personal meditations on "the unanswerable question of human suffering" (Newman, 1966). He died after a second heart attack in 1970 at age 65.

Ad Reinhardt was born in 1913 in Buffalo, New York, to poor German immigrant parents. After graduating from Columbia as an art major, he attended the National Academy of Art. He married for the first time at age 31. Reinhardt was discharged from the U.S. Navy in 1945, after being hospitalized for what was termed "anxiety" (Lippard, 1981, p. 42). Biographer Lippard writes of his compulsive, dogmatic personality, "No one seems to have felt they really knew him well or really were close friends of his. . . ." (Lippard, 1981, p. 136). Reinhardt died following a heart attack in 1967 at age 53.

Clyfford Still was born in 1904 in Grandin, North Dakota, to well-to-do parents. After graduating from Spokane University, he earned a Master's degree in Fine Arts at Washington State College. Still self-righteously eschewed the other abstract expressionists and the art establishment, guarding the privacy of his life with his wife and daughters and growing increasingly reclusive over the years. He refused to acknowledge the influence of any past artists, to align with any cultural traditions, or to exhibit his art in public galleries (Still, 1948; *New York Times*, 1980). Still died of cancer in 1980 at age 75.

Bradley Walker Tomlin was born in 1899 in Syracuse, New York, to a middle-class family. He graduated from Syracuse University, majoring in fine arts. Tomlin never married. The deepest attachment in his life was to artist Frank London. Tomlin shared a house with London and his wife for 20 years, and when London died in 1945, Tomlin experienced a period of sadness, loneliness and confusion (Chenault, 1971). Tomlin died following a heart attack in 1953 at age 53.

Adolph Gottlieb was born in 1903 in New York City into a comfortable home of Jewish immigrants. After finishing high school and attending classes at the Art Students League, he was trained as an art teacher at Parsons School of Design. He married at age 29. Quiet, shy and self-contained, Gottlieb always felt alienated from other people (Fitzsimmons, 1953). He once explained, "In the 25 or more years that I have survived as a painter, I have never had the slightest interest in being adjusted to society" (Gottlieb, 1956). Gottlieb died following a stroke in 1974 at age 70.

James Brooks was born in 1906 in St. Louis, Missouri, to a middle-class family. He attended Southern Methodist University for two years, and then studied in art schools for four years. He married for the first time at age 32, divorced four years later, and then remarried at age 41 (Portland Museum of Art, 1983). Brooks died in 1992 at age 85.

Willem de Kooning was born in 1904 in Rotterdam, Holland, to middle-class parents. When he was five, his parents divorced, and young Willem was assigned to his father because of their "extremely warm relationship" (Hess, 1968, p. 12). However, his mother fought the decision and eventually gained legal custody. After his father

remarried, the two rarely saw each other (Cummings, 1983, p. 11). De Kooning left both parents when he came to America at age 21, after graduating from the Brussels Academie Royale des Beaux Arts. He had left grammar school at age 12 to work as an apprentice to commercial artists and had subsequently studied at a fine arts academy in Rotterdam. De Kooning married at age 39. In 1950, he began to abuse alcohol (Gruen, 1989, pp. 213, 221), which often made him destructive of people and property (Gruen, 1989, pp. 225, 229). During the 1950s, he was treated by a psychoanalyst (Gruen, 1989, p. 203).

ACKNOWLEDGEMENTS
This paper is based on Schildkraut, J.J., Hirshfeld A.J. & Murphy, J.M. (1994), Mind and mood in modern art II: depressive disorders, spirituality, and early deaths in the Abstract Expressionist artists of the New York School. *Amer. J. Psychiat.*, **151**, 482–488. Copyright © 1994, the American Psychiatric Association. Reprinted by permission.

This work was supported, in part, by the Karen Tucker Fund.

REFERENCES

Akiskal, H.S. & Akiskal, K. (1988). Reassessing the prevalence of bipolar disorders: clinical significance and artistic creativity. *Psychiat. & Psychobiol.*, **3**, 295–365.

Akiskal, H.S. & Akiskal, K. (1992). Cyclothymic, hyperthymic and depressive temperaments as sub-affective variants of mood disorders. *American Psychiatric Press Review of Psychiatry*, Vol. 11, Eds A. Tasman & M.B. Riba. American Psychiatric Press, Washington, D.C.

American Psychiatric Association (1987). *Diagnostic and Statistical Manual of Mental Disorders, 3rd Edn (Revised).* American Psychiatric Association, Washington D.C.

Arnason, H.H. (1977). *Robert Motherwell,* pp. 230–237. Harry N. Abrams, New York.

Ashton, D. (1962). *The Unknown Shore: A View of Contemporary Art.* Little, Brown, Boston.

Ashton, D. (1976). *Yes, but . . .: A Critical Study of Philip Guston,* pp. 76–84. The Viking Press, New York.

Ashton, D. (1983). *About Rothko.* University of Oxford Press, New York.

Baur, J.I.H. (1957). Bradley Walker Tomlin. In *Bradley Walker Tomlin,* p. 11. Whitney Museum of American Art, New York.

Cavaliere, B. (1978). The subtlety of life for the artist. In *William Baziotes: A Retrospective Exhibit.* Newport Harbor Art Museum, Newport Beach, CA.

Chave, A.C. (1989). *Mark Rothko, Subjects in Abstraction.* Yale University Press, New Haven, CT.

Chenault, J. (1971). Bradley Walker Tomlin. In *Bradley Walker Tomlin: A Retrospective View,* p. 19. The Buffalo Fine Arts Academy, Buffalo.

Chronology of A. Reinhardt, in the Reinhardt Papers. Owned and microfilmed by the Archives of American Art/Smithsonian Institution, Roll N/69–99.

Csikszentmihalyi, M. (1988). The dangers of originality: creativity and the artistic process. In *Psycho-analytic Perspectives on Art,* Vol. 3, p. 217. Ed. M.M. Gedo. The Analytic Press, Hillsdale, N.J.

Cummings, P. (1983). The drawings of Willem de Kooning. In *Willem de Kooning: Drawings, Paintings, Sculpture, New York, Berlin, Paris,* p. 11. Whitney Museum of American Art, New York.

Davies, H. (Ed.) (1983). *The Prints of Barnett Newman,* pp. 13, 24. The Barnett Newman Foundation, New York.

Dawson, F. (1967). *An Emotional Memoir of Franz Kline.* Pantheon Books. New York.

Dissanayake, E. (1988). *What Is Art For?* University of Washington Press, Seattle.

Fitzsimmons, J. (1953). Adolph Gottlieb. *Everyday Art Quarterly,* No. 25. In Gottlieb Papers, owned and microfilmed by the Archives of American Art/Smithsonian Institution, roll N/69–72.

Flam, J.D. (1983). With Robert Motherwell. In *Robert Motherwell,* p. 22. Abbeville Press, New York.

Friedman, B.H. (1972). *Energy Made Visible.* McGraw-Hill, New York.

Gablik, S. (1984). *Has Modernism Failed?* pp. 11–35. Thames and Hudson, New York.

Gaugh, H.F. (1985). *The Vital Gesture: Franz Kline.* Abbeville Press, New York.

Gaugh, H.F. (1979). *Franz Kline: The Color Abstractions,* p. 43. The Phillips Collection, Washington, D.C.

Gottlieb, A. (1956). Art Action. Paper delivered to the P.A.A. Conference at Portland, Oregon, 1956. Reprinted in *Adolph Gottlieb*. M. Knoedler & Co., New York, 1985.

Gray, C. (Ed. 1968). *David Smith by David Smith*, p. 15. Holt, Rinehart and Winston, New York.

Gruen, J. (1989). *The Party's Over Now*. Pushcart Press, Wainscott, New York.

Guston, P. (1945). Letter to James Brooks November 11 1945. James Brooks Papers, owned and microfilmed by the Archives of American Art/Smithsonian Institution, roll N/69–132.

Hadler, M. (1978). William Baziotes: Four Sources of Inspiration. In *William Baziotes: A Retrospective Exhibit*, p. 77. Newport Harbor Art Museum, Newport Beach, CA.

Hess, T. (1968). *Willem de Kooning*, p. 12. Museum of Modern Art, New York.

Hess, T. (1969). *Barnett Newman*. Walker, New York.

Hess, T. (1971). *Barnett Newman*, p. 69. Museum of Modern Art, New York.

James Brooks (1972). Dallas Museum of Fine Arts, Dallas.

Jung, C.G. (1966a). On the relation of analytical psychology to poetry. In *The Collected Works of C.G. Jung*, Vol. 15, Eds H. Read, M. Fordham & G. Adler, p. 82. Bollingen Series XX. Princeton University Press, Princeton, NJ.

Jung, C.G. (1966b). Psychology and literature. In *The Collected Works of C.G. Jung*, Vol. 15, Eds H. Read, M. Fordham & G. Adler, p. 101. Bollingen Series XX. Princeton University Press, Princeton, NJ.

Kingsley, A. (1992). *The Turning Point: the Abstract Expressionists and the Transformation of American Art*, Simon & Schuster, New York.

Kligman, R. (1974). *Love Affair: A Memoir of Jackson Pollock*. William Morrow, New York.

Landau, E.G. (1989). *Jackson Pollock*. Harry N. Abrams, New York.

Lippard, L. (1981). *Ad Reinhardt*. Harry N. Abrams, New York.

Marcus, S.E. (1983). *David Smith: The Sculptor and His Work*, pp. 24, 137. Cornell University Press, Ithaca, NY.

Mattison, R.S. (1987). *Robert Motherwell: The Formative Years*. UMI Research Press, Ann Arbor.

Mayer, M. (1988). *Night Studio*. Alfred A. Knopf, New York.

McCoy, G. (Ed) (1973). *David Smith*, p. 25. Praeger Publishers, New York.

Merkert, J. (Ed) (1986). *David Smith—Sculpture and Drawings*, pp. 44, 48. Prestel-Verlag, Munich.

Monson, R.R. (1974). Analysis of Relative Survival and Proportional Mortality. *Comput. Biomed. Res.*, **7**, 325–332.

Mooradian, K. (1978). *Arshile Gorky Adoian*. Gilgamesh Press, Chicago.

Mooradian, K. (1980). *The Many Worlds of Arshile Gorky*, p. 9. Gilgamesh Press, Chicago.

Motherwell, R. (1951). What abstract art means to me: statements by six American artists. *Mus. Mod. Art Bull.*, **XVIII** (3), 12–13.

Murphy, J.M., Monson, R.R., Olivier, D.C., Sobol, A.M. & Leighton, A.H. (1987).

Affective disorders and mortality: a general population study. *Arch. Gen. Psychiatry*, **44**, 473–480.

Murphy, J.M., Monson, R.R., Olivier, D.C., Pratt, L.A. & Leighton, A.H. (1989). Mortality risk and psychiatric disorders: results of a general physician study. *Soc. Psychiat. & Psychiat. Epidemiol.*, **24**, 134–142.

Naifeh, S. & Smith, G.W. (1989). *Jackson Pollock: An American Saga*. Clarkson N. Potter, New York.

New York Times (25 June 1980). Clyfford Still dies: a leading painter. In Clyfford Still Papers, owned and microfilmed by the Archives of American Art/Smithsonian Institution, roll 68–72.

Newman, B. (1966). Artist's statement. Barnett Newman: *The Stations of the Cross: Lema Sabachthani*, New York, Solomon R. Guggenheim Museum. In Barnett Newman Papers, Archives of American Art/Smithsonian Institution, roll 3481.

O'Connor, F.V. & Thaw, E.V. (Eds) (1978). *Jackson Pollock: A Catalogue Raisonné of Paintings, Drawings and Other Works*, Vol. 4. Yale University Press, New Haven, CT.

O'Connor, F.V. (1980). *Jackson Pollock: The Black Pourings, 1951–53*. Institute of Contemporary Art, Boston.

Paneth, D. (1951–62). Portrait of Baziotes. *New World Writing*, June 1951–62. Transcript in Baziotes Papers, owned and microfilmed by the Archives of American Art/Smithsonian Institution, roll N/70–21.

Polcari, S. (1991). *Abstract Expressionism and the Modern Experience*, Cambridge University Press, Cambridge.

Portland Museum of Art (1983). *James Brooks—Paintings and Works on Paper*, 1946–82.

Potter, J. (1985). *To a Violent Grave: An Oral Biography of Jackson Pollock*. G.P. Putnam's Sons, New York.

Rand, H. (1980). *Arshile Gorky: The Implication of Symbols*, pp. 5, 8. Allanheld, Osmun, Montclair, NJ.

Rodman, S. (1957). *Conversations with Artists* pp. 93–94. Devin-Adair, New York.

Ross, C. (1990). *Abstract Expressionism: Creators and Critics*. Harry N. Abrams, New York.

Rothko, M. (1947–48). The Romantics were prompted. Possibilities I. Winter, 1947–48: 84. Cited in Chave (1989, see above), p. 185.

Runyan, W.M. (1984). *Life Histories and Psychobiography: Explorations in Theory and Method*. Oxford University Press, New York.

Sandler, I. (1970). *The Triumph of American Painting: A History of Abstract Expressionism*. Harper & Row, New York.

Schildkraut, J.J. (1982). Miró and the mystical in modern art: Problems for research in metapsychiatry. *Am. J. Soc. Psychiat.*, **II**(4), 3–20.

Schildkraut, J.J. & Hirshfeld, A.J. (1995). Mind and mood in modern art. I: Miró and "Melancolie", *Creativity Res. J.*, **8**(2), 139–156.

Schildkraut, J.J., Hirshfeld, A.J. & Murphy, J.M. (1994). Mind and mood in modern art. II: Depressive disorders, spirituality, and early deaths in the abstract expressionist artists of the New York School. *Am. J. Psychiat.*, **151**, 482–488.

Seldes, L. (1974). *The Legacy of Mark Rothko.* Holt, Rinehart and Winston, New York.

Solomon, D. (1987). *Jackson Pollock: A Biography.* Simon and Schuster, New York.

Still, C. (1948). Letter to Betty Parsons, 10 March 1948. In Clyfford Still Papers, owned and microfilmed by the Archives of American Art/Smithsonian Institution, roll N/68–72.

Storr, R. (1986). *Philip Guston.* Abbeville Press, New York.

Terenzio, S. (1980). Robert Motherwell and Black. Storrs, William Benton Museum of Art, University of Connecticut.

Wilkin, K. (1984). *David Smith.* Abbeville Press, New York.

Wysuph, C.L. (1970). *Jackson Pollock: Psychoanalytic Drawings.* Horizon Press, New York.

CHAPTER 19

ABSTRACT EXPRESSIONISM AS PSYCHOBIOGRAPHY: THE LIFE AND SUICIDE OF ARSHILE GORKY

KAREEN K. AKISKAL AND HAGOP S. AKISKAL

This chapter examines the life history and circumstances of the suicide of Arshile Gorky, from a psychological perspective. Our main aim is to document his cyclical melancholy which contributed to his becoming one of America's greatest painters. Widely acclaimed as "a pioneer in discovering the primary principles of America's new abstract art" (Rosenberg, 1962, p. 118), Gorky is now considered "the vital link between European modern art and American Abstract Expressionism" (Lader, 1985, p. 7). His psychobiography is instructive because he was neither European- nor American-born.

GORKY'S ARMENIAN FOUNDATIONS

Arshile Gorky was born Vosdanig Manoug Adoian in 1904, in Khorkom, near Lake Van (now in Turkey). His provenance from this historic heartland of Armenia was a constant source of inspiration for the artist (Mooradian, 1978, pp. 75–161)—as seen, for instance, in the *Image of Khorkom* (1936) and related paintings—depicting the fecund soil of his birthplace, its orchards and fruits and, in particular, the fertility-enhancing blue rock against which young Armenian women rubbed their bare breasts. The latter is

a variant of the pagan rite of phallus worship (Figure 19-1) one still observes in ancient shrines in "modern" Armenia, side-by-side with Christian symbols (Figure 19-2). As an adult artist, Gorky related to his student Ethel Schwabacher—who eventually wrote the artist's first biography—that the rock was in the garden of his ancestral home, and served as a "garden of wish-fulfillment" (Schwabacher, 1957, p. 66).

Art historians and critics unfamiliar with Gorky's Armenian roots have intimated Byzantine, Iranian and European influences to explain how an immigrant, who came to America at the age of 16, could ultimately play the unique role he did in the evolution of modern art in the USA. These influences have been rebutted by Karlen Mooradian (Mooradian, 1985), the artist's nephew, who has written extensively about Gorky's Armenian sources (Mooradian, 1978, pp. 163–234). The latter point of view, which has gradually gained respect, has led art historian Barbara Rose (Rose, 1979) to conclude that the artist's "exquisiteness . . . lyricism and love of nature . . . [were] related to his early experiences in Armenia". We submit that Gorky's Abstract Expressionism represents, in

221

19-1
*HAGOP AKISKAL
photographed in Tvin
(Republic of Armenia) with
a pagan symbol found
during excavations of this
ancient Armenian capital
(seventh century BC)*

extensive use of these childhood impressions of colors, forms and scents. It could be said that what Marcel Proust did for literature, Gorky did for painting. In Gorky's case, the vivid (visual) remembrance of things in the past was enriched by history (Mooradian, 1978, pp. 99–161), and to some extent myth, created by the artist and his family.

The present contribution goes beyond the foregoing historical and artistic analyses, to develop a psycho-biographical understanding of the artist and his *oeuvre*—and the myths surrounding them—based on the tragedies that befell his family and country of origin as well as his stormy personal life in the USA. Since a great deal has been written about the mature artist, the present psychobiographical account will focus more selectively on the artist's childhood and young adult years and, in particular, his temperament.

THE YEARS OF PURITY

Gorky said that to paint is to make a confession: *Hishoughoutiun* (Memory), of 1947; cited in Fondation Calouste Gulbenkian (1985) is one of a series of crayon drawings which summarizes his artistic conception: painting is reminiscence. This is a recurrent theme for the artist, and we encounter it again most prominently in a 1944 painting that depicts *How My Mother's Embroidered Apron Unfolds in My Life* (Figure 19-3). Of his childhood recollections and reverie surrounding this painting, the artist wrote:

"My mother told me many stories while I pressed my face into her long apron with my eyes closed. She had a long white apron like the one in her portrait, and another embroidered one. Her stories and the embroidery on her apron got confused in my mind with my eyes closed. All my life her

part, a fantastic recreation of this lost Eden of wish-fulfillment. Along these lines, in his authoritative monograph on the symbols in Gorky's art, Harry Rand (1991) states that the artist's Armenian background is "the intrinsic stuff of his art", that indeed the artist's "main subject matter was a deep-seated examination of his own history" (p. XXI). As an adult artist, especially during his abstract period, Gorky made *stories and her embroidery keep unraveling pictures in my memory"* (Levy, 1966, p. 34).

His mother narrated legends, spoke of Armenia's heroic past, mythology and culture—going back to pagan times—as well as her lineage from priests who created, patroned or safeguarded the art treasures of the monasteries and the churches of medieval Armenia. (In the Armenian Apostolic Church, like the tradition of Eastern Rite Christianity, priests were permitted to marry.)

The Van region (the ancient Vaspurakan) is one of stunning natural beauty. Decades later, the artist portrayed it vividly in such paintings as *Waterfall* (1942), and *The Scent of Apricots on the Field* (1944). Though a physically active child who explored the natural habitat of his parents' ancestral home and gardens, he did not speak until he was four years old. The child felt at one with Vaspurakan and its nature (its flowers, fruits, creatures, mountains and waters) and its colors became a permanent part of his imagination. As a mature artist, in 1944, he wrote: "Always I try to duplicate the colors of Armenia in my paintings", the very colors the artists of the Van School of miniature painting had used for centuries (Ltr. to Vartoush, in Mooradian, 1978, p. 285–287).

"Vosdanig" in Armenian means a person of noble descent, and the name was given to the artist after "Vosdan" (his mother's city of birth). It was the seat of a medieval Armenian kingdom: the ink drawing *Queen of Vosdan* (1945) reflects Vosdanig's pride in his origins. Indeed, his mother's family was the guardian of Charahan Sourp Nishan (the Church of Holy Sign of the Demon Seizer), after the Saint who had the special ability to exorcise evil and cure the sick.

19-2
KAREEN AKISKAL photographed with a Christian monument excavated near Tvin, dating back to the medieval era

The city of Van, the ancient capital of the Urartian Kingdom, dates back to 5000 BC (Belli, 1986). There, the young Vosdanig was exposed to both pagan and Christian spiritualism (Mooradian, 1978, p. 99). The pagan fertility rites illustrate "hylozoism", whereby the animate and inanimate are juxtaposed; both are pervaded by spirits which can interpenetrate and, thus, a rock can enhance the fertility of young

19-3
ARSHILE GORKY
*HOW MY MOTHER'S
EMBROIDERED APRON
UNFOLDS IN MY LIFE*, 1944
*Oil on canvas, 40 × 45 in
(101.6 × 114.3 cm)
Collection Seattle Art
Museum. Gift of Mr and
Mrs Bagley Wright.
Photograph by Paul
Macapia. © 1996 Agnes
Fielding/Artists Rights
Society (ARS), NY*

women. The genital organs—so pervasive in Gorky's paintings (see, for instance, *Good Afternoon Mrs. Lincoln* of 1944)—are not mere Freudian symbols. They derive from Armenia's fecund land which, literally, cross-fertilized Gorky's art. For the artist, Armenia was a womb with inexhaustible creative powers: "Nature in Armenia is an inexhaustible paint tube. And brushes once dipped in it can dance to their own songs" (Ltr. to Vartoush, in Mooradian, 1978, pp. 283–285)

The awe-inspiring pagan past of Van was present side-by-side with Christian symbols of the Churches of the Armenian Apostolic Faith. The most important of these was on Akhtamar Island (Lake Van), the church of Sourp Khatch (Holy Cross), built by King Gagik, and considered one of the greatest masterpieces of medieval architecture (Der Nersessian, 1977, pp. 80–122; Belli, 1986, p. 73; Thiery & Donabedian, 1989, pp. 130–139). Belonging to the family of a priest, the young Vosdanig was privileged to observe stone carving, murals and miniature paintings in this church, as well as the monastery of Varak (2 kilometers from the city of Van), which had one of the richest collections of manuscripts from the Golden Age (thirteenth–fourteenth centuries) of Armenian art.

Gorky's mother, Lady Shoushanig ("white lilies" in Armenian), was a woman of great aesthetic sensibility (Mooradian, 1978, pp. 99–161). Both her priest-father and her first husband (a revolutionary) were killed by the Ottoman authorities and she was left a widow with two children. She was subsequently given in matrimony to Setrak Adoian, himself a widower with two children. This marriage, which was one of convenience, gave birth to two children, Vosdanig and his younger sister (see *Portrait of Vartoush*, 1933–34). Other than receiving a pair of red slippers shortly before his father fled to the USA to avoid Ottoman conscription, the young Vosdanig had no significant interaction with him. (Indeed, in *Armenia's Van Dreams* of 1930, the father is depicted as a portrait). Lady Shoushanig was now to turn much of her attention to her young son, imparting to him all the culture she had inherited from the priest side of her family. She paid special attention to his artistic talents, which had become apparent at the age of four, approximately when he spoke his first words. She personally tutored him in artistic conceptions that had been passed through generations of manuscript illustrators, thereby bequeathing upon him the aspiration to devote his life to *Gegharvesd* (Aesthetics, 1946) and *Sdeghtzagordzutyun* (Act of Creation, 1946).

Two competing schools of medieval Armenian manuscript art (Machtot's Institute of Old Armenian Manuscripts, 1978) were to deeply influence the artist later in his career. The school that professed "purity" placed emphasis on expressing a biblical scene with few strokes against a minimum background; thus, a given story was rendered in essential, pure elements, creating what today we might call abstractions. The school that professed refinement (or maturity), executed with precision, elegance and richer colors, creating fluent movement and life against a background which is three-dimensional, and had what today we call perspective. Of the artists from the Armenian Renaissance, Toros Rosslin, whose work Gorky examined at various points in his life, had the greatest influence on him.

To graduate from childhood innocence and purity (depicted, among others, in *Youth's Comrades IV* of 1946) and to attain the coveted stage of artistic maturity and refinement, the artist had to cross a life-path full of agony. His biography and art are fully interwoven in this respect.

EARLY AGONIES

Vana Danjank (Agony of Van, 1945), and *Images of Haiyotz Dzor* (Vale of the Armenians, 1945) represent the artist's reminiscences of the atrocities that he and other Armenians suffered in the early part of this century. It was a turbulent period for Armenians living under Ottoman rule, especially in the Van and surrounding provinces (Walker, 1980, pp. 121–240). Instead of carrying out reforms that had been guaranteed by European powers, the Sultan brutally suppressed Armenians, accusing them of siding with the Russians. The tragedies in Gorky's life actually began before he was born. Mooradian (1978, pp. 99–109) narrates that the artist's maternal priest-grandfather fell in battle while defending the family monastery against Ottoman invaders. Subsequently his 16-year-old maternal uncle (the son of the priest) was stabbed to death. These tragedies drove the artist's grandmother—who up to that point had been a devout Christian—to torch the ancient monastery of Vosdan, permanently burning parts of it. She then left for another monastery where she died a tortured soul several years later. This defiant act against God—atypical for an Armenian woman—was nonetheless testimony to the intense emotionality which was part of Gorky's temperamental legacy.

By the time of Gorky's birth, rumor had already spread among the common villagers that the family was no longer protected by its patron saint, that indeed it was cursed (Mooradian, 1978, p. 100–136). By naming him Vosdanig, Gorky's mother was perhaps reasserting the family's traditional claim to a glorious past with both pagan and Christian roots. The young Vosdanig thus grew up in this family of tradition and defiance. As we shall see later, once in America, his origins and very name were to haunt the artist for much of his life. Neither could he forget the mountain women's wails at his grandmother's funeral (see *Orators*, 1947). During Hokejash (the church service for the soul of this grandmother), Vosdanig punished himself with self-imposed hunger. Whenever the young Vosdanig subsequently visited the family Church, he watched in great awe the columns closest to the Saint's tomb. For it was there that the villagers chained their loved ones who had lost their minds, awaiting a cure from the saint: this is depicted in *Charahan Sourp Nishan Hokiner* of 1946.

In 1908, Setrak Adoian emigrated to the USA (Rhode Island), leaving the family behind. Thus, Vosdanig (then four years old), his younger sister Vartoush and Lady Shushanig, were left to live at the mercy of his paternal uncle. By this time Khorkom, the village where the family had lived, was no longer safe, and they were to move to Aikesdan, on the outskirts of the city of Van renowned for its orchards. A photograph showing the eight-year-old Vosdanig and his mother, which was taken in 1912 and sent to his father, expresses their misery. In a retrospective self-portrait (1927), the artist depicted himself as a nine-year-old with a melancholy countenance which reflects the personal suffering for the young Vosdanig that was evolving in the midst of the larger tragedy for all Armenians (Mooradian, 1978, pp. 99–160). Indeed, within two years, in 1915, repeated massacres and deportations forced the entire family to flee on foot for Yerevan, in Caucasian (Russian) Armenia. A year later, in the midst of war and starvation, half-sisters Akabi and Satenig were to join their father in America, leaving behind Vosdanig, Vartoush and Lady Shushanig.

By 1918, their only shelter was reduced to a roofless room in snow-covered Yerevan. They lived there in utter poverty until 1919 when Lady Shushanig died from starvation in her son's arms: she was dictating a letter to her husband to tell him that she would ". . . never go to America, this is my earth and soon we will all of us be in Van again" (Mooradian, 1980, p. 31). These circumstances are immortalized in *The Artist and His Mother* (1926–1932), where he is joined to the mother, whose face bears a cadaveric pallor. In another variant on which the artist worked from 1929 to 1942 (Figure 19-4), the artist, now severed from the mother, appears ready to walk away from her to the creativity and greatness she admonished him to pursue. In both paintings, the artist is offering modest flowers to his mother. These two paintings represent a lasting tribute to Lady Shushanig to whom Gorky traces his artistic temperament. Thus, the artist's mother, who never came to America—posing in the National Gallery in Washington, D.C. and the Whitney Museum in New York—has gazed as the entire world passed by (Southgate, 1981). Her eyes tell the untold story of the tragedy of an entire nation. Gorky disliked being told he painted "Picasso eyes". He maintained that the large and expressive sad eyes in his paintings—so characteristic of Armenian miniature painting dating back to medieval times—are the very mark of Armenian suffering: "Our eyes . . . the eyes of the Armenian, speak before the lips move and long after they cease to" (Mooradian, 1978, p. 196). Indeed, Gorky's entire artistic *oeuvre* can be considered a visual representation of the suffering that could not be told in words.

The artist worked for over a decade on the twin oil canvases *The Artist and His Mother*. This is a long gestation period for an artist who barely lived 44 years. Attempting to give birth twice to his own mother (Cantor, 1991, pp. 51–71)—who had created him—is unparalleled in the history of painting. It was not enough that she lived in memory, he had to bring her back to life, to preserve "the last glorious breath of Van nobility" (Mooradian, 1978, p. 71).

It is nonetheless fair to state that this prolonged labor was only successful historically, to the extent that it gave birth to the mother. Gorky, the artist, was yet to be born. It is as if the artist was resurrecting an entire nation that had nearly perished in genocide. That the artist worked for so many years in giving birth to his own mother is itself an indication that he was dissatisfied with this labor. The prolonged suffering of this labor was nonetheless necessary for the artist, to delve deeper into his memories, to reach ultimately the maturity his mother had admon-

19-4
ARSHILE GORKY
THE ARTIST AND HIS MOTHER
c. 1926–36
Oil on canvas, 60 × 50 in (152.4 × 127 cm)
Collection of the Whitney Museum of American Art, New York. Gift of Julien Levy for Maro and Natasha Gorky in memory of their father (no. 50.17). Photograph copyright © 1995 Whitney Museum of American Art. © 1996 Agnes Fielding/Artists Rights Society (ARS), NY

ished him to covet. According to the critic Rosenberg (1962, pp. 97–118), maturity was reached in 1944 when Gorky painted *How My Mother's Embroidered Apron Unfolds in My Life* (Figure 19-3). That is when Gorky gave birth to Gorky.

As already suggested, the female genitals—so pervasive in Gorky's art—are not mere olfactory memories of his mother. They symbolize the female elements of the artist's own psyche—his own quest for immortality through creation.

IDENTITY CRISIS AND NOSTALGIA

Brother and sister, beginning a trip afoot through Tbilisi and Batoum, and thereafter by ship to Istanbul, Athens and Naples, arrived in New York on February 6 1920. The children were reunited with their father in Providence after a 12-year separation. Vosdanig attended technical high school, but soon conflict was to erupt between father and son over Vosdanig's intention of pursuing a painting career. Alienation between them was further deepened by the father's remarriage (Recollections of Vartoush, in Mooradian, 1980, pp. 23–66).

In 1921, Vosdanig moved to nearby Watertown, Massachusetts—where his half sister Akabi and her husband lived—to work in a rubber factory. This was to be short-lived, because he was dismissed for drawing on shoe frames. Although details about this period of his life are sketchy, it is believed that, for a while, he studied in the New England School of Design.

In 1925, he moved to New York City and took his first studio, and was employed as an instructor at the Grand Central School of Art. In addition, he tutored private students. In 1930, he moved his studio to Greenwich Village and soon thereafter made his first group exhibition at the Museum of Modern Art. Naturally endowed with talent, the artist was largely a self-taught painter. Although he surprised his contemporaries by his confidence and knowledge of art, he was a man of deep conflicts. As early as 1924, he signed *Park Street Church* with the name of Arshele Gorky, which a year later he adopted—with change of spelling to "Arshile". He had no relationship to the revolutionary Russian writer, Maxim Gorky; yet he did nothing to dispel the myth (curiously, Gorky was Maxim's pseudonym too!).

This assumption of a new non-Armenian identity has given rise to various explanations. These range from his disregard for facts—and a rich fantasy life, presumably characteristic of his Eastern heritage—to deliberate deception for social prestige and advantage in the art world. A closer examination of the etymology of the new name, however, suggests more fundamental psychologic needs, i.e. Gorky ("the bitter one" in Russian) and Arshile (derived from "Arshak," a well-known fourth century Armenian king known for his defiance). One could also invoke the concept of survival shame: the humiliation of belonging to a nation that was slaughtered with relatively little resistance or, more simply, an immigrant's shame of his humble origins. There may have been even deeper psychologic processes at work—distancing himself from his lost past and, perhaps, even an attempt to escape the "curse" that had been attached to his family name upon his grandmother's defiance of the Christian God.

Finally, Vartoush Mooradian, the artist's sister, has suggested that Vosdanig, as the descendant of a great family, felt he was not worthy of his name until he created significant art: "At that time", the artist confessed to her, "I will proclaim to the world my Armenian race" (Mooradian, 1980, pp. 23–66). So deep was his need to conceal his Armenian origins that even as late as 1940–41 his childhood "garden of wish-fulfillment" had to be named *Garden of Sochi* (a resort on the Black Sea he had never visited). The artist "explained" the symbolism involved after another variant in the Sochi series was acquired by New York's Museum of Modern Art: it refers to the Khorkom folk shrine of the magic fertility stone surrounded by the votive offerings of strips of brightly colored clothing hung in trees (Schwabacher, 1957, pp. 41–80).

Practical considerations also played an important role in motivating the artist in changing his name: Vosdanig

Adoian was unlikely to sell paintings! In the interview he granted to the *New York Evening Post* (1926) upon his appointment to the Faculty of the Grand Central School of Art in New York in 1926, Gorky was highly critical of the art scene in New York, which had an "antique craze" for old masters, denigrated modern art, and would only patronise "well known" signatures. In espousing a "universal art" that appealed to all mankind, the 22-year-old artist "with a wave of his long, thin hand ... disposed of the greatest city in the world", which he accused of dismissing such modern artists as Cézanne and Picasso.

The foregoing considerations paint the profile of a proud and defiant young man who is cognizant of his potential, but suffers from a deep sense of loss, humiliation and low self-esteem. That the change of name transcended his relationship with the art world and involved deeper psychological layers can be inferred from the fact that repeatedly, in writing to the women with whom he was infatuated, Gorky liberally "borrowed" ideas, verses and even passages from well-known poets and presented them as his own (Schwabacher, 1957, pp. 59–69). The suffering of "confronting the loss of home, culture, language, family, mother, and name, and confronting it deliberately day after day, was as necessary for the artist as it was unbearable for the man" (Morgan, 1991).

Not surprisingly then, the decade of 1925–35 is one of intense nostalgia for the artist, as exemplified most directly by a series of Adoian family portraits, including those of his sisters and mother. Contemporaneously, he had a brief, tempestuous romance with model Sirun Mussikian who, like the artist, was of Van origin. At the same time, Gorky did a series of drawings (Figure 19-5) entitled "Night-time, Enigma, and Nostalgia" (1931–34). This nostalgia was profound: Raoul Hague, an Armenian New York sculptor, relates how "when he spoke about Van, tears came into his eyes because he had Van in him" (Mooradian, 1980, pp. 148–151). Gorky's nostalgia was further intensified by the fact that he felt like an exile and, according to Saul Schary, another long-time artist friend, never understood America and Americans—even when he went to see a Western movie, it was because the mountains reminded him of his birthplace (Mooradian, 1980, pp. 203–208).

Gorky, as a boy, it should be recalled, not only received the intense female—maternal—attention that was customary in Armenia, but had an unusually close relationship with a mother who, without being a widow, had been left husbandless. Throughout his life the artist had strong yearnings for his mother (and motherland). He even contemplated a return to (then Soviet) Armenia, but was unable to do so for lack of funds. Sister Vartoush and her husband Moorad Mooradian (who was the artist's adolescent comrade from Van) returned to Armenia for a two-and-a-half-year period, but ultimately settled in Chicago.

In 1935, the artist married the fashion student Marney George, 10 years his junior. This stormy relationship soon ended in divorce because, in Marney's words, "Arshile wanted to form and mold me into the woman he wanted for his wife" (Schwabacher, 1957, pp. 59–61). In his *Portrait of Myself and My Imaginary Wife* (Figure 19-6), painted around this time, he indicates his need for an ideal "Armenian" wife who would combine the impossible attributes of being both a mother and a muse and, perhaps, even tend to his artistic and melancholy moods (Figure 19-6). This is what Marney had to say about Gorky:

19-5
ARSHILE GORKY
*STUDY FOR NIGHTTIME,
ENIGMA AND NOSTALGIA,
c. 1931–32*
*Pencil, 22¼ × 28¾ in
(56.5 × 73 cm)*
*The Museum of Modern
Art, New York. Gift of
Richard S. Zeisler.
Photograph © 1996 The
Museum of Modern Art,
New York. © 1996 Agnes
Fielding/Artists Rights
Society (ARS), NY*

19-6
ARSHILE GORKY
*PORTRAIT OF MYSELF AND MY
IMAGINARY WIFE, c. 1933–34*
*Oil on paperboard,
8⅝ × 14¼ in (21.7 × 36.2 cm)*
*Hirshhorn Museum and
Sculpture Garden,
Smithsonian Institution.
Gift of Joseph H.
Hirshhorn Foundation,
1966. Photograph by Lee
Stalsworth. © 1996 Agnes
Fielding/Artists Rights
Society (ARS), NY*

"It seems the very moment we were married the battle began . . . Ferocious as a giant, tender as a little child . . . Arshile tried to break the barriers [between us], first with tenderness, then with force . . . violence . . . It was a tragedy for us both" (Schwabacher, 1957, pp. 59–61).

This failed romance was followed with yet another, Gorky's infatuation with the painter Michael West. His exotic and feverish expressions of love in intensely passionate sessions both charmed and drove her away. Gorky, according to his student-biographer (Schwabacher, 1957, pp. 59–61), unaccustomed to American girls, was more in love with love; and the attempt to create a wife—like he created a painting—failed and, once again, left him "alone with his phantom companions".

The foregoing considerations document how the artist's temperament, coupled with nostalgic melancholic attachment to his past, may have contributed to his striving for unattainable love objects. Nonetheless, one must not underestimate the fact that the chosen objects themselves were from the art world, and of a certain temperament; hence interpersonal collision may have been unavoidable. Finally, poverty further destabilized these already precarious romantic bonds. It was the period of the Great (Economic) Depression in America, and the artist lived in utter poverty. Poverty was somewhat mitigated by the fact that during this time Gorky worked for the Civil Works Administration Public Works of Art Project and, during the early years of World War II, he was commissioned by the New Works Progress Administration's Federal Art Project to paint 10 murals for Newark airport (all but two subsequently destroyed by officials).

Moreover, in 1937, the artist was rewarded by his first museum purchase of a painting entitled *Painting* by the Whitney Museum of Art. Nonetheless, the artist's poverty was compounded by the fact that Gorky could not visit an art store without emptying all that he had in his pockets in return for the very best paint tubes and brushes available (Schwabacher, 1957, pp. 59–61). This prolonged period of poverty—which revived the artist's teenage years of deprivation and starvation—served to intensify whatever natural inclination he had for melancholy and moodiness.

MATURITY, CREATIVITY AND TERMINAL AGONIES

During a cross-country trip which involved exhibiting in San Francisco and visiting his sister in Chicago, Arshile Gorky married Agnes Magruder in Nevada in 1941. The marriage was apparently a happy one in the beginning and two children were born. Soon conflict was to break out because of Gorky's continuing poverty and his complete dedication to art (Schwabacher, 1957, pp. 84–145). Agnes, the daughter of relatively well-to-do parents, was considerably younger than he was and expected other things from life. Despite such conflicts, marriage did bring some stability to the artist's life: the two children were a continued source of joy, one of whom he named Maro (after a well-known Armenian revolutionary heroine) (Mooradian, 1980, p. 8).

Although he still maintained his Greenwich Village studio, the family made frequent visits to Hamilton, Virginia and Sherman, Connecticut. The mountains and pastoral scenery in these two states reminded the artist of his childhood setting (Rand, 1991, pp. 1–12). It was a return to nature, and provided the artist with the inspiration for such paintings as *The Water of the Flowery Mill* (1944). This creative period culminated in an exhibition at the Julien Levy Gallery (Levy, 1972, pp. 283–295). André Breton, the French surrealist critic who, because of the war had left Paris for New York, proclaimed *The Liver is the Cock's Comb* (1944, Figure 19-7), as the greatest painting produced in modern American art (Breton, 1945). Despite such critical acclaim, the artist felt that fame was still eluding him and that indeed success was—as indicated in the title of a painting from 1945—*Unattainable*.

Tragedy was to strike the artist unexpectedly in 1946, beginning with the studio barn fire in Sherman, which destroyed most of his recent paintings. This has been immortalized in several paintings such as *Charred Beloved II* (Figure 19-8).

Soon thereafter, he was operated upon for colon cancer and had a permanent colostomy placed on him.

For a man who valued cleanliness as much as Gorky did, this operation was a major source of shame, humiliation and demoralization. This suffering, immortalized in yet another masterpiece, *Agony* (1947), is depicted in Figure 19-9. The marriage apparently was also highly strained at this point in time, and Agnes was spending a lot of time in the circle of the European surrealist painters who had accompanied Breton or had come from South America. Despite these setbacks, the initial satisfactory recovery from cancer surgery seemed to have given Gorky a new creative vigor. In the summer of 1946 he completed 292 drawings, and throughout 1947 and early 1948 he painted some of his best paintings. The artist must have known his terminal status and gave the ultimate aesthetic expression to his multiple agonies. These paintings depict the strain of conjugal relationships (*Betrothal II*, 1947); grieving his father's death which occurred around

19-7
ARSHILE GORKY
The Liver Is the Cock's Comb, 1944
Oil on canvas, 73¼ × 98 in (186 × 248.9 cm)
Albright–Knox Art Gallery, Buffalo, New York. Gift of Seymour H. Knox, 1956.
© 1996 Agnes Fielding/Artists Rights Society (ARS), NY

19-8
ARSHILE GORKY
CHARRED BELOVED II, 1946
Oil on canvas, 53⅛ × 40 in
137 × 101.6 cm
*National Gallery of
Canada, Ottawa.
Photograph © Joe
Weneiberg. © 1996 Agnes
Fielding/Artists Rights
Society (ARS), NY*

this time, remembering his grandmother's funeral, which he had attended as a child (*Orators*, 1947); or erecting his own tombstone that the artist wanted to have made from the Armenian villagers' plough (*The Plough and the Song*, 1947).

On June 26 1948, Gorky sustained injuries in a car accident as a passenger in an automobile driven by his dealer Julien Levy. This led to the partial paralysis of his painting arm, for which he was hospitalized for weeks to undergo traction. The artist was in exquisite physical pain and was petrified by the prospect of the inability to paint. During this period he was described as a man who was in utter suffering, was agitated, and felt that there was no more reason for living (Levy, 1972, pp. 283–295). In mid-July, his wife walked out with both children. An entry in the artist's diary around this time reads as follows: "I have been so lonely, exasperated, and how to paint such empty space, so empty, it is the limit" (Levy, 1966, p. 35). A few days later, the artist confessed to painter Saul Schary: "My life is over. I'm not going to live anymore" (Mooradian, 1980, p. 207). On July 21 1948 he slashed the last incomplete painting with a knife, and hanged himself. His suicide note read: "Goodbye my 'Loveds".

GORKY'S TEMPERAMENT AND LIFE IN PERSPECTIVE

Gorky's terminal depressive state was profound "... more than ordinary gloom ... uncanny desolation ... exuding darkness over all of us" (Levy, 1972, p. 290). There are no other documented periods of clinical depression, neither has there ever been any frank record of manic excitement. Nonetheless, as described below, throughout much of his life, the artist exhibited extreme fluctuations in mood and behavior. While perhaps not meeting the full criteria for a major affective disorder, these fluctuations represent testimony to a life-long affective disturbance at the temperamental level.

The artist's temperamental inclination towards cyclic melancholy, alternating with intense cyclic activity, is documented in his letters in Armenian to his sister (Mooradian, 1980, pp. 249–327), which have many entries with statements such as: "Nowadays an extremely melancholy mood has seized me ... lately I have been well and am working excessively ... this constantly gives me extreme mental anguish" (February 28 1938). More-

over, the artist on numerous occasions drew himself in Christ-like pictures: "The agonies and torments in my mind impel me to recognize that I must have been born to suffer for art" (April 18 1938). Such self-descriptions—and frequent melancholy "poses" which so puzzled his contemporaries—were not attention-seeking devices, but the mark of a truly melancholic disposition.

Contemporaries of Gorky have provided testimonials to his being a "sad and melancholy person" (Rothko) or "mostly morose ... the natural bent of his temperament" (Schary). In these testimonials, based on interviews done on Gorky's contemporaries conducted by Mooradian (1980, pp. 92–217), painters and sculptors who knew Gorky documented the artist's strong penchant toward melancholy moods. They described the artist primarily with such traits as "very melancholy," a "sad and melancholy man" with "brooding mood", "mostly morose", a "very lonely person", "gentle and soft", "introverted", "serious", "self-doubting", "scrupulous", "immaculately clean", and "dressed well". Others remarked that "his eyes were very, very sad", and that he had an "extremely melancholy glance". These attributes are compatible with those of the classical melancholic or depressive temperament (Akiskal & Akiskal, 1992). Nonetheless, these were apparently interspersed with attributes of an opposite affective polarity such as "intensity", "volatile" and "dramatic" behavior, "lively and vigorous", and a "ferocious worker" (Mooradian, 1980, pp. 92–217). Indeed, some of his contemporaries described the "Gorky of gaiety" who was "dressed very elegantly", "attracted great crowds" and loved to "create an uproar", with such volatility that "he could flare up very strongly with that temperament", and

become "cantankerous". Indeed, "at parties he would get wild and start to dance and sing Armenian songs at the top of his voice". He was described as a man of "Messianic force" who "worked very fast" and "very sure" with little need for sleep at such times. The latter constellation suggests a strong cyclical if not cyclothymic element, arising periodically from the artist's melancholic temperamental background (Akiskal & Akiskal, 1992). He was thus "an intensely emotional man" whose mood was dominated by gloominess, and even when he was in a state of gaiety, he was described as having a "melancholy laughter" (Mooradian, 1980, pp. 99–217).

Rosenberg, (1962), commenting on Gorky's life and achievements, regarded him as a "monument of melancholy in the hall of modern American masters" (p. 14). The artist's entire life was devoted to art. His life was an endless series of tragedies and suffering, mostly due to repeated losses, so much so that "art took on, for Gorky, so total a function because there was so little else in his life" and that "with Gorky, to be an artist counted for more than to be himself" (Rosenberg, 1962, pp. 21–22).

Our examination of the life and suicide of Arshile Gorky Adoian illustrates the multi-factorial complexity of artistic creativity which obviously involved much more than any simplistic notion of mood dysregulation leading to artistic creativity. In this chapter, we have submitted the thesis that Gorky's abstract expressionism was born of the artist's lifelong agony and unsuccessful attempts to camouflage his Armenian origins: "I drip with Van" (Mooradian, 1980, p. 16). It was the search for a spiritual order—in life and in art—which aspired for purity. Out of the incompatible dualities of his identity, his tragic life and the search for such purity, he created brilliant art. He did not need the suffering that he endured in America: as an Armenian, he had already been privileged to experience suffering. The added insult of life tragedies, superimposed on his cyclothymic temperament, may have provided the impetus to transcend the limitations of mere existence and his infirmities, aiming for immortality through art. What is remarkable in great art is the ability to create in spite of the limitations of existence. Gorky, commenting on twentieth-century art, proclaimed genius to be in the qualities of "intensity . . . activity . . . [and] restless inner energy!" (Gorky, 1931). What he, himself, accomplished in art came from the rich inner resources that he had brought from Armenia: "Art is not in New York . . . art is in you" (*New York Evening Post*, 1926). Gorky's creative vitality derived from ". . . the themes which sprang from the depth of his own personality . . . and the experiences of his childhood . . . they were autobiographical; his art paradoxically was impersonal" (Schwabacher, 1957, p. 18). The intensity of his personal suffering—"unifying sadness and beauty" (Rose, 1976)—was transformed into Abstract Expressionism.

CONCLUSION

Based on existing biographical material, letters by the painter himself, other autobiographical material and statements by his contemporaries and family—some of which are available only in Armenian—this chapter has reconstructed the life of this pioneer giant of Abstract Expressionism in order to examine the relationship between his life and temperament on the one hand, and his art and artistic conceptions on the other. Special attention has been given to:

1. The painter's early life in historic Armenia, where he was born in 1904 as Vosdanig Adoian, and his emigration to the United States in 1920, shortly after the death of his mother from starvation in war-ravaged Armenia;
2. His burning nostalgia for his homeland of origin with its tragic history and myths, glorious past, masterpieces of both pagan and Christian art, as well as its nature and colors;
3. His adjustment problems in the USA and assumption of false identities (e.g. that he was a cousin of the Russian writer Maxim Gorky);
4. His cyclic melancholic temperament;
5. His stormy object relationships;
6. His bohemian life and life-long poverty;
7. The fire that burned his paintings;
8. The disfiguring cancer surgery;
9. The neck injury which led to partial paralysis of his painting hand;
10. The desertion by his wife who took his two children;

—all of which culminated in his untimely death by hanging in 1948 at the age of 44.

The psychobiography of Vosdanig Manoug Adoian is the essential link between his traditional Armenian background—barely known to the

West—and the avant-garde modernism of Arshile Gorky. Although he studied such masters as Rosslin, Uccello, Ingres, Cézanne, Picasso, Miró, Matta and other surrealists, as well as more modern painting techniques—"absorbing the best of all past art" (Rose, 1976)—the achievement of Vosdanig Adoian Gorky is his uniquely personal synthesis that transcended all schools, thereby creating Abstract Expressionism (Seitz, 1983, p. 32).

As with Joan Miró, whose art was inspired by his Catalan background, Gorky's painting arose from the intensity of his feelings for his native Armenia (Tashjian, 1995, pp. 261–301). The oral tradition of folktales of heroic deeds and tragedy—which so enthralled the young Vosdanig—are key to understanding the innovation he brought to modern painting. Because of the absence of his father, Vosdanig enjoyed near-exclusive intimacy with his mother, who bequeathed these traditions to her son's imagination. This exclusive relationship also served to intensify the feminine, creative and artistic elements of his psyche. The artistry of the embroidered apron—which lulled his impressionable youthful head on so many occasions—is indicative of an artistic temperament that was transmitted both genetically and culturally.

The white apron that the mother wears in the two famed "artist and his mother" paintings served as the artist's canvas on which his imagination recreated the lost motherland with its organic forms, in which the seeds implanted by Armenian peasants germinated into gardens of wish-fulfillment. Gorky believed in purity in art, where the personal is sacrificed for the universal. Yet, paradoxically, beneath his marvelous abstract creations lay his joy and suffering of a lost Armenia that could live only inside him. The artist's temperament, with a penchant for cyclic melancholy, intensified the profound nostalgia and the losses he experienced throughout his 30 years in the New World. Armenia was so foreign to the New World that he had to camouflage his origin and everything related to it—starting with his name. In the end, he lost everything, his life included, to give birth to the purest form of art, Abstract Expressionism.

REFERENCES

In this chapter, most titles and years of paintings are based on Jordan & Goldwater (1982: see below).

Akiskal, H.S. & Akiskal, K. (1992). Cyclothymic, hyperthymic and depressive temperaments as sub-affective variants of mood disorders. In *Annual Review*, Vol. 11, Eds A. Tasman & M.B. Riba, pp. 43–62. American Psychiatric Press, Washington, D.C.

Belli, O. (1986). *The Capital of Urartu: Van.* Net Turistik, Yayinlar, Istanbul.

Breton, A. (1945). The eye-spring: Arshile Gorky. *Le Surrealisme et la Peinture*, pp. 196–99.

Cantor, J. (1991). *On Giving Birth to One's Own Mother.* Alfred A. Knopf, New York.

Der Nersessian, S. (1977). *L'Art Armenien.* Arts et Métier Graphiques, Paris.

Fondation Calouste Gulbenkian (1985). *Arshile Gorky: Collection Mooradian.* Paris.

Gorky, A. (1931). Stuart Davis. *Creative Art*, **9** (3 September), 213–217.

Jordan, J.M. & Goldwater, G. (1982). *The Paintings of Arshile Gorky: a Critical Catalogue.* New York University Press, New York.

Lader, M.P. (1985). *Arshile Gorky.* Abbeville Press, New York.

Levy, J. (1966). *Arshile Gorky.* Harry N. Abrams, New York.

Levy, J. (1972). *Memoirs of an Art Gallery.* Putnam and Sons, New York.

Machtot's Institute of Old Armenian Manuscripts (1978). *Armenian Miniature—Vaspurakan.* Matanadaran, Yerevan.

Mooradian, K. (1978). *Arshile Gorky Adoian.* Gilgamesh Press, Chicago.

Mooradian, K. (1980). *The Many Worlds of Arshile Gorky.* Gilgamesh Press, Chicago.

Mooradian, K. (1985). The Wars of Arshile Gorky. *Ararat,* **XXIV**, 2–16.

Morgan, S. (1991). Becoming Arshile Gorky. *Artscribe,* **31** (October), 16–23.

New York Evening Post (1926). Fetish of Antique Stifles Art Here. September 15.

Rand, H. (1991). *Arshile Gorky: The Implications of Symbols.* University of California Press, Berkeley.

Rose, B. (1976). Arshile Gorky and John Graham: eastern exiles in a western world. *Arts Magazine,* **50**, 62–79.

Rose, B. (1979). Gorky—Tragic Poet of Abstract Expressionism. *Vogue,* **169** (October), 355, 386.

Rosenberg, H. (1962). *Arshile Gorky: The Man, the Time, the Idea.* Horizon Press, New York.

Schwabacher, E.K. (1957). *Arshile Gorky.* Macmillan, New York.

Seitz, W.C. (1983). *Abstract Expressionistic Painting in America.* Harvard University Press, Cambridge MA.

Southgate, M.T. (1981). Arshile Gorky, the Artist and His Mother. *JAMA,* **245**, 1813.

Tashjian, D. (1995). *A Boatload of Madmen: Surrealism and American Avant-garde.* Thames & Hudson, New York.

Thiery, J.M. & Donabedian, P. (1989). *Armenian Art.* Harry N. Abrams, New York.

Walker, C.J. (1980). *Armenia: The Survival of a Nation.* Croom Helm, London.

AFTERWORD

Joseph J. Schildkraut

The interrelatedness of mood disorders, spirituality and artistic creativity has been observed in the life and work of Joan Miró and many of the Abstract Expressionist Artists of the New York School. The literature, however, has mainly focused on the pairing of mood disorders with artistic creativity or spirituality with art. While plausible hypotheses have been put forth to account for these paired associations, further research grounded in neurobiology, genetics, psychology and ethology, as well as in art history, will be needed to document and explore the three-way association of mood disorders, spirituality and artistic creativity.

Although she does not specifically deal with depression in her pathfinding book on the evolutionary "survival value" of the arts, Dissanayake (1988) provides preliminary bridging insights concerning this three-way association. Relating art to ritual, religion, myth and the longing for transcendence in the face of life's ultimate mysteries, Dissanayake (1988, p. 144) suggests that the ". . . impulse to escape or find refuge from an isolate and imperfect reality in transcendent experience. . . . is a fundamental consequence and imperative of human biology". While mood disorders (mania as well as depression) may enhance the intensity of the "impulse", art is one of humankind's responses to this biological "imperative". When coupled with great talent, this response can lead to great art—art that reflects the human condition, art that is timeless and tragic.

Thus, recalling the themes found in Dürer's engraving "Melencolia I" (Figure 0-1)—isolation, loneliness, despair, depression, dissatisfaction with earthbound limitations, and the yearning to ascend to celestial heights—we are brought back to the issues with which Miró struggled in his life and which he captured in his art.

Homage to Joan Miró.

REFERENCE

Dissanayake, E. (1988). *What Is Art For?* University of Washington Press, Seattle.

INDEX

Index compiled by Annette Musker